T0336313

Capital County: Historical Studies of Pulaski County, Arkansas

Pulaski County Historical Society

2008

Capital County: Historical Studies of Pulaski County, Arkansas

Table of Contents

INTRODUCTION

In 1951 a group of people interested in local history formed the Pulaski County Historical Society. Two years later, the organization began to publish the Pulaski County Historical Review, bringing out a separate issue four times a year. In the first issue of the Review, the editor, Margaret Smith Ross, gave it a specific purpose: "Above all, we hope to demonstrate that history is fun."

Ross was an excellent choice to get the journal going and an archetype for later editors. She wrote a column on local history for the *Arkansas Gazette* and was an authority on Pulaski County history. Some of the best early articles in the Review were her meticulously-researched pieces on the early settlers and settlements of Pulaski County. In 1969 she published *Arkansas Gazette: The Early Years, 1819-1866*, which was not only the biography of a newspaper but also an excellent account of politics in Arkansas Territory in the antebellum period of statehood.

In 1957, J. H. Atkinson, another founder of the PCHS, took over as editor of the Review. Atkinson was a professor at what was then Little Rock Junior College, now the University of Arkansas at Little Rock. He had a strong interest in Arkansas history and was the co-author of a high school textbook on that subject. The third editor, Tom W. Dillard, was doing graduate work and employed at the Pulaski County Clerk's office in 1972 when he took over from Atkinson. While editor, he went on to teach at Hall High School in Little Rock. He later headed the state Department of Arkansas Heritage and the Butler Center for Arkansas Studies and played a major role in the successful effort to make Arkansas History a required subject in Arkansas public schools. He is now Head of Special Collections, University of Arkansas Libraries, in Fayetteville. Dillard edited the Review through 1978, then Richard Robertson took over for a year, after which Dillard did two more issues. Dillard's final two issues are particularly important because they were done in a new publication format that replaced the old typescript with printed text and added black and white pictures.

Martha Williamson Rimmer was editor of the last two issues of the *Review* that were published in 1980 and continued in that role until 2001. A native of Pine Bluff, she graduated from Rhodes College in Memphis and received a master's degree from the University of Arkansas, writing a thesis on Charles E. Taylor, the Progressive era mayor of Little Rock. In addition to finding authors and helping them to improve their submissions, she also devoted countless hours to a compilation that became *The Pulaski County Historical Review: Index to Volumes 1-45, 1953-1997*, published by the society in 1998. All the articles in this volume come from the years in which Rimmer edited the Review. In part this is because professional printing made them relatively easy to scan into electronic print. Limiting them to that period also makes a convenient stopping point for this book and a place from which a future volume may begin. The quality of the articles in this period owes much to Dr. F. Hampton Roy, who funded the F. Hampton Roy History Awards Contest in 1981, providing a financial incentive for historians to submit their work.

The articles in this book are remarkable in their quality. Martha Rimmer's account of Pulaski is not only a detailed and readable narrative but an important interpretation that shows, among other themes, the synergistic, if sometimes acrimonious, relation between Little Rock and North Little, the trials of African-Americans as second-class citizens but also their success at building a vibrant and strong society and advancing the cause of their political freedom, and the ways in which modern technology altered the city of Little Rock and improved the lives of its residents. All of the thirteen essays taken from the *Pulaski County Historical Review* have their own virtues and must be read to be appreciated. Selecting some at random, one can highlight Carolyn Yancey Little's account of Sampson Gray, which documents the economic and civic contributions of an early pioneer, Linda Pine's portrayal of the boisterous Little Rock volunteer firemen, and Mrs. Cotton's charming description of trolley cars and the people that rode them. It should also be noted that one of the hardest parts of getting this book done was choosing a selection of articles from the many ones worthy of re-publication. The articles that first appeared in the *Pulaski County Historical Review* are printed here as they appeared there, except that almost all the maps and pictures are not reproduced. An "Images of Pulaski County" section has been created for the book.

The origins of this volume go back to a Pulaski County Historical Society board meeting in the fall of 2004, when a discussion over the treasurer's report meandered into the idea of publishing a collection of articles from the *Review* that would give those excellent pieces of local history a wider audience. When Martha Rimmer agreed to write a historical overview of the county's history, the project began to acquire a life of its own, which was further sustained by a generous grant from the Arkansas Humanities Council. Jim Metzger was president of the historical society when this project began and his played a major role in seeing it through. Current president Jon Wolfe has continued that support. Stephen Recken, a member of the board, has made significant contributions. Other board members are Bob Razer, the long-time treasurer, Tim Nutt, who was then editor of the *Review*, Becky Parkerson, who took over from Tim, Sandra Taylor Smith, Lloyd Davis, Richard Clark, Alan Ward, and Brian K. Robertson. Special thanks go to the Arkansas Humanities Council for its generous support of this project. Amanda Paige scanned all the articles, Jim Ross gave the manuscript a careful read, and Cheri Thriver of Thriver Impressions provided excellent advice along with quality printing. This writer is also a historical society board member and has served as editor of the book as well as "chief cook and bottle washer" for the project.

Martha Rimmer and the other thirteen authors whose work is represented here know that Margaret Ross was right and "history is fun." Their readers will feel the same way.

S. CHARLES BOLTON

DEPARTMENT OF HISTORY

UNIVERSITY OF ARKANSAS AT LITTLE ROCK

NOVEMBER 2007

This project is supported in part by a grant from the Arkansas Humanities Council and the Department of Arkansas Heritage.

Pulaski County: The First 150 Years

Martha Williamson Rimmer

Despite the many fine articles in the "Pulaski County Historical Review", the several very good books about Little Rock, and a large bibliography of work on Arkansas history done in recent years, up until now there has not been a study of Pulaski County history as a whole. The following study, written especially for this book, fills that void admirably.

Located in the geographic center of Arkansas and home to its capital city, Pulaski County has developed through its history into the political, economic, and cultural center of the state. It is one of seven counties in the United States named for Casimir Pulaski, the Polish nobleman who was a hero of the American Revolutionary War. Count Pulaski was an experienced cavalry officer who, having been exiled from Poland after leading resistance efforts against the Russians, came to America to help George Washington and his Revolutionary army fight for this new country's independence. He played a key role in defending Charleston, South Carolina, against the British and later lost his life trying to drive the British from Savannah, Georgia, in 1779. While the memory of his service was still fresh, the states of Kentucky, Georgia, Missouri, Virginia, Indiana, and Illinois named counties for Pulaski between 1799 and 1843. In addition, in 1818 the government of Missouri Territory created a Pulaski County in its southern section, and the following year the county became part of the new Arkansas Territory formed by Congress as Missouri prepared for statehood.[1]

Pulaski was one of five counties established in the future territory of Arkansas between 1812 and 1819 while the area comprised the southern part of Missouri Territory. The first was Arkansas County in 1813, then Lawrence County in 1815, and finally Pulaski, Clark, and Hempstead Counties were all created in 1818. In 1819 these five counties made up the newly created Arkansas Territory. The physical size of Pulaski County in 1818 was many times greater than it is today, encompassing a large irregular swath through the middle of the territory that ranged westward from the White River almost to the Rocky Mountains. To encourage settlement in this new, undeveloped land that had been acquired in the Louisiana Purchase, the national surveying system was extended so that property locations could be systematically described and the distribution and sale of public land could begin. In 1815, surveyors established two lines from which the rest of the area could be measured, one running north from the mouth of the Arkansas River (designated the Fifth Principal Meridian for the purpose of the survey) and the other, which formed a baseline, running west from the mouth of the St. Francis River. These lines were the basis of the survey system used in what became Arkansas, Missouri, Iowa, Minnesota, and the Dakotas. There is a reminder of this system in the form of Baseline Road in modern-day Little Rock.[2] As the population increased and more governmental administration was added, large pieces of Pulaski County were reorganized into new counties, so that by 1875 Pulaski County was very close to the size and shape we recognize today.[3]

After Pulaski County was established in December 1818, the rudiments of local governmental authority were placed in the hands of several officials, appointed first by Missouri Territory and then in 1819 by the newly created Arkansas Territory. There was a court of five justices of the peace, a county clerk, and a sheriff, who were in charge of administering the law, keeping land records, collecting taxes, and in time, building roads and registering voters.[4] The county seat was located initially at Cadron, then two years later was moved to the new town of Little Rock. As the population grew, the county court would further subdivide the county into townships, through which it could keep up with its citizens by way of the census, and more efficiently tend to civil and political business. Over the years there have been as many as twenty different townships in Pulaski County, though today there are only Hill Township, north of the Arkansas River, and Big Rock Township, south of the river.[5]

BEFORE THE WRITTEN RECORD

The history of Pulaski County, however, began long before it became a political entity. The land in central Arkansas has a variety of geologic features that have been important to its human inhabitants throughout time. The most dominant feature is the Arkansas River, which flows southeasterly through the area on its way to the Mississippi River. In a geologic history of the county, *Pulaski County Historical Review* author Dr. Fred Henker described other topographical and physical features of note:

> To the north and west lie the foothills of the Ozark and Ouachita Mountains. Eastward are the residuals of the Mississippi Embayment and Gulf Coastal Plain, and in the southern part of the county is Granite Mountain, . . . In the center are quartz crystal deposits, and scattered around the county are old mining operations for lead, silver, copper, zinc, manganese, and even gold.[6]

The earliest native culture that archaeologists have been able to study was that of the Plum Bayou people, who before 700 A. D. began living along Plum Bayou near the Arkansas River in the area of today's Toltec Mounds State Park. Before these native people left the area around 350 years later, they had built eighteen ceremonial mounds and left remnants of their culture in the form of stone tools and clay pottery. Archaeologist Martha Rolingson has written that most of the Plum Bayou people lived out in the countryside in small communities or on farms away from the actual mounds. They earned their livelihood by hunting, gathering, or farming and "traded with other settlements as far as the Gulf of Mexico and the Great Lakes."[7]

EUROPEAN INFLUENCE

European explorations of the region began with the Spanish explorer Hernando de Soto, who had set out from Florida and crossed the Mississippi River into Arkansas in 1541. There is no consensus among scholars on De Soto's exact route through Arkansas or Pulaski County, though the U.S. De Soto Expedition Commission of 1939 concluded that De Soto came upon the Indian town of Coligua near Big Rock on the opposite bank from present-day Little Rock in September 1541. Others, who subscribe to the 1989 study done by Professor Charles H. Hudson of Georgia, locate Coligua nearer to Batesville and describe a more southerly route through central Arkansas. Regardless of whether De Soto "slept here" in Pulaski County or not, his main significance for our purposes is that his journey marked the beginning of European influence in our part of America.[8]

The French began to establish their presence in the region during the next century as explorers ventured down the Mississippi River from Canada, claiming the entire Mississippi Valley for France in the 1680s and setting up trading posts. In 1722 the French governor of Louisiana dispatched Bénard de La Harpe to explore the Arkansas River in the hope of discovering valuable mineral deposits. With a small group of men and supplies in three pirogues (canoes carved from logs), La Harpe began his expedition upriver. When he reached the large rock in the river bank that the Indians had told him marked the beginning of the mountains and is known today as Big Rock, La Harpe climbed to the top, calling it le Rocher Français, the French Rock, and claimed it for King Louis XV. Though La Harpe found only crystals and novaculite (a rock that makes excellent whetstones) instead of precious gems, he recognized the geographic significance of the future site of Little Rock and North Little Rock and recommended that a fort be established there. Several known Indian trails converged at this advantageous river crossing, which La Harpe no doubt recognized as a potentially important trade and transportation center.[9]

Among the reminders of the French hunters, trappers, and traders in the period that followed are the French names left on landmarks in the area. One example is "Maumelle," which is a distortion of the French word "mamelle," meaning breast, and was first given to the mountain that we know today as Pinnacle and later used to name a river, a lake, and now a town. The story goes that the shape of the mountain reminded a Frenchman of a woman's breast and his descriptive name stuck. Another is "Fourche" of Fourche Bayou and Fourche Creek, which comes from the French word for a branch of a stream. Sam Dickinson, an authority on this period, surmises that Bayou Meto, which begins in the northeast part of Pulaski County where early explorers hoped to find gold and silver, could have come from the French "metaux" meaning minerals, though others have offered differing French derivations.[10]

The Quapaw, also described as the "Downstream People," referring to their route down the Mississippi River from their land of origin, moved into Arkansas around the time of De Soto. These Native Americans established villages near the mouths of the Arkansas and White rivers, and hunted throughout a large area stretching into Pulaski County. According to Sam Dickinson in his article "Quapaw Indian Dances," reprinted in this collection, "seven archaeological sites in the county have been identified positively as Quapaw of the proto-historic period from 1500-1700." The Quapaw lived in rectangular houses with arched roofs that were sided with cypress bark and cane matting. They did some farming, though hunting for deer and buffalo was their chief economic activity. Contact with Europeans greatly reduced the size of their population, from an estimated 6,000 to around 600 by the time the Americans began arriving.[11]

By the time Pulaski County was created in 1818, the growing white population with its desire for good farm land prompted the federal and territorial governments to draw up a series of treaties with the Quapaw. The first required them to give up all claim to lands in Arkansas except for a specific area on the south side of the Arkansas River with boundaries running from "the Little Rock" to Arkansas Post. (A point on this Quapaw Line in the northwest corner of MacArthur Park in Little Rock is designated with a marker.) In 1824 the Quapaw ceded even this restricted area, and in 1833-1834 they agreed to leave Arkansas altogether and move to land in Indian Territory.[12]

Even though France gave her claim to Louisiana and the Mississippi Valley to Spain in 1764, following the Seven Years War in Europe, French hunters and trappers stayed, and some settled with their families. Margaret Ross, Arkansas historian and founding editor of the *Pulaski County Historical Review*, has identified several of these families in the Pulaski County area in the late 1700s. The earliest, from 1769 to 1784, was John Baptiste Imbeau, a French colonist who had married a Quapaw woman, and who with his family lived for a time below "the Little Rock" in what is now the industrial section of the city. Other Frenchmen in the period, such as Joseph Bartholomew and his family, Francis Coussatt, and Joseph Duchassin, lived in the vicinity of "the Little Rock," or farther up on the north side of the Arkansas River near Cadron Creek.[13]

AMERICAN SETTLEMENT

After 1804 and the acquisition of the Louisiana Purchase lands, American settlers began to drift into the area looking for land and fresh opportunities in this newly opened wilderness. There were several areas in the future Pulaski County where the early Americans found both fertile land and access to water. Around 1812 a settlement was established on the north side of the Arkansas River near Crystal Hill by Jacob and James Pyeatt and their families and is thought to have been the first real American community in the area. Another cluster of families settled a few miles upriver from Crystal Hill near the mouth of Palarm Creek. On the south side of the river a few settlers claimed lands along the Big Maumelle River and near Maumelle Mountain. Jacob Pyeatt put in a ferry that ran between his place on the north bank of the Arkansas River to that of Samuel Gates on the south bank.[14]

The Cadron Settlement, which was farther up the Arkansas River on the north bank along Cadron Creek and is now in Faulkner County, attracted around forty or fifty families beginning about 1808. The Cadron community became an important settlement in this pre-territorial period. It was the first seat of government for Pulaski County and was briefly considered for the territorial capital.[15]

Other enterprising American settlers also began to arrive between 1810 and 1813 and, since the Quapaw claimed all the land on the south side of the Arkansas River, they settled on the north bank across from the landmark "point of rocks," also known as "the Little Rock." According to Margaret Ross, among the earliest who can be documented were William Mabbet, Edmund Hogan, who established a ferry across from "the Little Rock," and Wright Daniel, who lived at the foot of Big Rock but operated a grist mill by a creek on the south bank.[16] They may have been among the first white inhabitants after La Harpe to recognize the natural potential of the "point of rocks" as a commercial and transportation center. Historian Dallas Herndon points out that "during the greater part of the year it was possible to ford the river at Little Rock, a feat rarely, if ever, practical at any other point farther south." Native Americans, French hunters and trappers, and settlers migrating down the Southwest Trail from Missouri had all found this recognizable spot to be a good place to cross.[17]

With the creation of Pulaski County in 1818 and the official establishment of Arkansas as a territory around six months later, the focus on the land near "the Little Rock" greatly increased. The land claimed by the Quapaw on the south side of the Arkansas River had been greatly reduced by treaty, opening the area west of the Quapaw Line and "the Little Rock" to American settlement. It did not take long before a few men, hoping to increase their fortunes, arrived and began to establish their property claims to the site and talk up its potential as a location for the soon-to-be-chosen territorial capital. Problems arose immediately over the legitimacy of the claims to the land. One group based its claims on certificates issued by the federal government to those in southeast Missouri and northeast Arkansas who had suffered a major loss from the New Madrid earthquake of 1811-1812. Several of these certificates, good for 160 acres of any public land, were purchased by speculators and used to claim the site for the future Little Rock. In opposition, another group of speculator-claimants based its right to the land on preemption claims, purchased from those early settlers who had lived on or improved the land prior to 1814. Controversy resulted, followed by lawsuits and shenanigans. At one point the New Madrid group transported all the existing buildings and shacks across the Quapaw Line out of reach of its opponents and made a bonfire of those that couldn't be moved. In the end, however, deals were struck and a compromise was effected, and the town of Little Rock began to grow and develop. Its central location in the new territory, along with some heavy political lobbying, persuaded the territorial legislators to make Little Rock the capital in 1821.[18]

Shortly thereafter, the county seat of Pulaski County also was relocated to Little Rock from Cadron. Reflecting the town's rustic environment, the county's governmental officers operated out of a log house for about ten years before they moved into a brick building located on today's City Hall property. In 1840 county government moved to the east wing of the then-new (now Old) State House where it stayed until the 1880s.[19]

In 1820, soon after the fortune seekers began squabbling over the town site, Little Rock saw the arrival of its first family, headed by Matthew Cunningham, a physician originally from Philadelphia, his wife Eliza, a cultured and well-educated woman from New York, and her two children. The Cunninghams were not a typical pioneer family, and one has to wonder what they saw in the very rudimentary settlement that Margaret Ross described as:

> not even a fair-sized village. Its population consisted of some twelve
> or thirteen men, and none of them were married except Dr.

Cunningham. ...There were only two buildings in town that might be classified as houses, and they were mere shanties.

Undaunted by the challenges, the Cunninghams stayed to make Little Rock their lifelong home, raising their family and serving the community. Dr. Cunningham was Little Rock's first mayor after the city was incorporated in 1831.[20]

Some months later, a second family arrived by keelboat from Kentucky. Maria Toncray Watkins, her husband, Major Isaac Watkins, their son, and a niece debarked in Little Rock in March 1821 after a long and difficult journey. In her diary Maria Watkins described her initial feelings about her new home:

O the disappointment to me, only one house and a few cabins, but two decent families. . . . I hope I may be as much resigned to death when it comes as I am now, but the Lord's ways are not our ways. I endure many privations in this place, the Sound of the Gospel of Jesus is not heard in this village. [21]

Despite this discouraging first impression, the Watkins family, too, made Little Rock its permanent home and left its stamp on its history.

The town soon began to develop into a community. William Woodruff moved his printing press and the *Arkansas Gazette* from Arkansas Post to the new territorial capital in December 1821.[22] Jesse Brown, a school teacher from Massachusetts, also came that year, built a log school house at the foot of Rock Street that became the Little Rock Academy, and began a career teaching Little Rock children.[23] With the encouragement of Maria Watkins, a Baptist church was established in July 1824 and soon built the community's first church building out of logs. (In 1832 this group decided to change its name to the Christian Church and went on to replace its log structure with a brick building in the 1840s, adding the town's first clock tower in the 1850s.)[24] As the decade of the 1820s progressed, other entrepreneurs arrived and established new businesses with additional amenities. Jesse Hinderliter built a tavern or grog shop several blocks south of the river at what is now the corner of Third and Cumberland, and Nicholas Peay opened the first hotel. The Peay Hotel at Markham and Scott was the forerunner of the Anthony House, which figured as prominently in Arkansas politics of the nineteenth century as the Hotel Marion did in the twentieth.[25]

FRONTIER TERRITORY

Although life in Little Rock was gradually improving, the settlement was still a very rough and wild frontier town in both appearance and atmosphere. In 1827, a young printer working for William Woodruff described his impressions of his new town and its citizens for his family in Boston:

> [Little Rock] contains about 60 buildings, 6 brick, 8 frame, the balance log cabins. The best building in the place is the printer's; it is built of brick and is as good an office as any in Boston. . . .The town has been settled about eight years, and has improved very slow. The trees are not cut down in the town yet; instead of streets we walk in cow trails from one house to another. . . . [Of the inhabitants, he says], a more drunken, good-for-nothing set of fellows never got together. . . . Of the female part of the community, I have not much to say, as there are five grown girls in the township and they are as ugly as sin and as mean as the devil.[26]

Outside of Little Rock in other parts of Pulaski County, pioneering settlers were also arriving, acquiring new land, and establishing farming operations. One prominent example is Samson Gray, who with other family members came from Tennessee in 1820 and settled on Bayou Meto in northern Pulaski County, in the present-day vicinity of Jacksonville. In her article on Samson Gray, reprinted here, Carolyn Yancey Little Kent writes about this rural wilderness and Gray's involvement in the development of the county's early roads and mail routes, particularly the building of the military road between Memphis and Little Rock in 1827. Transportation was a critical issue in this period, and overland routes that were at least cleared of trees and brush, avoided the swamps, and bridged the streams were vital to increased settlement. Throughout this period there was a steady flow of immigrants from the older, more populated states moving south and west through Arkansas toward Texas. The easiest route brought them to the Arkansas River at Little Rock where, with wagons, livestock and, perhaps, slaves, such pioneers paid a ferryman to transport them across the river and on their way.[27]

Another family from Tennessee that arrived during the early days of the territory and settled ten miles outside of Little Rock along this southwesterly route was that of Archibald and Margaret McHenry. The McHenrys built a sturdy, four-room log house, which still stands and has come to be known as the Ten-Mile House or the Stagecoach House. They became substantial, self-sufficient land owners and with the labor of slaves raised a variety of crops, cattle, and horses. This family and its succeeding generations were among the many solid citizens who contributed to the life and economy of early Pulaski County, and in the process helped transform the area from an unpopulated wilderness into an increasingly stable and prosperous territory, steadily progressing toward statehood.[28]

Other families followed these early settlers to Pulaski County. They cleared land, constructed sawmills and grist mills on nearby streams and bayous, planted corn and cotton, built homes and churches, raised their children, established cemeteries, helped build roads, served on commissions and juries, and in so doing developed the civic, social, and physical infrastructure of their communities.[29]

For Pulaski County the territorial years from 1819 to 1836 and beyond were a period of considerable growth and change. The population in 1820 of 1,921 persons grew to 2,395 in 1830, an addition of only 24 percent compared to the 113 percent increase during the same decade in the territory as a whole. If one considers the drastic reduction in the county's physical size that also took place during the 1820s, when huge areas of land were taken away to form the original Crawford and Conway counties and part of Jefferson County, this relatively slow growth rate is given perspective. During the 1830s when Arkansas's population more than tripled, growing by 221 percent, Pulaski County, which lost land to the formation of White and Saline counties, nevertheless grew by 123 percent, of which the increasing number of slaves formed a significant proportion (24 percent by 1840). The county's population seemed to stagnate in the 1840s (in part due to the separation of what would become part of Prairie County) but stabilized in the 1850s, when its growth rate equaled that of Arkansas as a whole. Though most of the county's growth came either from the birth of children to those already here or from migration from older southern states, the county also attracted a larger concentration of foreign-born settlers, mainly German and Irish, than anywhere in the state, chiefly settling in Little Rock. Jonathan J. Wolfe stated in an analysis of Pulaski County's population that the growth of Little Rock and its increasing importance as an urban center was "the most significant single factor in the development of Pulaski County . . . . It made the county unique."[30]

ANTEBELLUM LITTLE ROCK, THE CITY OF ROSES

Though Arkansas achieved statehood in 1836, its capital of Little Rock was still very much a frontier town during the 1830s and into the 1840s, only gradually developing the genteel trappings that would emerge in later decades. It was oriented toward the river where there was a constant bustle and traffic of goods and people. Keelboats were the chief mode of river transportation in this period, although after the Eagle made its way upriver to Little Rock in 1822 an increasing number of steamboats brought all manner of people. As a river town Little Rock attracted its share of "prostitutes, gamblers and con men," who congregated along the waterfront near the boat landing. It was not long before the streets in this area developed the reputation represented by their names, Battle Row and Fighting Alley, where, according to Margaret Ross, "there always seemed to be a brawl or free-for-all fight going on."[31]

The comings and goings of the town's rowdy element were tempered by the arrival of a more stable group of citizens – attorneys, merchants, craftsmen, doctors, and politicians – characterized by historian Carolyn Billingsley as urban pioneers, who "brought political, legal, and economic structure to the frontier and built towns that became focal points of populated areas."[32] Little Rock's developing urban environment formed the focal point of Pulaski County and of the new state's government. As such, Little Rock provided a wider variety of opportunities and cultural experiences than were available to people living on the rural frontier. By the 1840s the more prosperous of this elite group of urban pioneers had begun to build elegant brick homes with formal flower gardens, such as Albert Pike's mansion, still standing at Seventh and Rock streets, with its "extensive grounds" planted "with shrubbery and exotics of choice varieties." Other, somewhat more modest homes, described by landscape architect C. Allan Brown as built "upon generous city plots, allowing ample area for the necessary complement of outbuildings, livestock lots, and gardens," gave antebellum Little Rock a very attractive landscape that was the basis for its reputation as "The City of Roses." Harriet Jansma's article in this collection, "The Quaint Old Place Called 'Tanglewood'" gives a more detailed account of another urban homestead. Little Rock's first public garden opened in April 1840 on the block between today's Commerce and Sherman streets and Third and Fourth and was owned by the German businessmen Alexander and Henry George, whose family had immigrated to Little Rock in the 1830s. Called the "City Garden" or the "Dutch Garden," Little Rock's first park-like attraction featured, in addition to its plantings, the sale of "ice cream, wines, liquors, cake and other refreshments" and was a popular spot into the 1870s.[33]

Ellen Harrell Cantrell (mother of Deadrick Harrell Cantrell for whom Little Rock's Cantrell Road was named) remembered life as an eligible young lady in the capital city of the 1850s as one of leisure and romance. Even though when she first landed in Little Rock in 1849 there was no "carriage" to transport her to the hotel, "only drays, with their stout mules and [N]egro drivers, moving in and out among the cotton bales that covered the wharf," she found the "village" charming.

> The streets were partially grass-grown, with here and there an oak or elm standing midway. . . Roses were nestling everywhere . . . magnolia trees in profuse bloom, The aroma of forest trees which encompassed the city added to the charm . . . There were a few two-story brick residences, with long avenues, hedged with flowers or privet.

Of public buildings there were the state house, State and Real Estate banks, the United States arsenal, five or six very plain churches, and state penitentiary, while a hall, situated over a suite of two or three stores, served for a theater.

She was quickly accepted after her arrival as a member of Little Rock's top social circle, and remembered that the "gay young officers" posted at the town's federal military post greatly contributed to the parties and dances hosted by planters "down the river, where the invited guests would go on a flat boat, dance all night and return in omnibuses at daybreak."[34] Though the realities of life were harsher for most who lived in antebellum Little Rock, Cantrell's description depicts a town that had emerged over the course of three decades from a frontier wilderness into a center of commerce and government with many of the trappings of wealth brought by the cotton culture, not unlike other southern towns on the eve of the Civil War.

A significant element of the agricultural economy of this pre-war period was slavery. The number of slaves in Pulaski County followed the trend in the rest of Arkansas and had steadily increased between 1830 and 1860, when it reached 30 percent of the total county population of 11,699. An 1861 assessment concerning the ownership of slaves between the ages of 5 and 60 counted 325 owners in Pulaski County, of whom 51 owned more than 10 slaves and 5 owned more than 50. There were many fewer slaves in Little Rock than on the farms and plantations in the rest of the county, but their labor was depended upon in many well-to-do households. They were bought and sold and passed down to heirs along with land, livestock, and household goods. One example of an exception to this way of life was Nathan Warren, who, though an African American, was a free man and ran a successful confectionery business in Little Rock in the 1840s and early 1850s. Married to a slave of the prominent Chester Ashley family, Warren associated with both whites and blacks until the growing tensions that preceded the Civil War forced him to leave Little Rock.[35]

THE CIVIL WAR IN PULASKI COUNTY

The threat of war came early to the capital city. Two months before the Confederate firing on Fort Sumter in April 1861, Little Rock faced the possibility of hostile action to force the surrender of the Federal Arsenal, which had served as a quiet frontier outpost since its construction around 1838. In January 1861, with war pressures building in the cotton-growing sections of the state, rumors began to circulate that the Federal forces of Captain James Totten stationed at the U.S. Arsenal (located at Ninth and Commerce streets in present-day MacArthur Park where one of its buildings still stands) would soon be reinforced with additional troops. Angry at the news, armed militia men from pro-secessionist parts of the state streamed into Little Rock prepared to prevent the rumored reinforcements from landing and to take the Arsenal by force if neces-sary. Little Rock's citizens, not yet convinced of the inevitability of secession or war, were horrified at the prospect of such a conflict and urged Governor Henry Rector to intervene. Captain Totten, whose men were greatly outnum-bered by the growing mob, repeatedly requested direction from his superiors in Washington. Receiving none, he decided to accept the governor's offer of safe passage out of the state if he and his men turned over the Arsenal to the state and left for St. Louis. Relieved that bloodshed had been avoided, a group of grateful Little Rock women presented Totten with a sword as a parting good-will gift.[36]

Little Rock's feeling of relief was only temporary, however. The attack on Fort Sumter galvanized secessionist sentiment around the state, and by May 1861 Arkansas had joined the Confederacy. Along with the rest of the state, Pulaski County began to contribute its share of soldiers and support for the war effort. Civil War historian William W. O'Donnell described the county's role as "the breadbasket of the most populous section of the state" and as a "staging area" for the military. In 1862 after the Confederate retreat from the Battle of Pea Ridge in northwest Arkansas, Pulaski County and Little Rock received numerous wounded soldiers, caring for them in make-shift hospitals where they were nursed by the city's women and fed by the county's farmers.[37]

By 1863 news from the war front grew increasingly grim for Arkansas. The federal plan to gain control of the Mississippi and Arkansas rivers was being real-ized. With the Confederate losses at Helena and Arkansas Post and in light of Grant's strategic victory at Vicksburg, the Union had both the opportunity and the manpower to move on the Arkansas capital. In August 1863, Federal forces under General Frederick Steele marched from Helena toward Little Rock. Faced with an enemy superior in both numbers and materiel, General Sterling Price mounted what defense he could. In his book on Little Rock, Ira Don Richards described the city's defensive position: "situated on a bluff on the south bank of the river, the city had impressive natural strengths provided the opponent chose to come in the right direction, out of the north; but should Steele ford the river downstream and approach from the south, then extensive works would be nec-essary to repel attack." Price prepared for an attack from the north bank, but he did little or nothing to enable his troops to defend the city from an attack from the southeast on his more vulnerable side. Confederate troops engaged the Federals several times during late August and early September as they advanced: at Brownsville near present-day Lonoke; at Reed's Bridge on Bayou Meto in northeast Pulaski County; and at Ashley's Mills near present-day Scott. Confederate morale was low. Governor Harris Flanagin moved state offices and records to the southwest Arkansas town of Washington.[38] In late August, Dr. Junius Bragg, a Confederate physician in Little Rock, described to his wife the hopelessness that pervaded Little Rock:

> All those who are determined to keep distance between themselves and the Yankees have consummated their arrangements and appear ready to walk at a moment's warning. . . I consider it merely a question of time when Little Rock falls. . . . With these lights before me, I am forced to conclude that the great city of Little Rock is doomed to feel the weight of the oppressor's heel. . . . If the state would rise as it did two years ago, upon the bare rumor that she was being invaded, the foe would thunder in vain at the gates of her capital. As it is the danger now menacing her kindles no patriotic fire to blaze forth and consume the invader. Dull apathy sits upon the face of her people. Her chivalry has long since gone from her shores.[39]

The Confederate plight was only made worse by a quarrel that erupted between two of Price's cavalry officers, Generals John S. Marmaduke and L. M. Walker. Their duel four days before the main attack resulted in Walker's death and a further weakened defense. On the morning of September 10, 1863, Federal cavalry forces crossed the river downstream from Little Rock and fought off resistance at Fourche Bayou, while the infantry advanced on the north bank. By mid-day the Confederates acknowledged the futility of resistance and began their retreat. At 7:00 p.m. the city officially surrendered.[40]

Federal occupation of Little Rock set the scene for the third notable event that took place in Pulaski County during the war, one that has become among the most commemorated events associated with the war in Arkansas–the hanging of the accused Confederate spy David O. Dodd. At the end of December 1863, seventeen-year-old David Owen Dodd departed Little Rock to join his family in Camden, having spent the previous five days in the city tending to some business for his father. He was stopped on the road to Benton by a Union picket, arrested, and found to be carrying coded messages describing the strength of Federal forces in the capital. He was brought to Little Rock and held at the prison located on the present-day site of the Arkansas State Capitol. The military commission that tried him on these charges found him guilty of spying and sentenced him to hang on January 8, 1864. Despite pleas for mercy on account of his youth, General Frederick Steele refused to rescind Dodd's sentence. A scaffold was constructed on the parade ground of St. John's Masonic College adjacent to the

Arsenal, and the sentence was carried out. A huge crowd, estimated to reach 6000, gathered for the spectacle. Though the official ruling was that Dodd died instantly from a broken neck, other accounts report that instead the rope stretched and the boy suffered a slower death by strangulation. There is no doubt that young Dodd was a sympathetic figure. He had written his parents that he was "prepared to die," and by all accounts he died honorably and bravely: one Federal soldier at the execution recounted that Dodd met his death "with a coolness I never saw equaled; and while of course I believe he was mistaken, as were all who sought the dismemberment of the Union, yet no one could doubt his honesty and his lofty patriotism." In the years following the demise of the Confederacy, the execution of David O. Dodd became a popular subject of artists and poets. In 1911 a stained glass window was dedicated to his memory at the White House of the Confederacy Museum in Richmond, Virginia, and in 1934 his grave in Little Rock's Mount Holly Cemetery was enhanced with an obelisk and outlined in marble, honoring him as "the Arkansas Boy Martyr of the Confederacy."[41]

Though grieved and angered by Dodd's execution, the white people of Little Rock were also growing increasingly weary of the war's toll and in time returned to a state of co-existence with the Union troops. Federal occupation also meant an influx of former slaves into Pulaski County seeking protection and a livelihood. Carl Moneyhon's article in this volume on "The Little Rock Freedmen's Home Farm" describes the military's experiment in helping freedmen adjust to their new circumstances.

RECONSTRUCTION AND RECOVERY

The long four years of Civil War finally ended, and Arkansans faced an even longer struggle to recover from the devastation and to reconstruct their economy and society. By 1868 the Radical Republicans in the U.S. Congress were in control nationally and intent on quickly redressing the ills of the Old South while establishing civil and political rights for black citizens. In Arkansas the Republican Party, composed largely of native Unionists and Northerners, some of whom had come to the state seeking economic opportunities and some to help the freedmen, followed the Congressional Radicals' lead and passed a new constitution intended to put the state on the right track. Despite the accomplishment of some positive economic and social changes, many white Arkansans would remember this period of reconstruction largely for its political confusion, fiscal corruption, and social disruption.

Although Little Rock had not suffered the physical destruction that the rural sections of the county and other parts of the state experienced during the war, her citizens nevertheless faced an enormous upheaval in their way of life: eco-nomically, socially, and politically. Initially the capital city enjoyed a burst of building construction and renewed commercial activity that included the estab-lishment of new enterprises, credit associations, and banks. A newspaper in 1869 reported one hundred buildings, twenty-five of brick, under construction. A merchants' association boasted that Little Rock would soon rival Memphis for customers. The city was also at the center of an emerging transportation industry, and many in the capital wanted to take part in the land grants and bond sales that accompanied the flurry of railroad construction. However, the city's seeming prosperity was short-lived. The Panic of 1873 set off a national depression that dried up credit and caused many of these new endeavors to fail, dashing hopes and bringing economic stagnation that only added to the fiscal woes in the state.[42]

Another aspect of the post-war instability in Pulaski County was the surge in population that dramatically altered the social fabric of the county. The end of the war had seen an influx of new people, especially in Little Rock, more than tripling the city's population. Many newcomers were "outsiders," often charac-terized as northern carpetbaggers, who hoped to profit from the reconstruction, or southern scalawags, who were viewed by the majority of the population as having been disloyal to the Confederacy. Another significant proportion of new citizens were African Americans. Historian Ira Don Richards stated that "out of a population of 3,727 in 1860, 853 were blacks, but at the next census Negroes accounted for 5,274 of a total 12,380, an increase from 23 to 43 percent." [43] Many of these former slaves sought education, training, and assistance to learn how to take advantage of their new freedoms and rights. Integrating new people, new ideas, and new ways of doing things brought problems and challenges to the capital city as it struggled to reorder its way of life and build a new urban envi-ronment. Progress would come, but it would be neither fast nor easy.

Political turmoil also marked these early post-war years of Radical Reconstruction when the hard-line elements of the Republican Party were in the ascendancy and Democrats were splintered and weak. It was a period character-ized by fraudulent elections, Ku Klux Klan violence, and fiscal mismanagement on both the state and local levels.[44] Without delving into the minutiae of the complicated and confusing political configurations, it is safe to say that as the state's capital Little Rock was in the center of the storm. The Brooks-Baxter War that played out on the streets of Little Rock in 1874 is emblematic of the chaotic atmosphere of almost ten years of Reconstruction politics in Arkansas. The 1874 battle was the result of the disputed gubernatorial election of 1872 between Republican rivals, Elisha Baxter and Joseph Brooks. There had been fraudulent votes cast on both sides, but the legislature had declared Baxter the winner and he took office in January 1873.[45] Dissatisfaction with this decision continued to simmer, however, through the next year while the issue was in the courts. When political maneuvering influenced the court to rule in favor of the initial loser, Joseph Brooks, the situation took a violent turn. Brooks immediately stepped into action to wrest the government away from Baxter and take charge before his opposition could organize. According to historian and former *Review* editor, J. H. Atkinson,

> On the morning of Wednesday, April 15, 1874, Governor Baxter
> and his son were working quietly in the governor's office, upstairs in
> the west end of the Old State House. About eleven o'clock, Joseph
> Brooks, with about a dozen men, came up the stairs, entered the gov-
> ernor's office, and ordered the governor to vacate the office . . . .
> Baxter hesitated, but when Brooks indicated that, if necessary, force
> would be used to put him out, Baxter and his son left and went to the
> Anthony Hotel, two blocks east, on the corner of Scott and
> Markham."[46]

The battle was on; armed men from around the state, both black and white, chose sides and poured into the city. For the next thirty days, Little Rock was the scene of two armed camps, with Main Street serving as the dividing line between Brooks's militia supporters on the west side and Baxter's forces, complete with a rejuvenated Civil War cannon, "Lady Baxter," on the east side. U. S. troops stationed in the city patrolled Main Street and tried to keep the two sides from doing more than posturing. Though there was little actual bloodshed in Little Rock and only a few casualties, there was serious fighting in scattered skirmishes elsewhere in the state.[47] One "bloody encounter," recounted by Fred Henker, took place upriver from Little Rock near Natural Steps and Palarm Station. A group of Baxter's men on the steamboat Hallie, who were on a mission to intercept a load of guns, were waylaid and fired on by Brooks's forces on shore, killing the captain and seriously wounding several others.[48]

In the end, President Ulysses Grant supported Elisha Baxter and the furor subsided. Reports differ as to the total number killed and wounded during the conflict, though one authority puts the number at around 200 statewide. The divisions within the Republican Party that resulted in Baxter's victory allowed ex-Confederates to reassert their political influence and marked the end of radical Republican Reconstruction. Shortly thereafter, Arkansans selected delegates to a new constitutional convention that would replace the 1868 Constitution with the 1874 model that we are governed by today, and the next election put the Democrats back in office.[49]

Despite all the upheavals and instability of the post-war period, there were several positive aspects of Reconstruction that had an impact on Pulaski County's future and paved the way for an era of growth. In Little Rock there was a new atmosphere of urban development that fostered an increasingly diverse population, which included a mixture of social classes, ethnic backgrounds, and races. Among the newcomers to Little Rock society after the war were skilled African-American tradesmen, who settled in the capital and became the foundation of a new phenomenon in Arkansas's social structure, a black middle class. Isaac T. Gillam and his family are a good example of this emerging group. As a freedman, Gillam had joined the Union Army shortly after it took control of Little Rock in 1863. He stayed after the war, establishing himself as a blacksmith as well as a dealer in horses. He and his wife raised and provided good educations for their eight children, all of whom pursued professional careers, with several distinguishing themselves as educators. Gillam became involved in politics, receiving several local Republican appointments. He went on to win election to the Little Rock City Council and the state legislature, and serve as Pulaski County's coroner. Both a school and a city park bear the Gillam name. Though few black citizens would rise to the prominence of Isaac Gillam, his family's achievements and success were indicative of the more multi-faceted society that developed as Little Rock grew.[50]

An expanding population and economy also prompted the city's new Republican administration to raise taxes and, at least, make a start in improving the city's infrastructure and services, especially in the areas of police and fire protection. The miserable condition of the streets downtown received some attention, though the most lasting change was the renaming of the east-west running streets south of Markham. These streets became Second through Tenth, replacing such names as Cherry, Mulberry, Walnut, Orange, Elizabeth, Chestnut, Hazel, Holly, and Caroline. After military control was over at the end of the war, city officials began creating a professional police department that under Republican administrations would include black police officers and at least one black detective. Another step forward was the enhancement of the city's fire fighting capability by the purchase of a more effective steam-pumped fire engine for the fire department and the hiring of an engineer to keep it going. In "'Putting on their red shirts and bringing down the Engine,'" reprinted here, Linda Pine describes the 1860s and 1870s as a "golden period for the volunteer fire companies in Little Rock." Fire protection was essential in the urban environment, and until the city established a fully paid fire department in 1892 these colorful and sometimes rival volunteer companies of businessmen and tradesmen provided reliable and trained crews that could respond quickly to a very real and threatening urban danger.[51]

Another major advance that had its beginning in this period was a tax-supported public school system in Little Rock. Although the first public school in the capital city began operation with 52 students in 1853, it wasn't until after the war that Little Rock organized a public school system in earnest, electing a school board, building school buildings, and hiring a superintendent, principals, and teachers. Though segregated, these schools began to address the paucity of educational opportunities for most of the city's children. A private education had been available at St. Mary's Academy, operated by the Roman Catholic Sisters of Mercy since 1851, or from various private academies for those children whose parents had the means. Until such public schools as Peabody, Sherman, and Kramer were opened for Little Rock's white students, however, the majority of them had few opportunities. The education of black children–and some adults–that began immediately after the war was in the hands primarily of missionary teachers sent south by the Quakers and the American Missionary Association. During Reconstruction the new Little Rock school system began adding schools for African-American children. For example, Union School, which was begun by the Society of Friends of Richmond, Indiana, was incorporated into the new school system around 1870 and others such as Capital Hill and Arsenal soon followed.[52]

One of the most notable contributors to black education in Little Rock was Charlotte Andrews Stephens. The daughter of Methodist minister W. W. Andrews, who had started a school for freedmen in Little Rock during the Civil War, Charlotte Stephens began teaching in 1869 and was the first African American hired by Little Rock's new school system. She went on to study at Oberlin College in Ohio and over the course of her distinguished seventy-year career influenced many able black students at a variety of Little Rock's better-known black schools: First Ward, Union, Capital Hill, Gibbs and Dunbar.[53]

Perhaps the most revolutionary change to come to Pulaski County and Arkansas during this period was the construction of railroads. The impact of this new mode of transportation would transform the economy, hasten urbanization, and for Little Rock shift the focus of the business district away from its reliance on the river. Despite the serious financial consequences that resulted when the railroad companies defaulted on their state bonds, railroads made it possible for Arkansas to take huge strides toward modernizing its economic base. The first line to be finished was the Memphis and Little Rock Railroad, which had received its charter and federal land grants in 1853. Most of the track had been laid by the early days of the Civil War, except for a section extending from

DeValls Bluff on the White River to the eastern bank of the St. Francis River. After the war the company regrouped, repaired the war's damage, and closed the gap, so that in April 1871 trains began running all the way from Little Rock to Memphis. Three years later, two other companies, the St. Louis and Iron Mountain Railroad from St. Louis and the Cairo and Fulton Railroad from southeast Missouri (at a point on the Mississippi River opposite Cairo, Illinois,) had both completed lines through the state that ran from northeast to southwest by way of Little Rock to the Texas border near Fulton, Arkansas. The Cairo and Fulton had also opened an extension from the capital city to Fort Smith. Less than ten years after the war's end, Little Rock was connected to markets in St. Louis, Texas, and New Orleans.[54]

The only snag in this transportation progress was the absence of a bridge over the Arkansas River. Without a bridge, trains were halted at the river where the railroad cars were ferried across to the opposite bank and reassembled. In the spring of 1873 the Cairo and Fulton Railroad created the Baring Cross Bridge Company and began construction of the first bridge across the Arkansas River. The "Baring Cross" name was coined to recognize the momentous act of "crossing" the river, and the Baring Brothers bank of London, England, which provided the financing. The new bridge opened to cheers "from the assembled multitude" on December 21, 1873. Four years later a "highway deck" was added across the top of the bridge for foot and wagon traffic, at the following toll rates: "footmen, 5¢; teams of two animals, 15¢; teams of six animals, 25¢; sheep and hogs, 3¢ each."[55]

NORTH LITTLE ROCK, A RAILROAD TOWN

The convergence of railroad operations on the north side of the Arkansas River spurred the growth of a new community associated with the railroads. Named Argenta, the Latin word for the silver mined at the Kellogg silver and lead mine in the area, the town quickly boomed. An 1871 report in the *Arkansas Gazette* stated that "buildings are rapidly going up, boarding houses, groceries, saloons and blacksmith shops opened, and a general air of go-aheadiveness and enterprise pervades that little berg [sic]." Before the Civil War there had been another small settlement in the vicinity referred to as Huntersville that had developed around the terminus of the Memphis and Little Rock Railroad. However, during the war Union troops took control of the railroad and the little settlement, and when they left at the war's end Huntersville never revived. At two other times, enterprising businessmen made attempts to take advantage of the north-bank real estate by developing towns—one around 1838 was to be called DeCantillon and one at the end of the war was to be called Quapaw—but neither got much beyond the planning stage.

Over the next twenty years, Argenta's population and businesses grew with the railroads. Without a governing authority, the town soon gained a reputation as a rough and lawless place. In 1890, just as the community was deciding to incorporate and take charge of its affairs, business and political leaders in Little Rock seized the moment and engineered its annexation, making Argenta Little Rock's eighth ward. Under the laws of the time, the residents of Argenta had no say in their annexation and, not surprisingly, they reacted with outrage, feeling the action had been taken only to increase Little Rock revenues, but their protests were to no avail. Thus began an uneasy and tenuous relationship that over the next fourteen years produced few benefits or improvements for Argenta citizens. Dissatisfaction on the north bank simmered, and shortly after the turn of the new century a wily plot was hatched to redress the injustice. As one local observer, John Cook, reminisced, "North Little Rock's history really begins with the Faucette brothers, William C. and James Peter Faucette," who were two of the conspirators behind the secret 1903 legislative scheme that enabled the newly incorporated town of North Little Rock to annex its next-door neighbor Argenta away from Little Rock. Timothy G. Nutt details these maneuverings in his article in this book, "Floods, Flatcars, and Floozies: Creating the City of North Little Rock." This time the annexation results brought protests from Little Rock, but the actions could not be reversed. In 1904, the new north-shore town elected William C. Faucette as its first mayor and set an independent course, free from the controlling interests of its more powerful neighbor across the river. By reinstating the name "Argenta" in place of "North Little Rock," the new city fathers further underscored the town's separate identity. In the next few years Argenta annexed the neighboring community of Baring Cross, began operating its own electric utility and street railway, and in 1914 began building a handsome city hall. By 1917, the hard feelings that led to the separation had subsided sufficiently to allow Mayor James P. Faucette and the council to see the future economic advantages of a name associated with the capital city, and they reset the city's course by reclaiming the name "North Little Rock." [56]

The effect of the new railroad lines on settlement was evidenced not just in Argenta, but in all parts of Pulaski County. Communities such as Levy, Baring Cross, Jacksonville, Mabelvale, and Alexander all had their beginnings as stations on one of the rail lines. One of the earliest mentions of Jacksonville was in 1878 when Little Rock's Board of Health designated it as a quarantine station in an effort to keep railroad passengers who may have come from an area afflicted with yellow fever out of the city. [57] This new mode of transportation connected previously isolated areas to the outside world as never before and generated jobs and services that attracted new people coming into the state, helping fuel the county's growth in the late nineteenth century.

GROWTH BRINGS DIVERSITY

The postwar population growth that had subsided during Reconstruction began to pick up again by the 1890s. By the turn of the century, the county's population had almost doubled, from 32,066 in 1870 to 63,179 in 1900. A portion of this new population settled out in the rural areas of the county, spawning communities centered on farm, timber, or railroad operations. One example dating to this period is the African-American farming community of Sweet Home, southeast of Little Rock, lying adjacent to the earlier site of the Freedmen's Home Farm. The noted African-American lawyer Scipio A. Jones taught school there in 1885 through 1886, but the community is better known as the location of the state-operated Confederate Soldiers Home that from 1890 until 1940 housed Confederate veterans in need and their widows.[58]

Other agricultural communities were settled by an increasing number of foreign immigrants in the county. Two settlements in this period, Marche (Marshay) and Little Italy, were distinctly European. A group of around one hundred Polish families under the leadership of Count Timothy von Choinski and his wife settled in north central Pulaski County around 1878, establishing the agricultural community of Marche, which became known as "Little Poland." Julia G. Besancon-Alford describes the history of that community in an article reprinted here. Another immigrant group, this one from southern Europe, settled in Pulaski County after the turn of the century. Responding to a newspaper ad for land in Arkansas, five Italian families who wanted to return to an agricultural life after immigrating to Chicago settled near the Pulaski-Perry county line on land that originally had been granted to the Little Rock and Fort Smith Railroad. Feeling at home in the rolling hills of northern Pulaski County, these families built homes and farms where they began raising cattle, planting vegetable gardens, and establishing vineyards, and became the nucleus of the community known as Little Italy.[59]

Germany was the source of the largest group of immigrants. There had been a small number of German settlers in central Arkansas prior to the Civil War, but after the war there was a second wave that wanted to escape the iron rule of Chancellor Otto von Bismarck and responded to advertisements touting the state's virtues. Some were farmers who settled on homesteads west of Little Rock or clustered in southwest Pulaski County in the vicinity of Mabelvale and Alexander, where they built a Lutheran church and grew fruit, potatoes, and grapes for wine. Larger numbers settled in Little Rock, establishing trades and businesses and organizing their own distinctive social and cultural life. The contributions of these German newcomers included the organization of three churches of different faiths, the German Lutheran, Congregation B'nai Israel, and St. Edward's Roman Catholic, as well as a variety of social clubs, such as the Turnverein Society, and the publication of two German-language newspapers, the *Arkansas Staats-Zeitung* (1877-1918) and Das Echo, (1891-1936).[60]

Each of the immigrant groups added to the richness and diversity of life in the county through the establishment of churches and other institutions to perpetuate its own culture. Though the Germans were perhaps the most successful in this regard, an indication of Little Rock's increasingly diverse mix of peoples, both immigrant and native, can be seen in a religious affiliation survey taken of the white population in 1903. It showed the traditional dominance of Methodists and Baptists, but also included a wide-ranging variety of other faiths: Catholics were third in numbers, followed by Presbyterians, Episcopalians, German Lutherans, and Jews, plus a smattering of Congregationalists, Christian Scientists, Universalists, two Spiritualists, and one courageous (or perhaps whimsical) soul who identified himself as an "Infidel."[61] In just a few years a Greek Orthodox congregation would be added to this urban mixture. Immigrants from Greece chose the city life of Little Rock for their new home beginning in the late 1890s. By 1913, the community's numbers had grown sufficiently to enable them to attract a permanent Greek Orthodox priest and hold regular services, establishing the Annunciation Greek Orthodox Church. [62]

African-American churches, though not included in the survey, also flourished in this period. First Missionary Baptist Church, founded by slaves before the Civil War, built its brick church building at Seventh and Gaines in 1882.[63] Many others, mostly affiliated with Baptist and Methodist denominations, also organized in the 1880s and 1890s, forming a significant cultural as well as religious component of the black community. These decades were a growth period for churches in general, and Little Rock's increasingly urban climate provided a variety of choices. At the close of the Civil War Little Rock had only a dozen churches; forty years later, a 1905 map of the Little Rock/Argenta area listed eighty-nine altogether, with slightly more black churches than white.[64]

A NEW URBAN ENVIRONMENT

The stormy Reconstruction era was followed in the 1880s and 1890s by a period of relative political and economic calm that fostered growth and the development of a many-faceted urban environment in Pulaski County. Perhaps symbolic of this transformation was the new Pulaski County Courthouse, begun in 1887. During the county's first few years, its offices had been housed in very modest log and brick structures. From 1840 until 1882, the county used the east wing of the State House on Markham. When the state reclaimed the space for its own use, however, county officials finally began plans for a new courthouse to be built on the northwest corner of Second and Spring streets that would project a more appropriate image for the state's most populous county. Designed in the Richardson Romanesque style by architect Max Orlopp, Jr., and built between 1887 and 1889 for a cost of $100,000, the building was constructed of Fourche granite with bands of Batesville limestone and terra cotta detailing and featured an observatory in its clock tower with "a fine view of the city." This impressive new courthouse, combined with the federal building across Spring Street, other new state buildings, and a boom in residential and commercial construction, gave the state's capital city an air of prosperity and progress.[65] Little Rock was no longer the sleepy frontier village of antebellum days but was striving to be a bustling urban center of the New South. In fact, Little Rock's population had more than tripled in this period, from 12,380 in 1870 to 38,307 in 1900, comprising for the first time the majority of the county's residents.

With a growing population, the city began in earnest to expand its physical infrastructure and give attention to its quality of life. New technologies of the period produced many household conveniences as well. Little Rock was one of the first cities to have telephone service, beginning in 1879 when Western Union Telegraph Company opened the city's first telephone exchange. Electric arc street lamps brightened the streets at night as they replaced the older oil lamps, and Edison's incandescent light bulb brought electric lights inside homes and businesses. The 1880s also brought improvements in the city's sanitation and to its streets and sidewalks, as well as the addition of a public transportation system, and the convenience of running water. An expanded and reworked public sewer system piped waste to the Town Branch, an extension of Fourche Creek that ran through downtown, which in turn carried it along to the Arkansas River. Street paving and better sidewalks improved the longstanding condition of the streets, where the "dust was ankle deep in the summer and the mud bottomless in the rainy seasons," with mud holes so deep that one resident recalled it took "six mules to pull a loaded wagon out of the mire." City water also became available, though at first it was primarily suitable only for fire protection since it came unfiltered from the Arkansas River. A settling tank and filtration system, added in 1888, made the cloudy, often muddy, river water more palatable, and residents finally began to enjoy the benefits of convenient drinking water.[66]

Another major advance of this period was the streetcars that moved along steel railway tracks on set routes for an affordable fare. First powered by mules, then steam engines, and finally electricity in the 1890s, streetcars could transport people to jobs, shopping, school, church, clubs, and entertainment. Elle Cotton's article titled "Streetcars and Society" is a colorful account of this new-fangled way to get around. Commenting on this phenomenon of her girlhood in the late nineteenth century, Jessie Rose Smith, the daughter of Judge U. M. Rose, remembered,

> We had street cars in those days, drawn by little Texas mules, of a toughness and meanness hardly to be believed. They were so small you wondered how they ever pulled the cars, indeed, where there were hills it was necessary to have an extra pair to pull the car up, the mules then going down the hill to wait for the next car. Somewhere in my childhood there was built the dummy line, which was a distant ancestor of the modern Diesel engine shut up in a box car and belching out black smoke as it ran, pulling behind it one, occasionally two, passenger cars. . . . And we knew when it passed by! . . . It rattled and groaned and roared, but it did carry us at the soul-stirring speed of ten miles an hour.[67]

The streetcar was a boon to life in the city, making it possible to expand city boundaries, develop new neighborhoods, even a suburb, and absorb increasing numbers of people. Parks were added to the landscape. According to local historian James W. Bell, the first true park in Little Rock, Deuell's Park, opened in 1877 on Louisiana between 17th and 18th streets, only a block from the end of the newly opened streetcar line. It was owned and operated by the German Oscar Mueller and offered healthy "games and amusements" without "the annoyance of wood ticks." Streetcar companies also developed parks as destinations to attract their patrons. These offered more elaborate amusements such as balloon ascensions, roller skating, roller coaster rides, pavilions for dancing, and refreshments. West End Park, one of the largest, located on the present site of Little Rock Central High School, also had a bicycle track and a baseball field. City Park, Little Rock's first public park, opened in 1893 after several leading citizens arranged for the federal government to swap its Arsenal property for acreage on top of Big Rock where a new military post was built and named Fort Logan H. Roots. City Park continues to serve the public, having been renamed in 1942 for General Douglas MacArthur, who was born in the Arsenal's Tower Building.[68]

The streetcar suburb of Pulaski Heights is the legacy of Henry F. Auten, one of the "hardy group" of businessmen whom archivist, historian, and former *Review* editor, Tom W. Dillard described as "Northern expatriates arrived to seek their fortunes in post-Reconstruction Arkansas." Auten had the vision to see the development potential of the land west of Little Rock known as Pulaski Heights. He organized the Pulaski Heights Land Company in 1897 and bought 1300 acres of Heights property. He then secured the franchise to extend the streetcar line out Third Street to his scenic property, which he marketed as "300 feet above the city, with beautiful oak and pine shade, pure air, and constant summer breezes" and only "nine minutes from Main Street."[69] Cheryl Griffith Nichols writes in detail about Little Rock's first suburban neighborhood in "The Development of Pulaski Heights," in this collection.

The growth and modernization that had taken place during the closing decades of the nineteenth century had changed the way people lived, broadening the range of available opportunities and, for many, making the daily routine easier and more varied. This was true especially for middle and upper class white women who, like others across the nation, began to move beyond their domestic sphere. New opportunities and responsibilities included church and Sunday school work, social and literary club activities, and involvement in the local Woman's Christian Temperance Union and other social causes to improve the lives of women and children. Little Rock's Aesthetic Club, which in 1883 was the first of its kind in the city as well as in the state and among the first "west of the Mississippi," organized "to present programs of a literary, artistic, musical and timely trend," and to "assist in educational uplift, and to bring its members together for social enjoyment."[70] A few of the most independent and active among these "new," socially conscious women saw that to achieve many of their desired reforms would require legislation, so they joined with Clara McDiarmid and formed the Little Rock Suffrage Association to work for equal voting rights for women.

By the end of the nineteenth century Little Rock's more open and diverse urban climate also allowed a few women to step even further from their traditional roles to manage their own property, seek professional education in law or medicine, and even attempt a new career. Several Little Rock women were notable examples of those who began to make a place for women in the public arena. Dr. Ida Jo Brooks left a teaching career and her role as the first female president of the Arkansas Teachers' Association to go to medical school, after which she set up a medical practice specializing in psychiatry and went on to achieve several other "firsts" for women. As a widow, Bernie Babcock supported herself and her five children with a career as a writer, earning acclaim for her work as the editor of *The Sketch Book*, described as "the most beautiful magazine in the South." She also wrote numerous articles and books, the most successful of which was *The Soul of Ann Rutledge*, the first of a series of novels on

Abraham Lincoln. As a last example, the Reverend Athalia Johnson Irwin became the first ordained woman minister in Arkansas when she was called in 1904 to serve the small Universalist church in Little Rock. Her socially progressive sermons, excerpted in the Little Rock newspapers along with those from the larger mainstream churches, earned recognition and respect for herself and her liberal church in the religiously conservative city.[71]

PERSEVERANCE AGAINST THE FORCES OF SEGREGATION

As women's horizons and opportunities began to expand at the close of the nineteenth century, the opposite was true for African Americans in Arkansas, who experienced a decline in their freedoms and a restriction of their civil rights. Race relations in Arkansas as a whole began to deteriorate during the early1890s when the General Assembly passed segregation and disfranchisement measures that proved very effective in keeping black citizens away from the polls and out of the way. Within the urban atmosphere of Little Rock, however, with its diverse population, its varied economic opportunities, and its improving educational facilities, race relations, at least on the surface, were more accommodating and cordial. There was a growing black middle class, even an upper class, which was educated, sophisticated, and lived comfortably, often in racially mixed neighborhoods. From this group came the teachers and educators, the ministers, lawyers, physicians, and entrepreneurs who made up the elite of the African-American community and were able to maintain a working relationship with the white establishment.

Like middle class white women across the nation, many black women in Little Rock joined the club movement, forming literary groups and service organizations such as the Lotus Club, the Bay View Reading Club, and the Frances Harper Charity Club. These women, many of whom were teachers, such as Charlotte Stephens, mentioned earlier, and Carrie Still Shepperson, an English teacher and mother of internationally known composer William Grant Still, were responsible for the cultural activities of the black community and its musical, artistic, and dramatic presentations. Teacher and businesswoman, Josephine Pankey, whose name was given to a community on Highway 10 west of Little Rock, is another notable example. She succeeded in starting a school called "Riverside" in an isolated black community at the eastern edge of Pulaski Heights and through her real estate business was able to help many of her fellow African Americans to own their own property.[72] These examples represent all those African-American women in Little Rock who strived to prepare the next generation for participation in what they hoped would be a larger more open society. In Arkansas in general, Little Rock was something of a mecca in educa-tion for black students during this era, with a good high school at Gibbs, under the direction of Principal I. J. Gillam, and no fewer than three black colleges, Philander Smith, the oldest, Arkansas Baptist College, and Shorter College, on the north side of the river.

While women provided leadership in the educational and cultural world, men were often making their marks as entrepreneurs and professionals in the black community. One of the most prominent was Mifflin W. Gibbs, a businessman, lawyer, politician, and the first elected black municipal judge in America, for whom Little Rock's Gibbs School was named. Another notable leader of the early twentieth century was Scipio A. Jones, who like Gibbs was an attorney. He was also a political activist in the Republican Party and a key player in winning the legal appeal and eventual release of twelve black sharecroppers denied a fair trail and convicted of murder after the Elaine race riots in east Arkansas. A North Little Rock school was later named in his honor. A third outstanding leader representative of this period was John E. Bush, who began as an educator and was one of the most vigorous black leaders in the Republican Party, fighting for black rights even as the party became increasingly segregated and racist. Bush was also a successful businessman and one of the founders of the Mosaic Templars of America, an organization set up in 1882 to benefit the black com-munity as an insurance company, a building and loan association, and operator of a hospital. By 1918 there were chapters in twenty-six states and elsewhere in Central and South America.[73]

The Mosaic Templars national headquarters building in Little Rock at the cor-ner of Ninth and Broadway was an anchor of the black community, housing not only the Mosaic Templars, but also black-owned businesses and professional offices, as well as an auditorium used for entertainment, political gatherings, and high school graduations. The dedication of this building in 1913 was the occa-sion for the last of three visits to Little Rock by Booker T. Washington, the unof-ficial leader of the South's black middle class, who saw the Mosaic Templars and its imposing building as a monument to what blacks could achieve. In August 1911, just three months after the very successful celebration of the national United Confederate Veterans Reunion that brought over one hundred thousand visitors to Little Rock, "including some 12,000 veterans of the 'Lost Cause,'" (see Michael D. Polston's "Little Rock Did Herself Proud: A History of the 1911 United Confederate Veterans Reunion") Little Rock Mayor Charles E. Taylor welcomed 3000 delegates from Mosaic Templars chapters across the nation to the capital city. The next week two thousand convention delegates of the National Negro Business League were in town and, along with two hundred of

Little Rock's white civic leaders and businessmen, heard Washington speak at the Kempner Theater where he shared the podium with Governor George W. Donaghey.

The good relations displayed on these occasions were praised by both black and white leaders and gave the appearance of racial harmony. However, despite this surface equanimity, the forces of segregation were becoming more entrenched. Protests against the "separate coach laws" enacted in the 1890s and the 1903 streetcar boycott in Little Rock had been ineffective in stemming the tide of racial discrimination that was spreading into every aspect of life. As the twentieth century progressed, West Ninth Street with its numerous black-owned shopkeepers and businessmen came to be called the "Line" and served as the boundary between two increasingly separate societies. Peggy Harris describes the continued leadership of black women in a segregated society in "'We Would Be Building': The Beginning of the Phyllis Wheatley YWCA in Little Rock,'" in this volume.[74]

The period between 1880 and 1900 was the high-water mark for African Americans in Pulaski County in terms of their percentage of the total county population, which stayed around 46 percent of inhabitants. During the next two decades, their strength relative to whites sharply decreased, so that by 1920 only 33 percent of the county's population was black. This proportional decline would slowly continue through most of the twentieth century. Whether this trend was caused by growing urbanization in the county, fewer job opportunities for working class blacks, the increasing tension brought about by segregation, or migration to the North, cannot be said. However, at least during the early years of the new century, the divisions between black and white societies, as perceived by the prospering middle classes, were not yet as apparent as they would be later

A NEW CENTURY

The parade, boat races, and fireworks that celebrated the opening of the Free Bridge in 1897, the first non-railroad bridge across the Arkansas River, expressed the spirit of optimism with which Pulaski County citizens on both sides of the river viewed the promise of the new twentieth century about to begin.[75] The county's overall population continued to grow and become more urban, so that by the 1920 census Pulaski County numbered 109,464 persons, of which 72 percent lived in the cities of Little Rock and North Little Rock. Grander and taller public and private buildings were added to the cityscape. A host of manufactured goods filled the stores, and the first automobiles appeared on city streets. It was a new century and a new age.

In the capital city it was believed that whatever problems had accompanied the city's rapid growth and expansion–an infrastructure that had not kept pace, ill-equipped fire and police departments, public health concerns, a lack of recreation areas and green space, and an unsavory reputation as a "wide-open town"–all could be fixed. In this spirit, Little Rock citizens followed the lead of urban voters across the nation in this era and in 1911 ousted the so-called conservative "old guard" at City Hall, which was hampering the city's progress and, some thought, fostering corruption. In its place the voters installed a new, reform administration under the self-styled "progressive" mayor, Charles E. Taylor, who promised to make Little Rock "a bigger, better, cleaner and more progressive city." During Taylor's four terms as mayor of Little Rock (1911-1919), he reformed the way city government operated, expanded the scope of municipal responsibilities, and instituted many needed services and improvements in the public interest that changed Little Rock from a nineteenth-century river town into a twentieth-century modern municipality.

One of the first items on Taylor's and the city council's agenda was the inadequacy of the fire department's horse-drawn wagons and low-pressure pumping "engines," which had been ineffective in fighting two devastating fires that had engulfed what one newspaper labeled the "Hoodoo Block" between Sixth and Seventh on Main in 1911. The fire chief warned that without modern, motorized equipment that could reach beyond the second story of Little Rock's increasingly taller buildings, Little Rock could easily be the victim of a fire similar to the one that had destroyed much of San Francisco after its earthquake in 1906. Five- and six-story buildings were becoming common in the downtown area, and there were two buildings that could qualify as "skyscrapers," the ten-story Southern Trust Building at Second and Center, and the eleven-story State Bank Building (later known as the Boyle Building) at Main and Capitol. Recognizing the danger, the mayor and the council took action and, despite the large indebtedness the city incurred, purchased an aerial truck with a 75-foot extension ladder as well as several other motorized trucks and pumps, making Little Rock, according to one equipment manufacturer, "the first completely motorized fire department in the South." With the council's enactment of the city's first comprehensive building, electrical, and plumbing codes, plus the construction of a new Central Fire Station and several new fire stations that extended fire protection into the residential neighborhoods, Little Rock had significantly improved its fire safety, one of its most fundamental responsibilities, and invested in its own future growth and development.

In this same vein, the city went on to add many other "modern" improvements that increased the city's livability: many more miles of paved streets and sewer lines; more water mains and fire hydrants; more electric street lights downtown that burned all night, every night, regardless of how brightly the moon was shining; and a traffic ordinance that imposed some basic rules of the road for the increasing number of automobiles that often constituted a hazard on city streets. Taylor also instigated the construction of the West Third Street Viaduct into Pulaski Heights, a concrete overpass replacing the original rickety wooden bridge that had spanned the railroad tracks northwest of the State Capitol and made streetcar access possible for the city's first suburb. Safe and convenient transportation only added to the growth and popularity of Pulaski Heights, which was annexed to Little Rock in 1916 with easy majorities in both areas. Taylor's vision of a bigger and better Little Rock was being fulfilled.

The city's rapid growth, however, had also produced various threats to the public health that demanded attention. In particular, in the summer of 1911 the city confronted the possibility of an epidemic of typhoid, which in those days was a major killer. An inspector from the U. S. Surgeon General's office found numerous unsanitary conditions associated with the city's water, food supplies, and waste disposal. The city government responded by establishing a Health Department that was authorized to regulate and inspect dairies, slaughterhouses, and other food supply services and to regularly test drinking water. It also expanded the sewer system and began city-wide garbage collection and incineration, which as the mayor pointed out, was "far more sanitary than the former method of throwing this stuff into the river." This sanitation and public health program was a success; the number of typhoid deaths dropped to only seven in 1912, after having averaged thirty per year in the three previous years. The overall death rate from disease also dropped by nearly one-third in 1912 from the previous year and continued in following years to show a steady decline.

A third thrust of Taylor's administration was directed at the city's moral climate and its "wide-open-town" image. This undesirable reputation, stemming from the availability of gambling, prostitution, and alcohol, hindered the city's economic and cultural development. Pulaski was one of only nine Arkansas counties at the time where one could buy an alcoholic drink, and Little Rock's sixty-two saloons did a good business. Efforts at moral reform attracted many adherents nationwide in this period, especially from the middle classes. National prohibition efforts culminated in 1920 with the passage of the Eighteenth Amendment to the U.S. Constitution, but in Arkansas, prohibition had been achieved four years earlier on January 1, 1916. Before Arkansas prohibition took effect, Taylor and the police department clamped down on the rowdier saloons or "dives" and raided various gambling establishments, arresting "gamesters," confiscating wagon-loads of "gambling paraphernalia," and burning it at a public bonfire. Taylor's most conspicuous attempt at social reform was his suppression of prostitution and the closing of Little Rock's "red light district," which had comprised the area between Main and Rock streets extending from the Arkansas River to Third and contained nineteen known houses of prostitution. A twenty-six member Vice Commission studied the problem and recommended that the existing policy of toleration, which allowed the houses to stay in business if the "madam" paid periodic fines, be ended and that all houses of prostitution be closed on August 25, 1913. There are stories that on the designated day the women in question paraded colorfully out of town. Taylor and his supporters believed not only that their actions improved the city's moral climate, but also encouraged people to live more productive lives.

Another component of the Progressive vision of urban life was the addition of parks and green space that would improve mental and physical health and make the city wholesome and pleasant. With this in mind, community leaders hired a noted city planner, John Nolen, from Cambridge, Massachusetts, to develop a plan for Little Rock that included parks, playgrounds, parkways, shaded streets, and a civic center. A particular focus of the plan was development of the river front, which had been taken over by squatters and their shacks. Raising the money to implement Nolen's plan, however, proved impossible. Taylor recognized that the chief obstacle to financing this plan, as well as other improvements such as a civic auditorium and a badly needed city hospital, was the state's prohibition against cities issuing public improvement bonds. Despite Taylor's three statewide campaigns for a constitutional amendment to allow such funding, none was successful. As a result, it would be 1928 before Little Rock began city planning in earnest and 1983 before Riverfront Park would take shape along the river between Broadway and "the Little Rock."[76]

Just as municipal government was influenced by a strong mayor, county government, too, was dominated by its chief executive, the county judge. As Pulaski County's population grew, the constitutional stipulation that there must be a justice of the peace for every two hundred voters gradually enlarged the size of the quorum court to unwieldy proportions. By mid-twentieth century the number of quorum court members would reach into the hundreds. As a result, the administration of the county was largely in the hands of the county judge, who, with negligible legislative oversight, controlled expenditures on the county's roads, bridges, and public works projects and enjoyed considerable political power. Three judges of note in this period illustrate the transition that took place in county government as it grew and adapted from the post-Reconstruction era, characterized by conservative, patrician stewardship, to the rapidly changing economy and society of the twentieth century that demanded more politically astute, business-like leadership.

The first is Judge Wilbur F. Hill who grew up in Texas, served in the Confederate army under Albert Pike, and came to Little Rock in 1873 where he opened a law office. He served three terms as county judge (1884-1890) and was responsible for building the 1887 Pulaski County Courthouse, which was viewed as "a bright ornament" in his able administration. Judge William M. Kavanaugh, who was born in Alabama and grew up in Kentucky, came to Little Rock in 1886 where he became a very successful businessman, a proponent of the Southern Baseball League, and politically influential in local and state politics. He served two terms as county judge (1900-1904) and is best known for building what was then a county road that wound through the new development of Pulaski Heights and subsequently came to bear his name.

The third in this group was Joseph Asher, for whom Little Rock's Asher Avenue was named. Asher was born in Bohemia, located in what is now the Czech Republic, and immigrated to America with his father at the age of ten. Asher's background and approach exemplify the change from the older noblesse oblige mode of public service to the more professional, career-based style of governance. He came to Pulaski County in 1880 as a twenty-two-year-old school teacher and then joined the ranks of the county's civil servants, learning the ins and outs of county government before being elected county clerk and then county judge. During his four terms as county judge (1908-1916), Asher is noted for several progressive changes: improving road-building practices, purchasing the county prison farm, establishing a juvenile court system, and building the Classical Revival annex to the 1887 courthouse.

County government had expanded along with the rapidly growing population and by 1912 was spilling into every corner of the twenty-five-year-old courthouse. In response, the county constructed an annex building at the corner of Markham and Spring streets, adjoining the existing courthouse to the north. Designed by George Mann, the original architect for the State Capitol, it featured an impressive, central four-story rotunda with a stained-glass dome, marble walls and pillars, and twelve statues sculpted by Italian artists representing art, justice, agriculture, and machinery. Completed in 1914, the courthouse annex was a fitting contribution to the array of imposing public buildings in the capital city and expressed the county's confidence and maturity at the start of a new century.[77]

THE WORLD AT WAR AND THE DECLINE OF OPTIMISM

After war broke out in Europe in 1914, civic reform and modernization began to take a back seat to national concerns. As U. S. involvement grew closer, city and county leaders got caught up in the patriotic fervor of supporting the war effort. Little Rock's German National Bank changed its name, the German-language newspaper, *Arkansas Staats-Zeitung*, ceased publication, and anti-war sentiment was not tolerated. Activity at Fort Roots in North Little Rock immediately expanded as America entered the war in April 1917. With the news that new, larger army training camps were being planned to replace outdated posts such as Fort Roots, business and government leaders began an active campaign to secure one of the new cantonments for Pulaski County. They were successful, and by June 1917 plans were underway to build Camp Pike, named for the western explorer Zebulon Pike, on 13,000 acres near North Little Rock. By September 1917, recruits were arriving at the camp that was designed to accommodate around 50,000 troops at any one time.

One of the most notable incidents in Camp Pike's history was the outbreak of influenza in the fall of 1918, part of the worldwide and deadly "Spanish Flu" pandemic. The disease, which was particularly prone to hit crowded environments such as military bases, reportedly infected a thousand soldiers a day at Camp Pike when it first struck. The epidemic afflicted the general population as well, causing the State Board of Health to put the entire state under quarantine and forbid all public gatherings. It is estimated that in central Arkansas one in every four fell ill from the virus. With its military training role coming to an end shortly after the war was over in November 1918, Camp Pike served first as a demobilization center and later as a rehabilitation site for wounded soldiers. The camp then became a training ground for the Arkansas National Guard between the wars. It was renamed Camp Robinson in 1937 in honor of Arkansas Senator Joseph T. Robinson.[78]

The changes brought about by the Great War, as it was called, and the freedoms that accompanied a modernizing society proved unsettling for many, who found their optimism about the promise of the new century shattered. Some responded by taking a reactionary stance, reviving the Ku Klux Klan that had been dormant since Reconstruction:

> On February 11, 1922, at a secluded spot in Pulaski County, Arkansas, some three thousand men gathered around a fiery cross to witness the initiation of six hundred and fifty men into their order. Among them were state, county, and city officials, preachers, lawyers, doctors, merchants, laborers, etc. There were men who had barely reached their majority, and men whose hair was snowy-white. The roads were choked by the more than one-thousand automobiles that were used to transport the people to and from the ceremony.[79]

This version of the Klan differed in many ways from its predecessor during Reconstruction. It was white supremacist, but its enemies also included anyone and anything perceived as "foreign" including socialists and communists, Jews and Catholics, and violators of conventional public morality. Instead of secrecy and violence, its methods were primarily open and political. In 1922 the Pulaski County Klan successfully ran candidates for county judge, sheriff, and mayor of Little Rock, as well as other offices. By the election of 1924, however, dissension within the Klan ranks disrupted their electoral efforts, and they were never as successful again.[80]

Despite the regressive Klan activities, Pulaski County citizens generally tried to take advantage of the peace and hoped-for prosperity during the early years of the 1920s. Some enjoyed a large, new outdoor swimming pool and amusement park in Pulaski Heights' Forest Park. For others, baseball was a major pastime, with fans following such teams as the Little Rock Travelers, the Blue Devils, the City Sluggers, and the all-black Little Rock Quapaws. The first local radio station went on the air in 1926, and another modern marvel, the airplane, was the featured attraction at the 1926 National Balloon Elimination Race held on the World War I air depot fields east of Little Rock. Big crowds enjoyed not only the balloon race but also the airplane races, stunt flying, parachute jumps, and the exhibits of all kinds of aircraft, especially the "Cotton Dusting airplane." Many well known aviators were in town for the event, including Orville Wright himself.[81]

The potential of modern technologies and processes inspired some businessmen to risk investment in new business ventures. The Climber Motor Corporation, which manufactured automobiles in Little Rock from 1919 to 1924, producing two cars a day at its peak, is one example, as was Leonard Ottenheimer's company dealing in the production of women's wear that not only survived but grew into a successful manufacturing enterprise. Home construction boomed in Pulaski Heights in the 1920s, and in North Little Rock businessman Justin Matthews planned and developed the north shore's first suburb in Park Hill. By the 1930s Matthews was laying out plans for his Lakewood addition that would include the innovative feature of lakes and green space. Matthews hired Mexican artist Dionicio Rodriguez to create rustic concrete sculptures that were practically indistinguishable from natural wood to enhance the park areas included in his residential subdivisions. The "Old Mill" in Lakewood's Pugh Memorial Park is one of Rogriguez's masterpieces and was featured at the beginning of the 1939 film "Gone With the Wind." Commercial construction and infrastructure improvements also flourished at the beginning of the 1920s, with two new bridges to accommodate the increasing automobile traffic: the Broadway Bridge in 1922, and the Main Street Bridge replacing the old Free Bridge in 1924. The fourteen-story Donaghey Building, built in 1926 at Seventh and Main streets, was the state's and the county's tallest building for almost thirty-five years.[82]

In 1927 disaster struck in the form of the great flood that engulfed large areas of Arkansas and neighboring states. Inundation of low-lying lands in Arkansas along the Mississippi, Arkansas, and White rivers devastated the Delta areas of eastern Arkansas, as far west as Pulaski County, where at least one bottom-land plantation on a river loop near Palarm was virtually carried away. The higher ground of Little Rock and western Pulaski County was mostly spared the worst effects, but water overran much of downtown North Little Rock and caused enormous losses at such businesses as the Vestal and Son nurseries, the successful florist and plant mail order business that had been located along the river in nearby Baring Cross since 1893. The raging Arkansas River also caused the loss of the Baring Cross Bridge, the first to span the river over fifty years earlier. Despite the efforts of the Missouri Pacific railroad company to stabilize the bridge by parking a fully-laden coal train on it, the span was carried into the river at the height of the flood on April 21, 1927. The flood waters also threatened the steam-powered pumps that provided the area's drinking water supply from the river, and only a forty-eight-hour, Herculean effort of "state prisoners, county prisoners, free colored labor, free white labor together with the white-collar men working side by side" to strengthen and raise the levee surrounding the pumping station with sand-bags saved the day and prevented a "water famine" in Little Rock and North Little Rock.[83]

Shortly after this natural disaster, there came another horrific event in Little Rock, this time of man's own doing and, according to historians, "one of the worst incidents of racial violence ever to occur in Little Rock." Racial tensions had been inflamed by the accusation and arrest of a black man for the rape and murder of a twelve-year-old white girl, but police were able to protect the suspect from the vengeance intended by a white mob. The frustrated vigilantes then turned their fury on another black man, John Carter, who was thought to have assaulted two white women. Carter was hanged from a telephone pole and his body dragged through Little Rock before being set afire, after which the murderous mob rampaged through the black section of town. It was the first lynching in Little Rock in thirty-six years and the last, but the impact was devastating to the black community, especially the black business and professional class in the city who had always claimed good relations between the races. Their counterparts in the white community denounced the atrocity, calling it an aberration, but after a grand jury investigation brought no indictments black citizens were forced to confront the darkest realities of racial segregation and discrimination.[84]

In "Dr. J. M. Robinson, the Arkansas Negro Democratic Association and Black Politics in Little Rock, Arkansas, 1928-1952," John Kirk points out that following the racial violence in Little Rock a new organization of African Americans began to seek political voice through the Democratic Party from which black citizens had been excluded for decades. The earlier influence of blacks in the Republican Party had declined, and the state was under virtual one-party rule by the Democrats. Dr. John M. Robinson, a Little Rock physician and one of the founders in 1918 of the local chapter of the National Association for the Advancement of Colored People, was the leader in an effort to gain black participation in Democratic Party primaries by chipping away at the barriers that barred African Americans from voting. His organization, the Arkansas Negro Democratic Association, met with only limited success, but it was able to keep the effort alive until after World War II when greater strides were possible.

THE DEPRESSION YEARS: PRIVATE HARDSHIP, PUBLIC PROGRESS

The 1927 flood was followed by another blow from nature in the form of an extensive drought at the beginning of the 1930s that devastated Arkansas's agriculture-based economy and produced dust-bowl conditions farther west. This natural calamity coincided with the generalized economic collapse of the Great Depression that has come to be synonymous with the 1930s and resulted in bank and business failures, mortgage foreclosures, and lost jobs. Although statistics on unemployment and poverty are difficult to obtain for Pulaski County, the effect can indirectly be seen in the sharp decline in population growth. The county had steadily grown by a cumulative 118 percent from 1900 to 1930, but the increase was only 13 percent from 1930 to 1940. For the urban portion of the county, the decline in growth was even more marked, from 164 percent to less than 8 percent, and for the first time since the county's beginning, it became less urbanized.

The state had few resources to help its citizens in their distress, but after Franklin D. Roosevelt became president in 1933, the federal government began to step in with public works projects and relief for the unemployed that made a difference. The establishment of the Civil Conservation Corps (CCC) offered the state's young men between the ages of eighteen and twenty-five work on land restoration, park facilities, and forest conservation. The two hundred men who set up a CCC camp near the small, rural community of Jacksonville in 1935 worked on land improvement projects in the area and were a boon to the town's economy. CCC boys also made improvements to Little Rock's newest park, located on the southwest edge of the city on land given by John F. Boyle, constructing dams on Rock Creek and building roads and pavilions. Another work relief program administered by the Works Progress Administration (WPA) had an even more significant impact by putting thousands of men and women to work on numerous projects that left a lasting imprint on the county. In addition to the WPA Writers' Project that employed professional writers, artists, and historians, the Public Works Administration (PWA) and the WPA worked with city, county, and state officials in the construction of many needed civic improvements, as Lynda Langford describes in her article on projects in Pulaski County. A few of the most notable include: the construction for the University of Arkansas School of Medicine of a new building on McGowan Street, east of City (now MacArthur) Park, conveniently near City Hospital; additions to McRae Sanatorium that had opened in 1931 for black tuberculosis patients in Alexander; the first real improvements to Little Rock's sewer system since the 1880s; construction of Lamar Porter Field where Boys' Club baseball teams would play for years; improvements to the roads and grounds at Fair Park, now known as War Memorial Park, including the addition of permanent animal houses for the park's new Little Rock Zoo; construction of the Museum of Fine Arts, now known as the Arkansas Arts Center, and the long-awaited municipal auditorium at the corner of Markham and Broadway that was named for Senator Joseph T. Robinson, plus the restoration of several of the capital's historically significant but dilapidated and disreputable buildings into what became the Arkansas Territorial Restoration and is now the Historic Arkansas Museum.[85]

The WPA also played a role in two other notable permanent assets to Pulaski County in this period. In 1930 Little Rock bought an airfield from the U.S. government east of the city, which had been used for the 1926 balloon and air show and then for National Guard activities, and in June 1931 American Airways began the first scheduled commercial airline service. The WPA was responsible for construction of the first terminal building at the airport, which was named Adams Field in 1937, honoring George Geyer Adams, a city councilman and National Guard captain who was killed in an accident that year at the airport. Little Rock's publicly owned water system also was a beneficiary of the WPA, which provided a 1935 grant and loan that along with a bond sale allowed the city to purchase the water treatment facility from the Arkansaw [sic] Water Company and develop a new and better source for the city's water, relieving years of dependence on the Arkansas River. Construction was completed in 1938 on a dam on Alum Fork of the Saline River creating Lake Winona, on a new treatment plant at Ozark Point, and on a storage reservoir, all of which are still in use as part of the regional water system that serves most of Pulaski County.[86]

WORLD WAR II AND THE HOME FRONT – PROSPERITY RETURNS

For Pulaski County as for the rest of Arkansas, the end to the stagnation of the Depression began with the preparations for World War II. "Work relief" jobs began to be replaced with war jobs. In June 1941, the federal government approved the construction of two military supply plants for the county: the Maumelle Ordnance Works, to be located along the Arkansas River near the community of Marche, and the Arkansas Ordnance Works, a larger facility to make fuses and detonators near Jacksonville, which became more commonly known as the Jacksonville Ordnance Plant. With the opening of the ordnance plant, Jacksonville, which at the time was a village of only 400 persons, became a boom town. As its population swelled, the community struggled to meet the housing needs of its new residents and find space in its schoolrooms for their children. The plant eventually employed as many as 13,500 workers and became in many ways self-sufficient, with its own hospital, fire department, recreation facilities, beauty and barber shops, and other amenities. Despite the construction of dormitories and federally funded housing, most employees lived elsewhere in the county and commuted to their jobs. Shuttle trains and buses made several runs daily between Little Rock and Jacksonville, and highway traffic was so heavy that the road leading to Jacksonville was made one-way as needed to cope with the arriving and departing shift workers. One of the significant changes that the war brought to Pulaski County, as in the rest of the nation, was the dissolution of the cultural and social barriers that had kept women out of well-paid industrial work. A substantial majority of the Jacksonville workers were women, who in many cases were working for the first time away from the home or farm. The manufacturing plants in other parts of the country may have had the iconic "Rosie the Riveter," but she was matched in Arkansas by the female munitions makers.[87]

Another major economic boost for the county brought by the war was the reactivation and expansion of Camp Joseph T. Robinson, the former Camp Pike, as a military training base. Thousands of soldiers passed through the camp during the war, generating many needed support jobs in the county. Beginning in 1943, Camp Robinson also served as a prisoner of war camp, housing as many as 3000 German prisoners at any one time. The community supported both the soldiers and the ordnance workers through a recreational facility run first by the Little Rock City Recreation Council and later by the United Services Organization (USO), which had three facilities in Little Rock for white soldiers.

The USO's downtown center was located at Third and Main in Little Rock and sponsored a wide variety of activities and recreation choices.[88]

African Americans responded readily to the call to fight for freedom and democracy, but their first battle was against discrimination at home. At Camp Robinson, as at all military training facilities, black soldiers were segregated, having to sleep, eat, and socialize in separate quarters. Many black soldiers found their opportunities restricted to driving trucks in transportation units. A separate USO club for black servicemen and workers was established at the former Taborian Temple on Ninth Street in Little Rock, where the city's Phyllis Wheatley YWCA and other women's social groups helped organize dances and social events. Businesses and restaurants along Ninth Street, which the WPA Guide on Arkansas described as "Little Rock's Harlem," provided a welcoming atmosphere for black soldiers. The Dreamland Ballroom in Taborian Hall brought in musical shows and stars, and movie theaters, nightclubs, and billiards parlors offered other kinds of entertainment. Though Ninth Street provided a kind of haven for black soldiers from the frequent reminders of their inequality with white soldiers, even there order was in the hands of white military and civilian police. Racial violence intruded in 1942 when a policeman's rough treatment of a black soldier provoked reaction by a black sergeant, Thomas Foster, who was himself then shot and killed by a Little Rock police officer. Widespread protests spread within the black community, led by L.C. Bates, founder of the *Arkansas State Press*, a newspaper recently established in Little Rock. The shooter was not prosecuted, but the police department began hiring black police officers to patrol the area, though it refused to give them equal status with their white counterparts.[89]

Housing for the large numbers of military personnel and defense workers who moved to Pulaski County in the early years of the war was in short supply and prompted a variety of responses. Some large, older homes were divided into apartments. Several of Little Rock's first federal low-income housing units, which had been planned to replace Depression-era slum dwellings, were opened instead for use by new residents working in the war effort. The housing projects at Sunset Terrace and Highland Park provided 150 apartments for white families, and Tuxedo Court opened its 100 units to African-American families. Businessman Wiley Dan Cammack with the backing of the Federal Housing Authority built one hundred houses on property he owned just northwest of Little Rock's city limits, which he rented to military officers and their families. Unable to interest the city in annexing his development, Cammack incorporated the property, and the town of Cammack Village was born. Though the town has become completely surrounded by the City of Little Rock, it continues to administer its own city services, police and (volunteer) fire departments, community swimming pool, and park.[90]

Between the military production plants and the actual military base, the war effort constituted a substantial economic boost for the county. After the war, business leaders on both sides of the river began planning ways to attract new industries and employment opportunities to replace wartime jobs and continue the area's economic momentum. The seeds of social change that would move the county toward integration of African-Americans and women into the workforce and political world had been sown during the 1940s, but they would not bear significant fruit for another decade or more.

POST-WAR ECONOMIC DEVELOPMENT

At the end of the war, just as had happened at the end of the First World War, Camp Robinson served as a demobilization center and then was turned back to the Arkansas National Guard. Some of the adjacent federally owned land was declared surplus, and the city of North Little Rock bought nearly 600 acres for an airport and 870 acres for future development as a park, which was named for Dr. William M. Burns, a long-time civic leader who had served two terms as mayor in the 1920s. With a later addition of nearly 700 acres, Burns Park, which then comprised over 1,500 acres on the western side of the city, became one of the largest municipally owned parks in the country. This far-sighted move indicated North Little Rock's expansionist aspirations, as did its annexation of the communities of Levy, Park Hill, and Rose City in 1946 and the Lakewood development in 1951, which had been popular with home-buyers after the war. Between annexation and the influx of war-time workers, the 1940s were by far the period of greatest growth in North Little Rock's history, with the population more than doubling from 21,137 to 44,097 by 1950.[91]

North Little Rock's growth continued during the 1950s with its population increasing 32 percent to 58,032. The city's physical expansion, however, was blocked to the northwest by Camp Robinson and to the northeast by the incorporation of the city of Sherwood in 1948. Though significant westward growth could have come a decade later when the former Maumelle Ordnance Works property became available, a proposed industrial park in the area in the early 1960s never developed. Instead, businessman Jess P. Odom took the opportunity to develop a new concept in urban planning promoted by the U.S. Department of Urban Development by building a planned community, the federally-subsidized "New Town" of Maumelle, independent of North Little Rock. After 1960, North Little Rock's population growth virtually stopped, hovering around 60,000 for the remainder of the twentieth century. [92]

The most significant post-war economic development in northern Pulaski County was the establishment of a new, permanent military air base on the site of the closed Arkansas Ordnance Plant near Jacksonville. A cooperative effort by business leaders county-wide to raise funds and acquire the land, led by the Little Rock Chamber of Commerce, along with the political clout of Arkansas's congressional delegation secured this big economic plum for Pulaski County. In 1953, construction began on an air base that was to be part of the nation's military buildup during the Cold War struggle with the Soviet Union. Completed in 1955, the Little Rock Air Force Base quickly became one of the largest employers in the state and has had a substantial impact on the economic life of the county.[93]

On the south side of the river, post-war industrial development was promoted through a number of significant, long-term infrastructure improvements and additions. In 1946, Congress authorized plans for navigation improvements on the Arkansas River to facilitate commerce, control flooding, produce hydroelectric power, and provide recreation areas along the river. Though passage of the appropriations for the massive project that would be known as the McClellan-Kerr Navigation System was slow, construction finally began in earnest in 1963. By 1970 the 445-mile project was complete, enabling freight traffic to move up and down the Arkansas River year-round from the Mississippi River to Catoosa, Oklahoma, through a series of seventeen lock and dam facilities, including two (Murray and David D. Terry) within Pulaski County. In 1988 North Little Rock would build a hydroelectric plant at Murray Dam to supplement its energy needs.[94]

Recognizing the necessity of attracting new employers to provide jobs and hire returning soldiers, Little Rock business leaders began plans to develop a designated industrial area that could accommodate the transportation and energy needs of manufacturing plants. Due to their efforts, industry flourished on the south side of Little Rock in the early 1950s with the development of a large industrial park that became home to almost one hundred employers, including some major manufacturers. In 1959, hoping to take advantage of the anticipated shipping that would result from the McClellan-Kerr project, the city also authorized a port facility on the Arkansas River and an additional industrial park east of the airport. The airport itself, which had been under military control during the war, was restored to the city and regular air service was reinstated with three commercial carriers: American, Delta, and Braniff. In 1953, major improvements were made to the runways, with the first instrumented landing system coming a year later. The county's entertainment and sports scene also received a boost in the late 1940s with the construction of Barton Coliseum and War Memorial Stadium.[95]

By the mid 1950s, plans were also being made to relieve the automobile congestion that had accompanied post-war prosperity but was plaguing motorists as they commuted to work across the county's two bridges or tried to shop in Little Rock's downtown. Efforts to control the flow of traffic in downtown helped some, as did the opening of La Harpe Boulevard along the riverfront, connecting Little Rock's business district with Cantrell Road and the western suburbs. A four-lane highway (US 67/167) from North Little Rock to Jacksonville was constructed as part of the air base project. In 1956 the design of a modern, six-lane expressway bridge over the river was announced, which would prove to have the largest impact on traffic problems. The project was described in the newspaper at the time as having "elevated street crossings, sweeping access lanes, [and] curlicued traffic interchanges." Completed in 1961, this bridge was a piece in what ultimately became Interstate 30, part of the Interstate Highway System authorized by Congress in the mid-1950s. With the intersection of the state's two major expressways (Interstates 30 and 40) in Pulaski County, the importance of the county as the state's transportation hub and commercial center was ensured.[96]

In the immediate post-war years Little Rock's community leaders also supported the growth of another building block of a healthy economy, its educational institutions. Little Rock Junior College (LRJC), which had begun in the north wing of the brand-new Little Rock High School in 1927, experienced a boom in growth from returning veterans, who wanted to take advantage of the "GI Bill" to pay for their education. After averaging only about 250 students during the war years, enrollment at LRJC zoomed to over 800 for the fall semester of 1946, climbing to a record of 1350 students by 1951. The school quickly became overcrowded at its campus at 13th and State streets, and officials began looking for more room. The college's problems were solved when businessman Raymond Rebsamen stepped forward in 1947 to donate an 80-acre wooded tract located in what was then the southwest corner of the city at 33rd and Hayes streets. A building fund campaign was successful and, according to the college's historian Jim Lester, "not only produced the desired revenue but also created an atmosphere of common purpose between the community and the college that lasted for over 20 years." Construction of permanent buildings on the new campus was completed in 1949, and Jaycee, as it familiarly was called, continued to grow. In 1957 the junior college expanded its curriculum and became a four-year institution, renamed Little Rock University. Recognizing the significance of the institution, the city changed the name of Hayes Street to University Avenue in 1959. The area near the new campus had been sparsely populated before the arrival of the junior college, but within a few years Broadmoor, a 700-home residential development, and Town and County, the city's first shopping center, were built nearby. In 1969 Little Rock University merged with the state university system, becoming the University of Arkansas at Little Rock. [97]

The medical college of the University of Arkansas system also saw major growth and change after the war as it joined the city's trend of westward expansion. Founded by Little Rock physicians in 1879 as the Medical Department of Arkansas Industrial University, the school was housed in a series of increasingly functional buildings in downtown Little Rock—an old hotel, a three-story building at Second and Sherman, the Old State House after the new Capitol Building was completed in 1912, and in 1935 a new six-story building at Thirteenth and McGowan partially financed with Public Works Administration funds. In the late 1940s medical college officials began planning a new teaching hospital and educational building to be located away from downtown on Markham Street near the western edge of the city. Despite continued funding woes, ground was broken for construction of the facility designed by Edward Durrell Stone in late 1951 and was finally completed in 1957. With the addition of new colleges of pharmacy and nursing, the medical school was renamed the University of Arkansas for Medical Sciences, which better reflected its expanded mission. Thus, by the mid-1950s two important institutions of higher education were flourishing in Little Rock and in position to contribute to the vitality of Pulaski County for years to come.[98]

THE STRUGGLE FOR CIVIL RIGHTS

Along with breaking ground for new buildings, the medical college was also breaking ground for social change when its first African-American medical student, Edith Irby Jones, was admitted in 1948. Earlier in the year, the Board of Trustees at the University of Arkansas had altered its policy for the professional schools of law and medicine, admitting black students to study on campus instead of subsidizing their education out of state. The war years had heightened awareness of many aspects of racial discrimination that were rapidly becoming less tolerable and legally defensible. A series of U.S. Supreme Court decisions during the 1940s addressing voting rights and the actual inequities of the "separate but equal" philosophy of racial segregation began to force last-gasp attempts at parity for some still-segregated facilities and token integration for others. For example, in Little Rock the black community finally achieved two, long-sought recreational amenities when the city funded the development of Gillam Park in 1950 and the Dunbar Community Center in 1954. Other aspects of public life that slowly began to be integrated included the "Community Chest" charitable organization (1948), the public library (1951), the Pulaski County Medical

Society (1953), the city bus transit system (1956), and city employment.[99]

Attempts at parity were also made in the Little Rock public school system. In the mid-1940s salary discrepancies between black and white teachers had been reduced in response to a 1942 lawsuit, and by the 1950s per-pupil expenditures had been nearly equalized between the races. The school district also opened two new high schools: Hall High in 1957 in western Little Rock for white students and Horace Mann High in 1955 in the eastern part of the city for black students. Dunbar High School, which for twenty-five years had served as Arkansas's premier educational institution for black students, was converted to a junior high, and Little Rock High School, the architecturally acclaimed structure built in 1927 and located in a somewhat-integrated working class neighborhood, was renamed Central High and became the site where school integration was scheduled to begin. In 1955, the Little Rock School Board approved a gradual, phased-in integration plan presented by Superintendent Virgil Blossom in response to the 1954 Brown vs. Board of Education decision of the U.S. Supreme Court that had overturned the "separate but equal" concept for public schools. It provided for very limited enrollment of black students beginning in September 1957 at Central High School and the gradual expansion of the plan to additional schools at other grade levels over a seven-year period.[100]

The tragedy that subsequently unfolded at Central High during the 1957-1958 school year when mobs tried to prevent integration and Federal troops had to be ordered in to keep the peace and enforce the court's mandate is a long, sad story that can hardly be covered adequately in this account. There were many players in the drama, from the nine courageous black students under the guidance of Daisy Bates who first breached the doors at Central High, to Governor Orval E. Faubus and his politically motivated defiance, to the segregationist Capital Citizens' Council that fanned the flames, to the Women's Emergency Committee to Open Our Schools (WEC) that stepped in as a moderating force. The tragedy carried over to the next year, when all the Little Rock senior high schools were closed, and continued for many following years, as Little Rock's relatively moderate image of racial harmony suffered irreversible damage.[101]

The North Little Rock school district had also developed a gradual integration plan to begin with the high school in 1957, and there was an attempt by a few black students to enroll at the white high school that year, but the events at Central High brought a halt to progress north of the river. Desegregation in North Little Rock did not begin even in a limited way until the 1964-1965 school year. In Little Rock, however, the high schools re-opened in 1959 and desegregation proceeded, though very slowly. By the 1966-1967 school year only

16.7 percent of black students attended school with white students in Little Rock, and many schools were still completely segregated. Spurred by federal court orders, the Little Rock School District (LRSD) tried one student assignment plan after another in the 1970s and 1980s to satisfy the courts as well as its patrons, using a mixture of neighborhood schools, cross-town busing, county-wide "magnet" schools designed to attract white students into the district's schools, and other schemes to achieve an acceptable racial balance. During these years the Little Rock school population became increasingly African-American, reaching 70 percent in 1982. In an effort to counter this trend, the LRSD drew the schools in North Little Rock and Pulaski County into the fray by a lawsuit to consolidate the county's three districts. Though the consolidation decision was not upheld by the Eighth Circuit Court, the case resulted in the merger of fourteen county schools into the Little Rock District in 1987 to ameliorate the effect of "white flight" into the county. The protracted and controversial struggle to resolve all the issues involved in the integration of the public schools and gain compliance with the federal courts would continue for at least two more decades, hindering the county's subsequent development..[102]

Unlike some areas of the country that saw violent protests over other civil rights issues in the 1960s, the actions and protests against discriminatory practices in public services and commercial facilities in Little Rock were relatively mild, though effective. Still reeling from the 1957 crisis, the city's leaders responded to a lunch counter sit-in and protest march by black students in 1962 by opening discussion with the protesters and urging merchants and service managers to end racial restrictions. By the end of 1963, most businesses serving the public, such as restaurants, hotels, and movie theaters, as well as Robinson Auditorium and the city's parks and museums had become integrated with minimal controversy.[103]

THE CHALLENGES OF THE 1960S

In addition to civil rights issues, the county faced many other challenges in the 1960s, many related to growth. During the 1950s, Little Rock's population had only grown by 5 percent, the smallest rate of growth in its history, while the county as a whole had grown by 24 percent, with North Little Rock increasing by 32 percent and Jacksonville by a phenomenal 486 percent. In the 1960s, Little Rock bounced back, however, with growth outpacing the county. In 1955 after the cooperative success in securing the Little Rock Air Force Base, the mayors of the three municipalities along with County Judge Arch Campbell created the Metropolitan Area Planning Commission, which in 1970 became known as Metroplan, to continue to deal jointly with county-wide development issues. Its function was to address the metropolitan area's future needs for industrial growth, transportation improvements, and recreational opportunities, as well as create a Cold War era civil defense plan in case of an attack by the Soviet Union.[104]

Little Rock voters also sought more professional leadership in dealing with the various issues confronting the city and in 1957 approved the change from a mayor-council form of government to one directed by a city manager. Concern was mounting that the city's increasing expansion to the west was causing the transfer of retail commerce from Main Street and downtown to shopping centers, which were located nearer residential neighborhoods and provided easy access and parking. The success of the Park Plaza Shopping Center, which opened in 1960 at Markham and University, was symbolic of what was to come and prompted repeated attempts by investors to reinvent and revitalize the downtown area. Westward growth also meant the decline of housing quality in the central city. Deterioration of inner cities was a national problem, and federal funds were available to cities for "urban renewal" projects that involved razing slum areas and building modern and safe apartments and housing units. Little Rock's Dunbar Urban Renewal Project in 1961 was one of the first in the nation and the start of eleven such projects in the city. One assessment reports that over 5,500 families in Little Rock were moved to improved housing during the urban renewal program's fifteen-year life, though critics point out that many poor families were uprooted when neighborhoods were destroyed and rebuilt with houses they could no longer afford or with commercial buildings. North Little Rock faced similar challenges. According to a North Little Rock history, the federal government supplied funding for at least eight urban renewal projects in that city as well, and the North Little Rock downtown area also suffered from the development of outlying shopping centers, especially with the opening of McCain Mall in the early 1970s.[105]

As Little Rock continued to develop toward the west, other controversial issues arose, such as where and how to build an east-west freeway to ease crosstown traffic difficulties, the cost of expanding city services, and all the related problems that go with urban sprawl. Neglect and decay in the oldest sections of the city prompted concerned citizens to organize the Quapaw Quarter Association, which incorporated in 1968 to increase awareness of the buildings and houses that represented Little Rock's heritage and to work for the preservation of historic neighborhoods. The entire county began to experience some of the same problems, many of which would continue to present challenges to county and city leaders until the present day.

CONCLUSION

In many ways, the period from WWII through the 1960s was revolutionary for Pulaski County. The old social order of racial segregation was toppled, and the foundations were laid for a more egalitarian society with new opportunities opening not only for blacks, but for women as well. Progress toward an industrialized economy was being realized, and key institutions and infrastructure were falling into place, including the major interstate highways, the industrial parks, and transportation and communication systems. The county's major municipalities were now established, and growth patterns were clear. For Pulaski County the fundamentals of modern society had been set, and the ebb and flow of social and economic progress continued.

The year 1968 marked the sesquicentennial of Pulaski County's political formation and thus offers an appropriate point to conclude this historical survey. Over the course of its first 150 years, Pulaski County has been transformed from a sparsely settled wilderness into a predominantly urban metropolis with the benefits and complexities of modern society. With the advantages of its geography and early selection as the location of the future state's capital, Pulaski County and its people have adapted to the myriad changes brought by war and economic disasters, by a growing and diverse population, by social and racial upheavals, by the advances of science and technology, and by new forms of transportation from steamboats and railroads to highway systems and airplanes. On the whole, the county's enterprising citizens and public-spirited leaders have fulfilled Pulaski County's promise and responsibility as the cultural, economic, and political center of Arkansas.

NOTES

[1] "Casimir Pulaski, 1747-1779, A Short Biography," brochure (Chicago: Polish Museum of America).

[2] S. Charles Bolton, *Arkansas 1800-1860, Remote and Restless*, (Fayetteville, Ark.: University of Arkansas Press, 1998), 10-15, 24-27. Gerald T. Hanson and Carl H. Moneyhon, *Historical Atlas of Arkansas* (Norman, Okla.: University of Oklahoma Press, 1989), 26.

[3] D.Y. Thomas, *Arkansas and Its People*, 3 vols. (New York: The American Historical Society, 1930) 2:764-765. Russell P. Baker, "A History of Pulaski County Townships," *Pulaski County Historical Review* [PCHR] 31:3 (Fall 1983), 42-44.

[4] "Some Other Early Pulaski County Records," PCHR 6:3 (Sept. 1958), 42-45. "Officers of Pulaski County, 1818-1958," PCHR 15:1 (March 1967), 11. Dallas T. Herndon, *Centennial History of Arkansas*, 3 vols. (S. J. Clarke Publishing Company, 1922), 1:797.

[5] Russell P. Baker, "A History of Pulaski County Townships," PCHR 31:3 (Fall 1983), 23-48.

[6] Fred O. Henker, M.D., "A Geologic History of Pulaski County," PCHR 49:3 (Fall 2001), 62.

[7] Martha Ann Rolingson, "Toltec Mounds," pamphlet (Fayetteville: Arkansas Archeological Survey).

[8] Samuel D. Dickinson, "Up the Arkansas by Pirogue," PCHR 37:1 (Spring 1989), 2. Hanson and Moneyhon, *Historical Atlas*, 21. Michael B. Dougan, *Arkansas Odyssey* (Little Rock: Rose Publishing Co., 1993), 17-22.

[9] Dickinson, "Up the Arkansas by Pirogue," 3-13.

[10] Others have thought the word came from the French "metre" or meter, referring to the bayou's depth, or "mi-terre" for minor land, referring to its path lying on what the Quapaw considered less significant land, or "mi-terre" meaning mid or halfway, referring to the bayou's location between the Mississippi and Arkansas rivers. Ernie Deane, *Arkansas Place Names*, (Branson, Mo.: The Ozarks Mountaineer, 1986), 92, 112. J. H. Atkinson, "An Excursion To Natural Steps," PCHR 8:3 (Sept. 1960), 40. Dickinson, "Up the Arkansas by Pirogue," 9. Julia G. Besancon Alford, "Bayou Meto Township, Pulaski County's Northern Panhandle, 1818-1910," PCHR 39:1 (Spring 1991), 2.

[11] Dougan, *Arkansas Odyssey*, 26-29. Hanson and Moneyhon, *Historical Atlas of Arkansas*, 14. Bolton, *Arkansas 1800-1860, Remote and Restless*, 67.

[12] Ellis Doyle Herron, "The Quapaw," PCHR 11:1 (March 1963), 8,13. S. D. Dickinson, "The Quapaw Journey to Red River," PCHR 34:1 (Spring 1986), 14.

[13] Margaret Smith Ross, "Little Rock's Old Town," PCHR 37 (Fall 1989), 61 and Ross, "Squatters Rights: Some Pulaski County Settlers Prior to 1814," PCHR 47 (Fall 1999), 56-65.

[14] Margaret Smith Ross, "Squatters Rights Part II, Crystal Hill, Maumelle, Palarm, Settlers Prior to 1814," PCHR 4 (Sept. 1956), 33-50.

[15] Margaret Smith Ross, "Squatters Rights, Part III: The Cadron Settlement Prior to 1814," PCHR 4 (Dec. 1956), 51-65. Ernie Deane, *Arkansas Place Names*, p.138.

[16] Ross, "Little Rock's Old Town," 61. Ross, "Squatters Rights, Some Pulaski County Settlers," 61-65.

[17] Dallas T. Herndon, *Why Little Rock Was Born*, (Little Rock: Central Printing Co., 1933), 3. Alonzo D. Camp, "Ferries Over the Arkansas," PCHR 29:3 (Fall 1981), 52-53.

[18] Ross, "Little Rock's Old Town," 62. Bolton, *Remote and Restless*, 36-38. Dougan, Arkansas Odyssey, 67.

[19] Robert Johnston, "The Historic Pulaski County Courthouse," PCHR 24 (March 1976),1-3.

[20] Margaret Smith Ross, "The Cunninghams: Little Rock's First Family," PCHR 32 (Summer 1983), 29-33.

[21] Margaret Smith Ross, "The Watkins-Stevenson Family, Pulaski County Pioneers," PCHR 2 (March 1954), 5-16.

[22] Margaret Smith Ross, *Arkansas Gazette, The Early Years 1819-1866* (Little Rock, Ark.: Arkansas Gazette Foundation, 1969), 43.

[23] Margaret Smith Ross, "Jesse Brown, Pulaski County Pioneer," PCHR 2 (December 1954), 5-12.

[24] Ross, "The Watkins-Stevenson Family, 8. Mary Janie Woodruff, "Little Rock's First Church," PCHR 40 (Winter1992), 81-86.

[25] William B. Worthen, "Louise Loughborough and Her Campaign for 'Courage and Fineness'," PCHR 40 (Summer 1992), 26-27. F. Hampton Roy and Charles Witsell, Jr. with Cheryl Griffith Nichols, *How We Lived: Little Rock As An American City*, (Little Rock, Ark.: August House, 1984), 54.

[26] Margaret S. Ross, "Young Hiram Whittington Arrives In Little Rock and Writes to His Family Back in Boston," PCHR 17:3 (Sept. 1969), 45-48.

[27] Camp, "Ferries Over the Arkansas," 52-60. See also Carolyn Yancey Kent, "Builders and Keepers of the Bayou Meto Bridge," PCHR 51:3 (Fall 2003)58-69.

[28] Margaret Smith Ross, "The McHenry Family, Pulaski County Pioneers," PCHR 3:1 (March 1955), 3-9. See also Nancy Newell, "The McHenrys: A Frontier Family in Early Arkansas," PCHR 47:2 (Summer 1999), 22-37.

[29] For a good example of one family who settled near Hensley, see Hilda Hicks Adams, "The Campbells Came to Arkansas, Hurrah! Hurrah!" PCHR 35:3 (Fall 1987), 50-59. German immigrants settled in the 1830s in the Primrose Community, see Jefferson, M. Dorough, "George Daniel Peil and Early German Immigrants in Pulaski County," PCHR 31:3 (Fall 1983), 55-57.

[30] Jonathan J. Wolfe, "The Peopling of Pulaski, Pulaski County Population Sources and Composition, 1830-1860," PCHR 21:3 (Sept. 1973), 51-62. Bolton, *Remote and Restless*, 15-21.

[31] James E. Youngdahl, "Steamboats on the Arkansas," PCHR 11:3 (Sept. 1963), 35-39. Ross, "Little Rock's Old Town", 63-64. Worthen, "Louise Loughborough and Her Campaign," 27.

[32] Carolyn Earle Billingsley, "Charles Anthony Caldwell: Pioneer on the Urban Frontier," PCHR 42:4 (Winter 1994), 91-99.

[33] C. Allan Brown, "The Legacy of the 'City of Roses' " PCHR 31 (Summer 1983), 22-28. Dan Durning, "Those Enterprising Georges: Early German Settlers in Little Rock," PCHR 23:2 (June 1975), 21-37.

[34] Ellen Harrell Cantrell, "Little Rock in 1849," PCHR 2:3 (Sept. 1954), 7-9.

[35] Wolfe, "Peopling of Pulaski," 53. "Slaveowners and Slaves in Pulaski County, Arkansas, in 1861," PCHR 8:2 (June 1960), 22-28. Margaret S. Ross, "Nathan Warren, Free Negro Confectioner," PCHR 3:1 (March 1955), 10-11. See also Margaret S. Ross, "Nathan Warren, A Free Negro of the Old South," *Arkansas Historical Quarterly*, 15 (Spring 1956), 53-61.

[36] Carl Moneyhon, "1861: 'The Die Is Cast,' " in Mark K. Christ, ed., *Rugged and Sublime, The Civil War in Arkansas* (Fayetteville, Ark.: University of Arkansas Press, 1994),1-6; Dougan, *Arkansas Odyssey*, 632. James R. Eison, "The Arsenal in Little Rock," PCHR 16:2 (June 1968), 19-20. "Seizure of the U. S. Arsenal, February, 1861," PCHR 5:1 (March 1957), 1- 15.

[37] Dougan, *Arkansas Odyssey*, 197. William W. O'Donnell, "Pulaski County in the Civil War," PCHR 35:4 (Winter 1987), 77-79. Martha Bridges, "The McAlmont Family of Little Rock Views the Civil War," PCHR 26:3 (Sept. 1978), 46-47.

[38] Thomas A. DeBlack, "1863: 'We Must Stand or Fall Alone,'" in Mark K. Christ, ed., *Rugged and Sublime, The Civil War in Arkansas* (Fayetteville, Ark.: University of Arkansas Press, 1994), 59-96. Ira Don Richards, *Story of a Rivertown, Little Rock in the Nineteenth Century* (Benton, Ark.: Ira Don Richards, 1969), 70.

[39] "Two Civil War Letters: Little Rock in 1863," PCHR 9:2 (June 1961): 17-21.

[40] O'Donnell, "Pulaski County in the Civil War," 80. DeBlack, "1863: 'We Must Stand or Fall Alone,'" 92-94. Richards, Story of a Rivertown, 73-75.

[41] Nancy Newell, "The Trial and Execution of David O. Dodd," PCHR 40:3 (Fall 1992): 50-62. Charles G. Williams, "A List of Confederate Citizen Prisoners Held at the U.S. Military Prison at Little Rock, Arkansas," PCHR 36:4 (Winter 1988), 82, 84. Dougan, *Arkansas Odyssey*, 541, 561. James Reed Eison, "A Radiance That Will Illuminate the Name," PCHR 38:1 (Spring 1990), 16-21. Sybil F. Crawford, *Jubilee, The First 150 Years of Mount Holly Cemetery*, (Little Rock, Ark.: Mount Holly Cemetery Assoc., 1993), 95.

[42] Richards, *Story of a Rivertown*, 90- 91.

[43] Richards, *Story of a Rivertown*, 81.

[44] Richards, *Story of a Rivertown*, 82-89.

[45] J. H. Atkinson, "An Exciting Campaign for Governor in 1872," PCHR 15:3 (Sept. 1967), 35-42.

[46] J. H. Atkinson, "Two Governors for Thirty Days," PCHR 15:3 (Sept. 1967), 43-48.

[47] Richards, *Story of a Rivertown*, 89-90.

[48] Fred O. Henker, "Natural Steps, Arkansas," PCHR 47:1 (Spring 1999), 15.

[49] Dougan, *Arkansas Odyssey*, 259-263.

[50] Tom W. Dillard, "Isaac Gillam: Black Pulaski Countian," PCHR 24:1 (March 1976), 6-11.

[51] Richards, *Story of a Rivertown*, 83, 86-87. Jim Lynch, "Governmental History of Pulaski County," PCHR 22:1 (March 1974), 15. Margaret S. Ross, "Little Rock's Street Names," PCHR 1:2 (Sept. 1953), 14. Roy, Witsell, and Nichols, *How We Lived*, 137.

[52] Selma Plowman Hobby, "The Little Rock Public Schools During Reconstruction, 1865-1874," PCHR 15:2 (June 1967), 17-27.

53 Fon Louise Gordon, "Black Women in Arkansas," PCHR 35:2 (Summer 1987), 26-28.

54 Weaver Bruce Cook, "Emperor Without an Empire: The Story of Roswell Beebe and the Cairo and Fulton Railroad," PCHR 33:3 (Fall 1985), 50-62. Robert L. Gatewood, "Asa Peter Robinson, Builder of a Railroad and a Town," PCHR 28:4 (Winter 1980), 2-18.

55 A. Hall Allen, "The Baring Brothers and Their Famous Bridge," PCHR 30:3 (Fall 1982), 54-58.

56 John Cook, "Reminiscences of Argenta," PCHR 33:4 (Winter 1985), 82-86. Helen D. Best, "North Little Rock Progressivism, Parts I and II," PCHR 21:4 (Dec. 1973), 87-91 and 22:1 (March 1974), 1-12. Lynch, "Governmental History of Pulaski County," 15-16. Walter M. Adams, *North Little Rock, A Unique City* (Little Rock, Ark.: August House, 1985), 93-139.

57 Herndon, "Pulaski County," in *Centennial History*, 1:798. *Weaver* Bruce Cook, "Emperor Without an Empire," PCHR 33:3 (Fall 1985), 61. See Sarah C. Hudson, "Little Rock's Leadership: The First State Board of Health," PCHR 33:2 (Summer 1985), 32.

58 Byrd Gibbens, "Some Men of Sweet Home," PCHR 47 (Fall 1999):46.

59 Christopher A. Dorer, "Little Italy: A Historical and Sociological Survey," PCHR 51:2 (Summer 2003), 43-54. See also Sybil Smith, "Notes on the Italian Settlers of Pulaski County," PCHR 38:3 (Fall 1990), 51-57.

60 Marguerite Keller Henry, "Some Early German-Speaking Settlers in Pulaski County," PCHR 37:4 (Winter 1989),70-81. Dan Durning, "Attracting the German Immigrant, A German Immigrant Describes Arkansas' Advantages to His Countrymen," PCHR 28:1 (Spring 1980), 2-8.
"A Sketch of Congregation B'nai Israel," PCHR 4:1 (March 1956), 3-7. Carolyn Gray LeMaster, A *Corner of the Tapestry*, (Fayetteville, Ark.: University of Arkansas Press, 1994), 58-62. Floyd W. Martin, "Eight Downtown Little Rock Churches: An Architectural History," PCHR Part I, 34:4 (Winter 1986),74-89; Part II, 35:1 (Spring 1987), 16-22; Conclusion, 35:2 (Summer 1987) 38-45.

61 "1903 Religious Census," PCHR 23:3 (Sept. 1975), 58-59.

62 James and Helen Hronas, "A History of the Annunciation Greek Orthodox Community of Little Rock, Arkansas," PCHR 39:3 (Fall 1991), 61-71.

63 Martin, "Eight Downtown Churches," 82-84.

64 Roy, Witsell, and Nichols, *How We Lived*, 168. "The 1905 'New Handy Map of Little Rock,'" PCHR 34:4 (Winter 1986), 90-92.

65Robert Johnston, "The Historic Pulaski County Court House," PCHR 24:1 (March 1976), 1-5.

66 David M. Ernest, "Changes in Little Rock Residence Patterns 1820-1939: The Chester Ashley Mansion/Oakleaf Hotel Example," PCHR 45:3 (Fall 1997), 48-49. Roy, Witsell, and Nichols, *How We Lived*, 134-135.

[67] Mrs. Hay Watson Smith, "Life in Little Rock in the Gay Nineties," PCHR 5:4 (Dec. 1957), 69-74.

[68] James W. Bell, "The Early Parks of Little Rock: Parts I & II" PCHR 30:1 & 2 (Spring & Summer 1982), 17-21 and 44-47. Lisa D. Thilo, "Fort Logan H. Roots, North Little Rock, Arkansas," PCHR 46 (Spring 1998), 2-17.

[69]Tom W. Dillard, "H.F. Auten, A Man Who Could Not Stand Still," PCHR 29:1 (Spring 1981), 11-18.

[70]Sloan Powell, "Pilgrims Journeying to the Shrine of Knowledge and Sociability: The Aesthetic Club in Little Rock, Arkansas, 1883-1900," PCHR 46:2 (Summer 1998), 26-27. See also Mary F. Worthen, "The Aesthetic Club: Oldest Women's Club in Little Rock," PCHR 25:2 (June 1977) 23-29.

[71] Tom W. Dillard, "Clara A. McDiarmid," PCHR 26:2 (June 1978), 27-28. Peggy Harris, "Homemaker To Homeowner: Little Rock Women in the 1920s," PCHR 39:2 (Summer 1991), 26-27. Paula Kyzer, "Promoting Political Responsibility, The League of Women Voters of Pulaski County," PCHR 39:3 (Fall 1991), 50-60. Dr. Ida Joe Brooks, "Women In Medicine," PCHR 44:4 (Winter 1996), 90-93. Marcia Camp, "The Soul of Bernie Babcock," PCHR 36:3 (Fall 1988), 50-62. Martha W. Rimmer, The Left Lane on the Road to Salvation: Universalism Comes to Arkansas," PCHR 49:2 (Summer 2001), 30-32.

[72] Fon Louise Gordon, "Black Women in Arkansas," PCHR 35:2 (Summer 1987), 26-28. "Pulaski Profiles: Josephine and Samuel H. Pankey," PCHR 38:3 (Fall 1990), 58-59. Aubrey F. Williams, "Letter to the Editor," PCHR 39:1 (Spring 1991), 24.

[73] Joe Neal, "Fraternal Cemetery: Reflections on a Southern Negro Graveyard," PCHR 25:1 (March 1977), 5-7.

[74] Todd E. Lewis, "Booker T. Washington and His Visits to Little Rock," PCHR 42:3 (Fall 1994) 54-65. Berna Love, "West Ninth Street, The Line," PCHR 42:3 (Fall 1994), 69. Tom W. Dillard, "Perseverance: Black History in Pulaski County, Arkansas – An Excerpt," PCHR 31 (Winter 1983), 62-73. Charles J. Rector, "Lily-White Republicanism: The Pulaski County Experience, 1888-1930," PCHR 42 (Spring 1994), 2-18.

[75] Charleen Lanier Hardeman, "My Grandfather – the Mayor, James Alexander Woodson," PCHR 30:2 (Summer 1982), 49. James W. Bell, The Little Rock Handbook, (Little Rock, Ark.: James W. Bell Publisher, 1980), 27.

[76] Martha Williamson Rimmer, "Progressivism Comes to Little Rock: The Election of 1911," PCHR 25:3 (Sept. 1977), 49-60. Rimmer, "Progressivism in Little Rock: The War Against Vice," PCHR 25: 4 (Dec. 1977), 65-72; Rimmer, "Little Rock's Third Street Viaduct," PCHR 41:3 (Fall 1993), 72-73. Rimmer, "Riverfront Park – A Progressive Vision," 31:1 (Spring 1983), 10-14.

[77] Ben F. Johnson III, Arkansas in Modern America, 1930-1999 (Fayetteville, Ark.: University of Arkansas Press, 2000),163-164. "The Old Pulaski County Court House and the Man Who Built It," and "Kavanaugh Boulevard and the Man for Whom It Was Named," in PCHR 16:1 (March 1968), 9-16. Herndon, Centennial History of Arkansas, 2: 687-688. Johnston, "The Historic Pulaski County Court House,"4.

[78] Michael D. Polston, "'Time Does Not Count Here.' Letters of an American Doughboy Stationed at Camp Pike," PCHR 33:4 (Winter 1985), 74-81. Tracy Nieser, "The History of Camp Pike, Arkansas," PCHR 41:3 (Fall 1993), 64-71. Dougan, *Arkansas Odyssey*, 353, 378.

[79] Bob Riley, "The Party That Almost Was. . ." PCHR 19:3 (Sept 1971), 33.

[80] Todd E. Lewis, "From Bull Mooser to Grand Dragon of the Ku Klux Klan: James A. Comer of Little Rock," PCHR 43:2 (Summer 1995), 33-41.

[81] James Reed Eison, "White City," PCHR 40:2 (Summer 1992), 34-35. Robert A. Diffee, "Arkansas's Early Aviation Heritage," PCHR 43:3 (Fall 1995), 61. Jim Lester and Judy Lester, *Greater Little Rock* (Norfolk, Virginia: The Donning Company, 1986), 152-173.

[82] Jacob E. Odle III, "Little Rock in 1919, A Post War Southern City," PCHR 22:3 (Sept. 1974), 48. Carolyn Gray LeMaster, "The Ottenheimers of Arkansas: An Excerpt," PCHR 49:2 (Summer 2001), 39-47. Sybil F. Crawford, "Dionicio Rodriguez: The Faux Bois Sculptor," PCHR 50:1 (Spring 2002), 15-18. Roy, Witsell, and Nichols, *How We Lived*, 186-187. Anisa Baldwin Metzger, "The Donaghey Building and Its Impact on the History of Arkansas," PCHR 49:3 (Fall 2001), 67-69.

[83] Dougan, Arkansas *Odyssey*, 411. Betty Rowland Wittenberg, ed., "June Rise in February: Excerpts From the Diary of Nancy Mooney Rector, "PCHR 52:2 (Summer 2004), 61. Tom W. Dillard, "The Luther Burbank of Arkansas: Joseph W. Vestal and the Company He Created," PCHR 49:3 (Fall 2001), 50-61. Allen, "The Baring Brothers and Their Famous Bridge," 57-58. "1927: The Arkansas turns ugly . . . real ugly," *Arkansas Democrat*, Special Little Rock Bicentennial section, Sunday, 1 Nov. 1981, 22-23H.

[84] John Kirk, "Dr. J. M. Robinson, the Arkansas Negro Democratic Association and Black Politics in Little Rock, Arkansas, 1928-1952," PCHR 41:1 (Spring 1993), 4. James Reed Eison, " 'Dead, But She Was in a Good Place, A Church,'" PCHR 30:2 (Summer 1982), 30-42.

[85] "The History of Jacksonville," at http://www.jacksonville-arkansas.com/community/history.html (accessed 2 Feb. 2006). Jonathan, J. Wolfe, Medical Education at the Old State House, 1912-1936, (Old State House Museum, 2002), n.p. Lester and Lester, *Greater Little Rock*, 183. Worthen, "Louise Loughborough and her Campaign," 26-33.

[86] Randy Tardy, "June 15, 1931: Little Rock gets off the ground," *Arkansas Democrat*, Special Little Rock Bicentennial section, Sunday, 1 Nov. 1981, 17H. "About Central Arkansas Water," http://carkw.com/history/history.asp (accessed 1 March 2006).

[87] Lynda B. Langford, "The Work Projects Administration in the Pulaski County District, 1935-1943," PCHR 35:1 (Spring 1987), 2-15. Phillip G. Basinger, "A History of the Jacksonville Ordnance Plant," PCHR 24:3 (Sept. 1976), 47-55.

[88] "Prisoners of War at Camp Robinson – A Document," PCHR 39:4 (Winter 1991), 74-78. Langford, "The WPA in the Pulaski County District, 11.

[89] *Arkansas; A Guide to the State*, comp. by WPA Writers' Program in Arkansas (New York: Hastings House, 1941), 171. Berna Love, "Backing the Attack: Black Arkansans'

Fight Against Germany, Japan and Jim Crow," PCHR 42:3 (Fall 1994), 66-73. Johnson, *Arkansas in Modern America*, 88-90.

[90] Roy, Witsell, and Nichols, *How We Lived* Roy, 206. Johnson, *Arkansas in Modern America*, 61. Bell, *Little Rock Handbook*, 59.

[91] Aubrey J. Hough, Jr. et al, "William M. Burns, M.D. Physician, Politician and Futurist," PCHR 37:1 (Spring 1980), 18-19. Adams, *North Little Rock, The Unique City*, 193,196, 215.

[92] Bell, *Little Rock Handbook*, 65. Roy, Witsell, and Nichols, *How We Lived*, 216. "History of Maumelle," http://maumelle.dina.org/living/history.html (accessed 28 Feb. 2006).

[93] Adams, *North Little Rock, The Unique City*, 196. Johnson, *Arkansas in Modern America*, 33. Dougan, Arkansas Odyssey, 574-575. Lester and Lester, Greater Little Rock, 206.

[94] See Robert Dunn, "The Corps and the Arkansas River 1833-1946," PCHR 39:1 (Spring 1991), 20-22. Dougan, *Arkansas Odyssey*, 574-575. NLR Utilities, http://www.nlrchamber.org/government/utilities.aspx (accessed 24 March 2006).

[95] Lester and Lester, Greater Little Rock, 204, 210. Roy, Witsell, and Nichols, *How We Lived* , 210-211. Tardy, "Little Rock gets off the ground," *Arkansas Democrat*, 1 Nov. 1981, 17H. "About Little Rock National Airport," http://lrn-airport.com/about/history.asp (accessed 22 March 2006).

[96] Bell, *Little Rock Handbook*, 42, 47, 48, 67. "Other Days, 50 Years Ago, March 22, 1956," *Arkansas Democrat-Gazette*, 22 March 2006, 6B.

[97] Jim Lester, *The People's College, Little Rock Junior College and Little Rock University*, 1927-1969 (Little Rock, Ark.: August House, 1987), 69, 73-79. Roy, Witsell, and Nichols, How We Lived, 212-215.

[98] J. H. Atkinson, "The Present Little Rock University: How It Began," PCHR 14:1 (March 1966), 6-11. W. David Baird, *Medical Education in Arkansas*, 1874-1978 (Memphis, Tenn.: Memphis State University Press, 1979), 229-258. "UAMS Growing For You," http://www.uams.edu/growing/history/timeline.asp (accessed November 2006).

[99] Peggy Harris, "'We Would Be Building,' A History of the Phyllis Wheatley YWCA," PCHR 44:3 (Fall 1996), 60-63.

[100] UALR Report on the History of the Little Rock School District, http://www.ualr.edu/lrsd/chap2.html (accessed March 2006). Johnson, *Arkansas in Modern America*, 134-148. Col. A. J. Almand, "John Parks Almand," PCHR 37:2 (Summer 1989), 36-41.

[101] Terry D. Goddard, "Race, Religion, and Politics: Rev. Wesley Pruden of Arkansas, Modern Day Jim Crow," PCHR 52:4 (Winter 2004), 107-118. Lola Dunnavant and James Reed Eison, ed., "Steel Helmets Under a September Sun, Little Rock Central High, 1957-1958," PCHR 37:2 (Summer 1989), 22-34 and "Long Halls Growing Darker, Little Rock Central High 1958-1959," PCHR 37:3 (Fall 1989), 46-59. Laura A. Miller, "'At Any Rate': Irene Gaston Samuel and the Life of a Southern Liberal," PCHR 45:1 (Spring 1997), 6-10.

102 Cary Bradburn, *On the Opposite Shore*, *The Making of North Little Rock*, (City of North Little Rock, 2004), 203-207. UALR Report on the History of the Little Rock School District

103 Johnson, *Arkansas in Modern America*, 151.

104 Metroplan, www.metroplan.org/Metroplan50.pdf (accessed 5 April 2006). Bell, Little Rock Handbook, 55-56.

105 Bell, *Little Rock Handbook*, 47-48. Roy, Witsell, and Nichols, *How We Lived*, 220. Martha Walters, "Little Rock Urban Renewal," PCHR 24:1 (March 1976), 12-16. Johnson, *Arkansas in Modern America*, 157-159. Bradburn, *On the Opposite Shore*, 228.

Quapaw Indian Dances

Samuel D. Dickinson

Samuel Dorris Dickinson earned a degree in anthropology from the University of Arizona and did graduate work at the Universidad Nacionale de Mexico and the University of Texas. However, his first job, in 1944, was as an associate editor of the Arkansas Gazette, and he later held a similar position at the "Arkansas Democrat" and finally at a newspaper in Shreveport, Louisiana. Meanwhile he was translating French and Spanish colonial documents into English and making other contributions to early Arkansas history. The following article is one of his many publications.

Dancing, perhaps the oldest of all art forms, was an important cultural expression of the Quapaw Indians of Arkansas just as it was of other primitive peoples throughout the world. The dance was both a ritual and a recreation. Through it, magical processes were set in motion, the gods were praised and invoked, aesthetic yearnings were satisfied, and pleasure was found in physical movement coordinated with songs, the beat of drums, the shaking of gourd rattles, and the piping of cane flutes.

When Jean-Bénard de La Harpe ascended the Arkansas River in 1722, he saw no Indian villages in what today is Pulaski County.[1] However, this county was within the hunting grounds of the Quapaws as attested by treaties with the United States.[2] Furthermore, seven archaeological sites in the county have been identified positively as Quapaw of the protohistoric period from 1500 to 1700.[3]

Fortunately for students of aboriginal life, European travelers during the colonial period witnessed dances in the Quapaw villages in the area of the confluence of the Arkansas River with the Mississippi. Several of them kept journals in which they referred to these performances, and from their remarks we can deduce what the dances were like in other Quapaw encampments. It is highly unlikely that there was any marked variation in each type of dance, from village to village, because of the ritualistic character.

Customarily the Quapaws honored deputations from other tribes and parties of friendly strangers by dancing and singing the calumet. Sometimes the dance was done for a single important visitor as in the case of Jean-Bernard Bossu, who in 1770 came a third time to visit them.[4]

Père Jacques Marquette, in discussing this dance among the Illinois tribe, friends and ally of the Quapaws, compared it to the opening of a ballet in France.[5] He and Louis Jolliet, the Sieur de La Salle and Henri de Tonti, Henri

Joutel and his companions were honored in this fashion in the Quapaw villages. No visitor left a complete account of this Quapaw dance, but from what was written about performances elsewhere it is possible to form a picture of the entire rite.

Joutel, for instance, gave only a partial description of it in his report of his party's journey from Texas to the Illinois country by way of Arkansas Post in 1687. Apparently he did not want to repeat himself. He indicated that the Quapaw dance was the same as the one performed for him and his men earlier in the Cahinnio Caddo village[6] a few miles west of the Ouachita River, probably near the modern city of Camden.[7] The following is what he recounted about the Cahinnio ceremony.

The Cahinnios, as the Quapaws would do later, mistook Robert Cavelier, La Salle's brother, a priest, for the leader of the group that Joutel headed. Consequently, they chose him to represent the whites in the dance. The elders of the tribe, followed by young men and women, all singing at the top of their voices, came to the cabin occupied by the visitors. They were led by the master of ceremonies who carried the calumet, decorated with feathers. He probably was a medicine man or *jongleur* as the French would say. After entering the cabin they sang for about fifteen minutes and then conducted Cavelier outside to a place arranged for the ceremony. Herbs were placed under his feet and they washed his face. He then was told to sit down on the ground, and the elders sat around him.

The master of ceremonies pushed two forked sticks, painted red, into the ground in front of Cavelier and placed another, also painted red, in the forks. Over this crossbar he draped first a dressed buffalo hide and then a tanned deer skin on which he laid the peace pipe. The singers resumed, and gourds containing pebbles were shaken in rhythm with the songs.

Two girls, directed by the master of ceremonies, put a collar on one side of the calumet and an otter skin on the other. Facing each other, they sat down on each side of Cavelier, and the master of ceremonies extended Cavelier's legs over theirs, to the priest's embarrassment. Meanwhile, an elder tied a red feather to Cavelier's hair. The singing went on throughout the night, but about nine o'clock Cavelier asked to be excused. He was led back to his cabin to rest if not to sleep.

At dawn the master of ceremonies returned for him and had him again sit near the calumet. Those singers who had not exhausted themselves continued while the master of ceremonies took up the pipe, filled it with tobacco and lit it. Ten times he offered and withdrew the calumet before he allowed Cavelier to take it and smoke it. Next the pipe was presented to the other whites, and after all of them had drawn a puff the Indians smoked.

By nine o'clock the hot sunshine was making Cavelier uncomfortable, and he let the Indians know he had had enough. They led him back to his cabin and gave him the calumet, wrapped in deer skin, and the painted sticks. The calumet, he was informed, was an emblem of peace. By showing it anywhere among the Cahinnios' allies, he would be hospitably received.[8]

Joutel, knowing that the Indians always expected gifts after the calumet ceremony, gave the Cahinnios an axe, four knives, and some beads. Père du Poisson, a Jesuit missionary to the Quapaws in 1727, was reluctant to let the Indians dance the calumet for him, as he knew that they would want presents that he did not have to give. He wrote:

> Two days after my arrival the village of the Southouis sent two savages to me to ask if I would permit them to come to sing the *Calumet* in full regalia – that is, with all the body painted in different colors, wearing tails of wildcats at the places where artists paint wings in the pictures of Mercury, carrying the Calumet, or pipe of peace in their hands, and with their bodies ornamented with rattles which announce their arrival from afar.[9]

Not having examined a copy of the original French from which this translation was made, the author cannot be sure, but suspects that "wildcats" should be raccoons. *Chat sauvage*, literally "wild cat," in colonial Louisiana French means raccoon while *chat du bois*, literally "forest cat," is the American wildcat or lynx.[10]

The rattles probably were small sheet brass bells or copper or brass tinkling cones of European origin that the Quapaws obtained either directly from whites or more likely through trade with the Tunica Indians who had got them from Europeans. Bossu reported that the Quapaws attached bells to their legs.[11]

After repeatedly refusing, Père du Poisson finally allowed the young men to perform the dance of discovery "without design," that is, without rewarding them. He said all the villagers except the women came at dawn and they danced, sang, and made speeches until noon. This dance portrayed the search of an enemy; it was similar to the commencement of the war dance. "Their dances, as you may imagine," he wrote, "are bizarre. The exactitude with which they keep time is as surprising as the contortions and the effort they make."[12]

In 1751, when Bossu for the first time visited the Quapaws, young warriors greeted him by dancing the calumet. Regrettably, he failed to describe it, though he commented that the Quapaws used dances for many different purposes. He wrote, "There are dances for religion, medicine, rejoicing, formalities, war, peace, marriage, death, entertainment, hunting and impudicity; the last has been suppressed since our arrival in America."[13]

Nevertheless, the Quapaws evaded the French prohibitive order by secretly staging the dance at night. The men and women who took part, so Bossu said, swore never to disclose what they did or saw. To confirm their oath they struck a post with a tomahawk.[14]

A post also was employed in ceremonies preliminary to going on the warpath. It represented the enemies, and hitting it was symbolic of an attack on them.[15] Presumably in this case they were the French officials who had forbidden the dance, and who openly the Indians dared not defy.

The Indians danced nude. They assumed erotic poses; they sang lewd songs and made obscene gestures. That is, according to the viewpoint of the whites. But the Christian European attitude toward sex differed greatly from that of the pagan Indian. The sexual dance was an orgy, in European eyes. It was not that at all, in the minds of the Indians. It was a fertility rite.

Believing in the efficacy of imitative magic, they applied their idea that like will produce like through ceremonies to bring a desired result. Since copulation is necessary for reproduction, they thought that by means of a sexual rite they could induce Nature to make plants and animals multiply for their subsistence. What the Europeans found offensive in the dance of impudicity, the Quapaws considered sacred, a means of controlling the sun, earth and rain for the benefit of man.

The war dance likewise was meant to exert magical influence by imitating combat. As usual, the music was provided by singers, drummers, and shakers of rattles. Young braves, who were to perform the dance, painted their body and face red, for that is the color of blood, and they would not be content until they shed the blood of their tribe's foes.

Bossu mentioned only two dancers, one representing the Quapaws and the other the enemy.[16] Judging by descriptions of this same dance done by other Indians,[17] it is thought that the entire corps of warriors participated, and they were divided into pairs of contestants acting like the two Bossu described.

At the start, the brave representing his tribe, danced about as if searching for the enemy. On discovering him, he crouched to spy on him. Suddenly he leaped up, uttering a shrill war cry, and then he struck at his adversary. The latter fell to the ground and stiffened his limbs as in death. Triumphantly the victor went through the motions of scalping his enemy.[18]

Bossu recorded this war chant:

> I am going to war to avenge the death of my brothers, I shall kill, I
> shall destroy, I shall plunder, I shall burn the enemies, I shall lead
> back slaves, I shall eat their heart, I shall make smoked meat of their
> flesh, I shall drink their blood, I shall bring back their scalp and their
> skulls to make cups — and other such things which only betoken
> vengeance, cruelty and slaughter.[19]

Though this song might have been nothing more than boasting and a magical
way of frightening the enemy, it does raise the question of cannibalism. The
author knows of no proof that Quapaw warriors ceremonially ate their enemies'
flesh and drank their blood in order to gain the powers of their slain foes.
However, Arkansas Territorial Governor George Izard in his report to the
American Philosophical Society in 1827 said, "Human sacrifices were, till a few
years ago, frequent among them. On their departure from the Cadeaux country,
they burnt to death an orphan child belonging to the tribe in order to propitiate
their dieties."[20] This question of cannibalism probably never can be resolved,
because of our scanty knowledge of the Quapaws, despite their long association
with whites. Evidently they were cleverer in keeping secrets than the whites
were in observing and understanding.

The Quapaws entertained Bossu with various dances during his third sojourn
among them. The first was held at night by the light of pine torches planted in
the ground. The Indians danced until daybreak.

He termed their dance of the wild animal hunt a type of play. "They have several tunes for this dance," he wrote, "and they used *chichikois* or pots covered with
parchment which they strike with a stick, tipped with wool wrapped in skin, to
keep time and accompany the sound of reed flutes."[21] This same kind of drum
was used by the Louisiana coastal Chitimacha tribe.[22] Bossu continued:

> The performers shout and make a *terrible* hubbub, calling to each
> other and speaking among themselves about the animals they are
> hunting. They are completely covered with skins of tigers (panthers),
> bears, wolves, stags and wild bulls (buffaloes), and they wear bonnets
> of the same shape as the heads of these animals. They carry in their
> hands sticks, lances and darts, clubs or axes with which they threat-
> en to kill the beast they are pursuing.

> Some of them, acting as if they already have dislodged the animal, run
> after a man in the same way that ferocious animals pursue a savage in
> a wilderness to devour him.

The pursuer must be very agile and swift of foot. The fugitive is similarly excited and moves like a man surrounded by implacable monsters. He runs, he struggles, he strikes here and there at these sham animals, which after some good sport seize him and appear to eat him. This dance is full of action, cries, howling. It closely resembles the war dance or scalp dance which I described in my preceding *Travels.*[23]

Baron Lahontan, who might have descended the Mississippi River as far as the Quapaw villages in 1689, as he claimed, wrote in his *Travels* that these Indians staged neither a comedy nor an opera for him, but they did provide a spectacle which he facetiously classed as "one of those Spanish entertainments called a bull fight." The Quapaws conducted the baron's party in a procession from the riverbank where they had landed to a place a league away. There they performed a dance showing how to capture buffaloes.[24] It must have been a version of the dance of the hunt of wild animals that Bossu saw many years later.

By 1806 when Thomas Ashe and two companions reached Arkansas Post or Ozark, as he called it, the Quapaw tribe was much smaller than it had been on the occasions the Indians danced the calumet for early French explorers. White man's diseases had taken a dreadful toll. Members of several other tribes that had dwindled and broken up had found a home with the Quapaws. Ashe said there were about 900 Indians, "composed of remnants of various nations," camped near the white settlement. Some of these Indians hunted far up the Arkansas River, even in the plains country, and brought their peltries back to Arkansas Post to trade for supplies.

It was October, and the time had come for the Indians to mark the change from autumn to winter. They honored their sun god in four seasonal festivals.

Just before dawn they separated into groups – warriors, young men and women, mothers with their infants. Each group formed a quadrant. At first light the warriors held their weapons aloft toward the sun, the young men and women offered ears of corn and branches of trees, the mothers lifted up their babies. Everyone was silent until the sun was above the horizon. Then they burst into a song praising their god. They paused after each verse. Ashe wrote that an excellent interpreter gave this translation:

Great Spirit! Master of our lives!

Great Spirit! Master of everything visible and invisible, and who daily makes them visible and invisible!

Great Spirit! Master of every other spirit, good or bad, command the good to be favorable to us, and deter the bad from the commission of evil!

Oh! Great Spirit! Preserve the strength and courage of our warriors and augment their number, that they may resist the oppression of their Spanish enemies, and recover the country and the rights of their fathers!

Oh! Great Spirit! Preserve the lives of such of our old men, as are inclined to give council and example to the young!

Preserve our children, multiply their number, and let them be the comfort and support of declining age!

Preserve our corn and our animals, and let not famine desolate the land!

Protect our villages, guard our lives! Oh Great Spirit! When you hide your light behind the western hills, protect us from the Spaniards, who violate the night, and do evil which they dare not commit in the presence of thy beams!

Good Spirit! Make known to us your pleasure, by sending to us the Spirit of Dreams. Let the Spirit of Dreams proclaim your will in the night, and we will perform it through the day! And of it say the time of some be closed, send them Master of Life, to the great country of souls, where they may meet their fathers, mothers, children and wives, and where you are pleased to shine upon them with a bright, warm and perpetual blaze!

Oh Grand, Oh Great Spirit! hearken to the voice of nations, hearken to all the children, and remember us always, for we are descended from thee!

Right after this appeal the quadrants broke up and formed large circles within circles. They danced and sang until about ten o'clock when they dispersed to rest and entertain themselves in their camp and in the nearby white village. At noon they reassembled in circles and again addressed the sun with these words:

Courage! nations, courage! The Great Spirit looks down upon us from his highest seat, and by his own power and greatness.

Grand Spirit! how great are his works and how beautiful are they!

He is good; is the Great Spirit, he rides high to behold us. 'Tis he who causes all things to augment and to act. He even now stands for a moment to hearken to us!

Courage! nations, courage! The Great Spirit now above our heads will make us vanquish our enemies; he will cover our fields with corn, and increase the animals of our woods. He will see that the old will be happy, and that the young augment. He will make them put up their voice to him while he rises and sets in their land, or while his heat and his light can thus gloriously shine out.

Dancing and more singing followed for the next two or three hours. Food then was served to everyone. Ashe ate with them, and he said he enjoyed the barbequed pork and stewed venison. The Indians rested until watchers announced that the sun was starting to set. Hurriedly the throng formed parts of circles, facing the west. Once more they held up their offerings and sang:

The nations must prosper; they have been beheld by the Great Spirit. What more can they want? Is not that happiness enough? See how he retires, great and content, after having visited his children with light, heat and universal good!

Oh, Great Spirit! Sleep not long in the gloomy west, but return and call thy people once again to light and life; to light and life; to light and life!

The Indians danced and sang until eleven o'clock, at which time the celebration ended. Each of the four solar festivals was alike, and they were called Days of Adoration. If one of these days was gloomy, the Indians built a great fire and danced and sang around it.[25]

With the exception of the references to Spain, this account sounds authentic. The Quapaws had no reason to be hostile to Spain, for under Spanish rule they had enjoyed more freedom than they were to know under the new United States government. The anti-Spanish remarks probably were interpolations made by either Ashe himself or the interpreter.

Red single and concentric circles and semicircles were favorite designs painted on Quapaw funerary pottery. Occasionally quadrants formed the decoration. Since these designs correspond to figures in the ceremonies Ashe observed, they, too, probably symbolize the sun.[26]

Thomas Nuttall while in a Quapaw village in 1820 saw two huge painted wooden mask and cone-shaped caps made of pelts and painted. He was told that these things were worn by dancers in festivals. In the spring and fall the Quapaws went to homes of white settlers and performed a "contribution dance" for which they expected gifts. They wanted salt and provisions most of all.[27]

During the period of French and Spanish exploration the Quapaws had desired presents of beads, trinkets, axes and other articles of European manufacture – luxuries to them – but they would settle for a feast as Père du Poisson learned. By 1820 the necessities of life were harder to come by, and they danced for them.

White settlements were increasing, game was declining, white government officials were cunning, tribal chieftains drank too much liquor, and ultimately all the ancestral hunting grounds would come into the possession of the whites. Against these evils the magic of old dances and songs could not prevail.

NOTES

[1] Baron Marc de Villiers du Terrage, *An Explorer of Louisiana Jean-Baptiste Benard de La Harpe* (1683-1765), ed. and trans. Samuel Dorris Dickinson, (Arkadelphia, Ark.: Institute for Regional Studies, Ouachita Baptist University, 1983), 32-33.

[2] John Hugh Reynolds, "The Western Boundary of Arkansas," *Publications of the Arkansas Historical Association*, vol. 2, (1908): 214-215.

[3] Michael P. Hoffman, "Protohistory Of The Lower And Central Arkansas River Valley In Arkansas," read at the Mid-South Archaeological Conference, Memphis, Tenn. 1983.

[4] Jean-Bernard Bossu, *New Travels In North America 1770-1771*, ed. and trans. Samuel Dorris Dickinson, (Natchitoches, La.: Northwestern State University Press, 1982), 38.

[5] Père Jacques Marquette, *Voyages of Marquette In The Jesuit Relations*, (Great Americana, Readex Microprint Corporation, 1966), 137.

[6] Henri Joutel, *Historical Journal Of Monsieur De La Salle's Last Voyage To Discover The River Mississippi, From France To The Coast Of Texas*, ed. Isaac Joslin Cox, (New York: A. S. Barnes & Company, 1905), vol. II: 198.

[7] S. D. Dickinson, "Historic Tribes of the Ouachita Drainage System in Arkansas," *The Arkansas Archeologist, Bulletin of the Arkansas Archeological Society*, 21 (1980): 6.

[8] Joutel, Journal of La Salle, 185-188.

[9] W. H. Falconer, "Arkansas and The Jesuits In 1727-A Translation," *Publications of the Arkansas Historical Association*, 4 (1917): 371.

[10] Jules Faine, *Dictionnaire Français-Creole*, (Ottawa, Canada: Editions Leméac, 1974), 113.

[11] Jean-Bernard Bossu, *Nouveaux Voyages aux Indes Occidentales*, (Paris, 1768), 111.

[12] Falconer, "Arkansas and The Jesuits," 372.

[13] Bossu, *Nouveaux Voyages*, 111.

[14] Ibid.

[15] Antoine Simon Le Page du Pratz, *History of Louisiana* (London, England: T. Becker, 1774; Harmanson Reprint, New Orleans: Pelican Press, 1947), 353.

[16] Bossu, *Nouveaux Voyages*, 116.

[17] Le Page du Pratz, *History of Louisiana*, 354.

[18] Bossu, *Nouveaux Voyages*, 116.

[19] Bossu, *Nouveaux Voyages*, 115.

[20] David W. Bizzell, "A Report On The Quapaw, The Letters Of Governor George Izard To The American Philosophical Society, 1825-1827," *Pulaski County Historical Review* 29:4 (Winter 1981): 72.

[21] Bossu, *New Travels*, 81.

[22] John R. Swanton, *Indian Tribes of the Lower Mississippi Valley and Adjacent Coast of the Gulf of Mexico*, Smithsonian Institution, Bureau of American Ethnology Bulletin 43, (Washington, D.C., 1911), 350.

[23] Bossu, *New Travels*, 81.

[24] Baron Lahontan, *Voyages Dans L'Amérique Septentrionale* (Amsterdam, 1728), 267.

[25] Thomas Ashe, *Travels In America* (London, England: Phillips, 1808), 305-308.

[26] S. D. Dickinson and S. C. Dellinger, "A Survey of the Historic Earthenware of the Lower Arkansas Valley," *Bulletin of the Texas Archaeological and Palaeontological Society*, 12 (Sept. 1940): 84.

[27] Thomas Nuttall, *Journal of Travels into the Arkansa Territory*, (Cleveland, Ohio: Arthur Clark Co., 1905), 290.

SAMSON GRAY AND THE BAYOU METO SETTLEMENT, 1820-1836

Carolyn Yancey Little

Carolyn Yancey Little, who is now Carolyn Yancey Kent, was a registered nurse in Jacksonville when she became interested in local history while helping Girl Scouts with their merit badges in history. This article, which began as a project for a writing class at the University of Arkansas at Little Rock, tells the story of a leading figure among the early settlers of Pulaski County. Kent continues to contribute to local history, writing articles for the Encyclopedia of Arkansas History and Culture, doing research for the Arkansas Chapter of the Trail of Tears Association, and working on her own oral history of people who worked at the ordnance plants in Pulaski County during World War II.

Samson Gray and the settlement on the Bayou Meto[1] in northern Pulaski County played a vital role in the development of Arkansas Territory. Even though Samson was a leading figure in territorial Arkansas, he has received very little mention in previously published accounts. As will be shown, Samson Gray was involved in the development of early roads, was mail contractor for a large portion of the state, was deeply involved in territorial business, and was also a political associate of the Conway-Sevier dynasty that controlled early politics. He numbered among his friends Ambrose Sevier, Governor John Pope, William E. Woodruff and Chester Ashley. His enterprising spirit put him in the middle of most aspects of territorial life, and only his early death cut short his influence.

Samson Gray was twenty-five when he came to Arkansas Territory "with a large number of his connexions, in the winter of 1820-21, and settled the place (then a wilderness)."[2] A wilderness was a good description of Arkansas Territory in 1820. A few scattered settlements along the waterways were the only breaks in the virgin land. An early missionary described Arkansas as a "perfect terra incognita. The only way to get there was unknown: and what it was, or was like, if you got there, was still more an unrevealed mystery."[3] A correspondent to the *Arkansas Gazette* in 1821 described the population as existing in small detached settlements or "squads which is always so destructive to the minds, morals, prosperity and harmony of the people of any country." The writer said Arkansas needed weekly mail and two good wagon roads.[4] Overland travel was slow and uncertain. Foot and horseback travelers followed Indian trails, but most of these trails were so narrow that wagon travel was impossible.

The waterways furnished the roads for Arkansas's population, but there were problems here also. Flooding and high water hindered travel during rainy seasons, and dry weather could lower the water level so much that boats could not navigate the streams. By 1821 steamboats were common on the Mississippi and a few had made the trip up the Arkansas River to Arkansas Post, but it was not until 1822 that a steamboat came up the river to Little Rock.[5]

Moving into unsettled wilderness areas and pioneering were nothing new to Samson and his family. Samson's grandfather had moved to Mecklenburg County, North Carolina, in 1766 when that county and Samson's father, Jacob, were both two years old.[6] Samson was born to Jacob and Mary Gray in Mecklenburg County, 16 November 1795.[7] Samson's parents moved to Williamson County, Tennessee, in 1804 when that county was only four years old and purchased a seventy-five-acre tract of land on Little Harpeth River for three hundred dollars.[8]

Jacob Gray and his seven children cleared the land and developed the plantation that was their home for the next sixteen years. His four daughters married and began to raise their families. Jacob and his family were a close-knit group with the married girls and their husbands living with Jacob and Mary or nearby. Education was important to this family. Jacob could read and write, and he saw that his children could read and write. Samson must have shared his father's views on education, for in 1817 he purchased a set of medical books for his brother.[9] Jacob was moderately successful during the early years in Williamson County, Tennessee. He was able to earn a comfortable income for his family and to afford slaves to help with the plantation.[10] He served on jury duty when called and was elected foreman of the grand jury one term.[11] The panic of 1819 proved disastrous for Jacob. In 1819 and 1820 the dockets of the court of pleas and quarter sessions of Williamson County carried several lawsuits for debts that were decided against Jacob,12 and on [12] April 1820 he sold his plantation for twelve hundred dollars.[13]

Jacob began to make plans to move his family during the summer and fall of 1820. On 1 November he made arrangements for the sale of his "articles" with the agreement that the profits would go to Samson.[14] On 7 August 1820, Abraham Secrest, one of Jacob's sons-in-law, sold his fifty acres on Little Harpeth River.[15] Abraham took a note for part of the sales price of the property, and on 29 December 1820 he assigned his interest in the note to Samson.[16] With Samson in charge of the affairs in Williamson County, Tennessee, Jacob and Abraham left for Arkansas Territory to find a new home. Samson stayed in Williamson County until 31 March when he was able to settle the family accounts[17] and leave for Arkansas Territory.

It is not certain which members of the migrating family came first and which came later with Samson, but the Arkansas territorial population increased significantly by the time the entire group of settlers had arrived. The elder members of the migrating party were Samson's uncle, Shared Gray, and Samson's father, Jacob Gray, Sr.; Samson's mother, Mary, may have come to Arkansas, but more likely she died in Tennessee before the migration. Other members of the party were: Samson's sister Sarah, her husband Charles Legate, and their six children; his sister Nancy, her husband Abraham Secrest, and their five sons; his sister Elizabeth, her husband Francis Secrest, and two children; his sister Jane and her husband George Wooten; and Samson's two younger brothers Jacob, Jr., and Thomas W.[18] There were at least four Negro slaves in the group; two belonging to Jacob, Sr., and one each for Samson and Abraham.[19]

Shared Gray had served as a magistrate and had owned and managed the local ordinary or house of public entertainment on Twelve Mile Creek in Mecklenburg County, North Carolina[20] until he retired to Williamson County, Tennessee, in 1815.21 Shared was not very active in the affairs of the settlement after coming to Arkansas. At sixty-two he was available to offer advice from his experiences as a magistrate and to witness legal documents. He also served as doorkeeper to the Territorial Legislative Council in 1833.[22] Jacob Gray, Sr., was fifty-eight when he came to Arkansas Territory. After the arrival of his eldest son, Samson, he retired to the background and passed control of the family to his son.[23]

The family continued as a close-knit group after arriving in Arkansas, and as the younger members of the party married they joined the group. Abraham Secrest and Samson were both very dominant men. Before coming to Arkansas they had both been involved in incidents in Williamson County where they indicated they would stand up for their ideas. Samson was arrested and charged with assault and battery, and Abraham with public fighting. Samson pleaded guilty and paid his fine. Abraham pleaded innocent and was judged not guilty.[24] Abraham and his family were the first ones to break with the settlement, but they only moved about four miles away and continued to keep in contact with the others.[25] Thomas W. became restless and returned to Williamson County, Tennessee. In 1824 he married a Williamson County girl. Thomas and his wife went to Kentucky for a while, but they were back in Arkansas by 1833.[26]

The "place" were Samson and his "connexions" settled was located between Bayou Meto and the Bayou of the Two Prairies about twelve miles north of Little Rock.[27] By 1830 Samson had made five hundred dollars worth of improvements on 160 acres of land in the Southeast Quarter of Section Thirty, Range Three North, Ten West, in Pulaski County, Arkansas Territory.[28] The settlement, which was on the edge of the Grand Prairie, was described as upland and bottom land from the bayous, with only sparse timber, and suitable for growing cotton and corn.[29]

In 1821 the settlers at Bayou Meto were just getting settled when the Territorial Legislature, the Superior Court, and the United States Land Office all moved to Little Rock. William E. Woodruff moved his printing press from Arkansas Post and began to publish the *Arkansas Gazette* in Little Rock that year. The Bayou Meto settlers, at first, were dependent on the Bayou Meto for transportation, but by 1823 Francis Secrest was paid by the county for "viewing and making a road" toward Little Rock.[30]

When the cotton crop began to see a profit, Samson began to speculate in land. The United States government had used large tracts of land in Arkansas to satisfy the government's obligation to soldiers who had fought in the War of 1812. Many of these soldiers were not residents of Arkansas and had never registered their land in the territory. On 11 November 1823 the *Gazette* published an act passed by the Arkansas Territorial General Assembly to regulate the collection of taxes on military bounties. The act made it the duty of the county sheriffs to enter and list all bounty land on the tax books that had been drawn three years prior to June 1, 1824. The act further provided that the owners had four months after the land had been entered by the sheriff to pay the taxes. If the taxes were not paid the land would be sold. If the land had been transferred, it became taxable at the date of transfer.[31] In the same issue of the *Gazette*, Woodruff offered his services as agent to take care of the land interests of non-residents. By 10 August 1824 Woodruff was doing so well as land agent that he made the agency permanent and named it Arkansas Military Land Agency. The land agency eventually brought Woodruff far more wealth with fewer problems than the *Gazette*.[32] Woodruff soon extended his land services to residents and included all types of land transactions.

Samson recorded his first land transaction in 1823 in Pulaski County.[33] He soon expanded to other counties and hired Woodruff as his land agent. In 1826 Woodruff billed Samson for taxes in Pulaski and Conway Counties, for Frank Secrest's taxes, and for purchasing four tracts of land. For his services, Woodruff charged six dollars and fifty cents commission.[34] Woodruff also printed the forms necessary for the land transactions, which he sold as well as paper and garden seeds to Samson.[35] The arrangement between Samson and Woodruff seemed to work out well. Woodruff was located in the territorial capital where he could keep an eye on what was going on. Each fall his paper published the list of lands to be sold for unpaid taxes, so he knew when choice land was available. If Woodruff's clients did not pay their obligation, he still had the land. By 1829-30 Samson had land in Independence, Conway, St. Francis, and Phillips Counties, as well as 2,880 acres in Pulaski County, three slaves, five horses, thirty head of cattle, and one stud horse.[36] Sometime in 1830 Samson purchased eight more slaves and is listed on the 1830 Arkansas Territorial census with eleven slaves.[37]

By 1825 Samson's financial picture had improved, and he was able to charge supplies against the cotton crop at John McLain's in Little Rock. On 19 June he charged sugar, a pitcher, a set of small plates, a set of large plates, six bowls, a set of knives and forks, a barrel of "flower," and some yard goods. On 6 July Samson's brother charged to Samson's account ten pounds of coffee. On 1 August Samson's father charged to Samson's account yard goods and thread. On 5 August Samson charged two-and-one-fourth yards of material, one vest "patron," one-half yard velvet, one dozen vest buttons, one piece of tape and thread, and ribbon.38 The women at the settlement must have been rushed making Samson's new suit in time for his marriage to Maria Gray on 7 November 1825.[39] Maria was not a member of the settlement and was not related. The 1850 Prairie County, Arkansas, Federal Census lists her place of birth as Illinois.[40] After the marriage a man named Vinum Gray moved to the Bayou Meto settlement. Vinum was not related to Samson unless he was a brother to Maria. Vinum and Samson became close associates, and in 1830 Samson paid taxes for Vinum.[41]

Samson and Maria's wedding was an occasion for celebrating at the settlement By evening some of the men had become intoxicated, and there was a quarrel between a Scotsman and a discharged soldier. The ex-soldier drew a knife and stabbed the Scotsman, causing his death. The incident ended the celebrating, and the ex-soldier was arrested by the sheriff and taken to jail in Little Rock.42 The *Gazette* called the crime murder, but at the October term of the Superior Court, the charge was entered as manslaughter and the accused was sentenced to three months in jail and fined five dollars.[43]

Samson continued to charge items at McLain's in 1825 and 1826. The charges included large amounts of yard goods, calico, needles, thread, spices, coffee, tobacco, sugar, pantaloons, three vests, shoes, and other items that might be called luxuries, such as one yard silk, a flat iron and a candlestick.[44] In 1826 and 1827 Samson started an account with Scott and Armstrong for additional supplies. Here he also charged a large amount of yard goods. The settlement used large amounts of cloth for its clothing needs. The settlement was beginning to lose the rough frontier look and take on the trappings of society. Among Samson's charges at Scott and Armstrong were: more dishes and kitchen items, two chamber pots, hinges, screws, cupboard locks, tea, lace, lampblack and one leghorn bonnet.[45]

In 1823 the Arkansas Territorial Legislature passed a resolution asking the United States government for an appropriation to open a road from Memphis to Little Rock.[46] In 1824 the United States Congress passed "an Act to authorize the surveying and making of a road from a point opposite to Memphis, in the state of Tennessee, to Little Rock, in the territory of Arkansas." The act stated that the President would appoint three commissioners to explore, survey, and mark the course. Fifteen thousand dollars was appropriated for paying the commissioners and for building the road. The commissioners were to be paid three dollars, and their assistants one dollar and fifty cents for each day they were engaged in determining the course of the road.[47]

The lack of a road linking Little Rock with the east was an acute problem for the territorial population. Samson's house on the edge of the Grand Prairie became a natural stopping place for travelers. In January of 1823 three men attempting to cross the Grand Prairie walked ninety miles in cold weather. The men waded through water and ice covering the prairie. Their fire-building material got wet early in the journey. They arrived at Samson's suffering from exposure and severe frost bite and in a state of delirium. [48] One of the men died a few days later in Little Rock because of his ordeal.[49]

In 1825 a new settler from Kentucky was forced to leave his keelboat with his belongings at Arkansas Post because of the low water levels in the Arkansas River. The settler crossed the prairie to reach Little Rock. He reported that there were only two settlements on the route, one in the prairie and the other the residence of Samson Gray located about eighteen miles from Little Rock. The settler reported that there were only nine families in Little Rock with a population of about 150.[50]

As late as 1827, the road situation had not improved. A political candidate sent messengers to Memphis to have circulars printed because Woodruff had refused to print the circulars on the *Gazette's* press. On the return journey the men quarreled over the route and separated. One man lost his saddle, but was able to find the route with considerable difficulty. The other man took a different direction and soon found himself in the swamps between the prairie and the Arkansas River. He wandered around for four days before reaching a house on the river. He had only berries and crayfish to eat and had lost his saddle, his horse, his bridle, and his hat. The briers and bushes had torn off most of his clothes. Only the circulars survived the trip unhurt.[51]

On 15 February 1825 the *Gazette* carried the report of the commissioners on the Memphis and Little Rock Road. The road would cross the Bayou of the Two Prairies about 120 miles from Memphis, cross Bayou Meto about five miles farther, and then cover the ten and a half miles remaining to the Arkansas River opposite Little Rock. The report indicated that both the bayous would require bridging. The land in the area of the bayous was described as thinly timbered with large bodies of good cotton. The area from the Bayou Meto to Little Rock was heavily timbered with some bottom land.[52] This route would pass by Samson Gray's settlement in Pulaski County. Much of the cotton land in the report belonged to Samson.

On 10 May 1825 the *Gazette* announced that there had been a change in plans concerning the road; the Memphis and Little Rock Road was to be built by contracts and not by federal troops as first announced. The President reported that no troops were available. The army would send a quartermaster to let contracts and to supervise the construction.[53] The *Jackson (Tenn.) Gazette* reported on 15 March 1826 that a Lieutenant Griffith had arrived and was making contracts for the road. When Woodruff reported the news from Tennessee, he was upset that people from central Arkansas had not been notified and thus not given a chance to bid on the road. On 25 July 1826 Woodruff reported that a correspondent stated that the citizens of Arkansas had had very little notice that contracts for the road were being made, even in the counties near the Memphis side, and no Arkansas bids were accepted for the project. The writer stated that people from Tennessee had been granted contracts for sixty-four miles of the project at $160 per mile and that the entire appropriation would be used building the road the first sixty-four miles from Memphis. Woodruff was critical of how the lieutenant had had handled the contracts and reported that the citizens were very dissatisfied and were of the opinion that someone else should have been appointed.[54]

An additional appropriation of $9,000 was approved in 1827, and a new superintendent, Captain Charles Thomas, was put in charge. The *Gazette* reported on 12 March 1827 that the first sixty-four miles of the Memphis and Little Rock Road were complete. On 20 March 1827 the *Gazette* carried the announcement that sealed proposals would be accepted for erecting bridges over several streams on the route including the Bayou of the Two Prairies and the Bayou Meto. The announcement carried detailed descriptions of the specifications for the bridges and gave bidders until 15 May to submit their bids. Bidders were required to submit a bond with two good securities. No advances were to be made. All bridges would be paid for on completion.[55]

On 12 June 1827 the *Gazette* ran an advertisement for bids for the roadbed. The bids would be taken under the same conditions as the bids for the bridges and would be open until 1 August.[56] Samson formed a partnership with two other businessmen and submitted two proposals, one for the bridges across the Bayou of the Two Prairies and the Bayou Meto and one for the roadbed construction from the Bayou of the Two Prairies to Little Rock. The bid from Samson's firm was the lowest, and it was awarded the contracts.[57] Problems with the road developed in August, and all contracts were suspended. Captain Thomas reported that it was impossible to follow the original survey between the St. Francis and White Rivers; in fact, he could not find the route marked by the commissioners. An alternate route was approved, and the road work resumed.[58] The new route did not change plans for the road from the Bayou of the Two Prairies to Little Rock. In December 1827 Thomas made two additional contracts with Samson for a bridge over a cypress swamp near Little Rock and for a small portion of the roadbed that no one else had bid on.[59]

Captain Thomas, in a letter to the quartermaster general in March 1928, reported that all work was progressing well and that Samson Gray would finish his contracts March 12, a delay of twelve days, because of recent flash flooding. Thomas requested a remittance to pay several contractors including $1620 to Samson Gray for contracts for "sundry bridges and sections of the road."[60] The road was cleared of all timber, with stumps cut as low to the ground as possible, and all brush wood and rubbish removed. The road was twenty feet wide. The bridges were built of timbers with strong log abutments. The hills were cut down and the low places were filled with earth.[61]

No official announcement was made concerning the opening of the road, but on 9 December 1828 Woodruff printed a letter to the editor from a citizen of Crittenden County. The writer reported that "emigration by way of the Military Road has increased fourfold this season. The press of wagons is so great at the ferry at Memphis, that many have to wait several days before they can cross over."[62] On 3 June 1829 the *Gazette* reported that travel between Little Rock and Memphis on the Military Road had not been interrupted by high water this season, and travelers on horseback passed through daily. Carriages could also pass along with little difficulty.[63] Another report on 9 September 1829 states "this road (Little Rock and Memphis Road) has been passable for horsemen and light wagons for considerably more than a year past, and it is occasionally traveled by heavily laden carriages, but not without encountering great difficulty." [64]

Samson was busy in 1827. Not only was he building the last fifteen miles of the road from Memphis to Little Rock, but he also was submitting bids for contracts for mail service on two routes. His bids were approved 11 October 1827 for mail service from Batesville to Little Rock and from Little Rock to Crawford Court House. The contracts called for Samson to furnish service over these routes from 1 January 1828 to 31 December 1829, for $580 for each route.[65] The route from Batesville to Little Rock covered 124 miles and called for weekly service. The mail would leave Little Rock every Saturday at 6:00 a.m. and arrive at Batesville at 6:00 p.m. on Monday. The route from Little Rock to Crawford Court House was by Standlee's Mills, Cadron, Conway Court House, Peconery, and Dardanells. The mail would be carried once every two weeks. The route covered a distance of 145 miles. The mail would leave Crawford Court House every other Tuesday at 2:00 p.m. and arrive at Little Rock by Friday at 6:00 p.m.[66]

The United States Post Office Department oversaw the contracts and had a long list of regulations concerning mail carriers and service. The Postmaster General could alter the times and route but would have to pay any additional expenses the changes occasioned. Seven minutes delay was allowed for opening and closing the mail at all offices. For every fifteen minutes delay in arrival time, the contractor forfeited ten dollars. If the delay continued until the departure time of any mail and a trip was lost, the forfeit would be double the amount allowed per trip. The Postmaster General could reduce the penalty for unavoidable accidents. Only a free white person was to be employed as a mail carrier. The list of regulations included detailed instructions on submitting bids, regulations for mail carried in stages, and provisions for cancellation of contracts. If contractors could improve the service or carry the mail faster, they would be given due consideration.[67]

Several members of Samson's family were involved with the mail service. His brother-in-law, George Wooten, helped with the business details. A son of Abraham Secrest worked as a cook at the mail stop and stage house that Samson opened on Bayou Meto.[68] A son of his brother-in-law, Charles Legate, became a mail carrier at age thirteen.[69] By 1830 several more routes had been added to the mail service contracts including routes to Cane Hill, Languille in St. Francis County, Grande, and Arkansas Post. Samson hired sub-contractors at some of the stops to arrange for food and lodging for the riders and their horses.[70] The mail stop at the Bayou Meto became a popular stopping place for travelers. Samson bought whiskey by the gallon from Jacob Reider in Little Rock and sold it by the bottle to customers at the Bayou Meto stage house. He also sold coffee, sugar, and other supplies and provided blacksmith services when needed.[71]

By 1832 Samson added a United States Mail Stage. The stage ran from Little

Rock to Arkansas Post every Saturday evening. The stage would leave Arkansas Post on Tuesday morning and reach Little Rock by 10:00 a.m. Thursday. The fare was ten dollars, and each passenger was allowed fourteen pounds of luggage.[72] Samson's mail now came addressed to Samson Gray, Bayou Meto, A.T. (Arkansas Territory).[73] The Bayou Meto settlement was now recognized as a community, and the settlers did not have to get their mail in Little Rock.

In 1830 Samson booked steamboat passage for himself and Allen Martin to Lake Port on the Mississippi River.[74] In the spring of 1831 Martin announced his candidacy for the Legislative Council from Pulaski County. On 20 April 1831 the *Arkansas Advocate* printed a letter, "the caucus," from "one of the people." The letter said the "ranks of the coalition" were behind Martin's candidacy and that Martin had been "palmed upon them [the people] by caucuses."[75] Martin answered the charges in the Gazette on 8 June 1831 in a letter "to the voters of Pulaski County." In the letter Martin referred to himself as " a plain, unvarnished farmer, who bends to no man, and wishes none to bend to him." He called himself an honest man and an independent citizen who was not a member of either of the two Little Rock parties.[76] In spite of his claims of being a plain, unvarnished farmer, Martin was a surveyor who had helped survey the Memphis Road and served as Pulaski County surveyor from 1825 to 1827 and in 1829 and 1830.[77] In 1830 Martin owned seven slaves.[78]

Martin was elected in 1831. In 1833 he announced for re-election. *The Advocate* was again critical of Martin's connections. On 26 June 1833 the *Gazette* printed a copy of the circular that Martin had been using in his defense. Martin claimed that he had very little ambition for public life, but when called by his neighbors and solicited by his friends, thought "it my duty ... of offering my humble name to you for your suffrages." Included in the circular were letters from William E. Woodruff, Chester Ashley, and Samson Gray. Their letters claimed they had not solicited Martin for this election, but Samson admitted that he had requested Martin to run in 1831, and Ashley admitted he was pleased that Martin was a candidate.[79]

Samson's involvement with the "reigning dynasty" that controlled Arkansas's territorial politics[80] was deeper than Martin's candidacy. On at least two different occasions Samson executed notes, with Ashley and Woodruff signing as his securities.[81] Author William F. Pope described Samson as a man of large influence who with Woodruff had been instrumental in getting Ambrose Sevier elected as Territorial Representative to Washington.[82] In 1832 when Shared Gray and Jacob Gray, Sr., applied for pensions for their revolutionary war service in the Carolinas, they named Ambrose Sevier as a man who could attest to their credibility.[83] Sevier was described as "an intimate associate of Samson Gray and in his [Samson's] company had mingled with the common people everywhere."[84] Samson's mail contracts had brought him into contact with a lot of people around the territory. Samson introduced Sevier to the many acquaintances he made and also gave financial support. In 1832 and 1833 Sevier signed several drafts for money he drew from Samson.[85]

In 1831 and 1832 Samson entered into contracts with the United States government to supply rations to Choctaw Indians who were migrating across Arkansas. The Choctaw Indians had signed treaties with the United States relinquishing their land in Mississippi for land in Indian Territory west of Arkansas.[86] Samson and his associates furnished large quantities of corn, beef and salt to the government for removal operations. One of his partners was Samuel Rutherford. Rutherford was hired by the government to act as a guide for the Indians and was under contract as a supplier. Samson also rented teams of oxen to pull wagons, sold fodder to feed stock, and used the hides from the beef cattle to trade for more rations and fodder.[87] The contractors were accused of frequently combining bids to force the government to pay inflated prices for the rations they supplied. Disagreements about weights and measures of rations from the private contractors were frequent problems.[88] Woodruff justified the supplier's prices and remarked "we hope they may realize from them [government contracts] a handsome profit."[89]

The United States Congress passed an act in 1831 granting ten sections of unappropriated lands to Arkansas to raise funds for the erection of a public building in Little Rock. On 2 April 1832 a group of citizens of Arkansas Territory petitioned the United States Congress, that since the Territorial Legislature had made no provisions for selecting the ten sections, that a law authorizing the governor to select the land be considered. There were 109 signers to the petition, including Woodruff, Ashley, Rutherford and Samson Gray.[90] Sevier was able to get the United States Congress to pass an act authorizing Governor Pope to handle the ten-section grant. The way that Pope discharged this duty and the construction of the State House were issues in 1833.[91] Pope appointed Ashley as superintendent of construction for the State House. In July the *Advocate* was critical of the State House construction and declared that all work had been suspended due to lack of funds. The *Gazette* countered with a statement signed by one hundred citizens of the territory that the work was progressing. Among the signers were Ashley, Rutherford and Samson Gray.[92]

On 16 October 1832 Governor Pope on a return trip from Kentucky took the overland route from Memphis to Little Rock. Pope and his party stopped overnight at the home of Samson Gray and left the next morning for Little Rock. Pope was met by David Rorer on the Arkansas River opposite Little Rock. Rorer had the ferry privileges at that site and after entertaining the governor for four hours saw Pope safely across on Rorer's ferry.[93] On 24 October 1832 the *Advocate* ran an editorial reminding the people that at the last session of the United States Congress $20,000 had been appropriated for repairs on the section of the Memphis and Little Rock Road from the St. Francis River to Little Rock. The editor informed the readers that contracts for the road repair had been given out to a few of Pope's personal and political friends, Rutherford, Gray and Rorer. The editor stated, "We are far from censuring those gentlemen for taking this profitable contract, even privately, they have all of late handled much of Uncle Sam's money - they doubtless know the use of it, and the pleasure its possession affords." The editor further stated that "kissing goes by favor" and asked the readers to judge the motives of the governor.[94] On 31 October the *Advocate* ran an editorial titled "$20,000 Just Going! - Gone!!" The editor added two more names to the list of contractors to "share in the spoils" and asked the question "What portion of this $20,000 is Governor Pope to receive?"[95] On 28 November 1832 the *Advocate* ran a letter "To His Excellency John Pope Governor of Arkansas Territory." The letter was signed CACHE. The letter was very critical of the governor's handling of the ten sections and of the road contracts.[96]

The *Gazette* did not answer the charges of the *Advocate* until 5 December 1832. The editor stated that the United States Congress granted $20,000 for repairs on the Memphis and Little Rock Road and placed the fund under the superintendence of the governor to handle in a manner that would give the best possible road for the money. Woodruff claimed that Rutherford, Rorer, Samson Gray and others were acting as agents of Governor Pope and that it would be foolish to hire his enemies to act as his agents. Woodruff said that all the men except Rutherford lived on the road and had a personal stake in seeing the work done right. The article further stated that Samson Gray was the only agent who could be considered a particular personal friend of the governor and described Samson as "a man of industry, and some practical sense and experience in such business."[97]

The controversy involving the road did not keep Samson Gray and Samuel Rutherford from getting started on the project. On 28 October 1832 the *Gazette* had carried their advertisement for "Laborers Wanted." The subscribers wanted thirty laborers for immediate employment to work on "that part of the Memphis and Little Rock Road commencing five miles north of the latter place and extending to the Mouth of Cache, on White River." The pay was sixteen dollars a month, and the work was expected to last six to eight months.[98] The advertisement for laborers ran in the *Gazette* for twenty-four weeks in 1832 and 1833.[99]

Samson was not only involved with territorial business, he also became involved with some of the social side of territorial life. The snag boat, *Archimedes*, came to Little Rock in 1834. The people rushed to the Arkansas River to view the boat. The captain allowed some of the citizens to come aboard while he demonstrated the abilities of the boat for his passengers and the people on shore. A large cottonwood tree, which was buried in the mud and had caused problems for boats on the river, was pulled out, sawed off at the roots, and dropped in the river to sink after being sawed into smaller pieces. The citizens were so pleased that a ten-man committee including Woodruff and Samson was named to express their gratitude. The committee planned a public dinner for the captain of the snag boat at the Eagle Hotel to honor him for his services in improving "inland navigation of our infant Territory." [100]

On 19 August 1834 the *Gazette* carried the story of yet another business venture for Samson. "Gray's White Sulphur Springs" was described as a "place of some note and considerable resort for persons laboring under the effects of recent illness, and particularly of affection of the liver and enlargement of the spleen." The springs were situated two or three miles southwest of Little Red River and forty-five miles northeast of Little Rock. Samson had erected cabins and built a road from Bayou Meto to the springs. Woodruff reported that a considerable number of people had visited the springs that summer and few, if any, had returned without deriving benefit, and some had been cured. The accommodations were described as being in a rude state but were comfortable for the season. Samson also boarded visitors, and the fare was described as far better than could be expected in so thinly settled a country.[101] As early as 13 June 1834, Samson was trading for supplies for Sulphur Springs. He got a coffee mill, eggs, chickens, butter, planks, nails, oil, sugar, molasses and a sailor knife from E. Gregory. In return he supplied Gregory with beef and ham and gave him credit for four meals and board from 17 June to 7 August.[102]

The development of the resort at Gray's White Sulphur Springs was the last business venture for Samson. On 11 November 1834 the *Gazette* carried the news that Samson Gray had died at his residence "11 miles from this place on Sunday evening last, after a painful illness of several months." Woodruff described Samson as a useful and enterprising citizen, a kind neighbor, a sincere friend, and a useful member of society.[103]

Samson was only thirty-eight when he died. He had by his enterprising spirit been deeply involved in the development of Arkansas Territory. He died before Arkansas became a state and before his friend and associate, Ambrose Sevier, became the first United States senator from the state of Arkansas. Samson established two settlements during his lifetime. The Bayou Meto settlement was named a Territorial Post Office in 1835, but business was so slow that the office was discontinued in 1836.[104] In the three years after his death, his brother Jacob, Jr., his uncle Shared, his brother-in-law Abraham Secrest, his brother-in-law Charles Legate, and his father Jacob, Sr., died.[105] His wife decided that his four sons needed a father, and she married one of the laborers who had been hired to work on the Little Rock and Memphis Road.[106] The old cohesive spirit was gone, and the settlement on the Bayou Meto began to break up. The members of the settlement began to move away and scatter.

Samson had acquired a large estate before his death, but he had also acquired many debts. Woodruff was eventually named administrator of the estate after the first administrators were not able to continue. On 2 May 1837 the *Gazette* carried in the report of the Circuit Court that an act authorizing the administrator of the estate of Samson Gray to sell real property of the estate had been passed by the Arkansas General Assembly in 1836, and the Circuit Court was now ordering a sale to be held. The debts of the estate were $4883.64. Woodruff was instructed to sell land belonging to the estate until the amount of $6,000 had been collected.[107] During the time Samson's estate was in probate, White Sulphur Springs[108] and the land in the Southwest Quarter of Section Thirty, Township Three North, Range Ten West, that contained the house where Samson lived at the time of his death,[109] was rented by the year, and his slaves were offered for hire.[110]

By 1841 the White Sulphur Springs were offered for sale. Woodruff had the land surveyed and divided into thirty-nine lots ranging from 63/100 of an acre to ten acres. The 63/100 of an acre lot containing the spring sold for twenty-one dollars. The one-acre lot containing a stable sold for forty dollars. The one-acre lot containing the dwelling house that Samson had built sold for one hundred eighty-five dollars.[111] Although Samson had purchased and developed the White Sulphur Springs land and built the road to the springs, he was not given credit for the venture, and the area was named Woodruff's addition to the town of Searcy.[112]

Samson Gray was honored by two townships that bore the Gray name: one, Gray Township, in Pulaski County[113] and the other, Gray Township, in White County.[114] All physical evidence of the Bayou Meto settlement has passed away with time, however. Even the Gray family cemetery has been destroyed and only lives in the minds of some early Jacksonville citizens who played there as children.[115]

Acknowledgment: The author wishes to thank [former Deputy Pulaski County Clerk] David W. Bizzell for his guidance and help in researching this article.

NOTES

This article originally appeared in the *Pulaski County Review*, 32 (Spring 1984): 2-16.

[1] Many variations of the spelling of Bayou Meto are found in territorial documents. In this paper the contemporary spelling will be used.

[2] *Arkansas Gazette*, 11 November 1834.

[3] Cephas Washburn, *Reminiscenses of the Indians* (Richmond: Presbyterian Committee of Publication, 1869) 89, cited by Walter Moffatt, "Transportation in Arkansas, 1819-1840," *Arkansas Historical Quarterly*, 15 (1956):187.

[4] *Arkansas Gazette*, 29 December 1821.

[5] Moffatt, "Transportation in Arkansas," 194.

[6] Jacob Gray, Application for Revolutionary War Pension, Military Service Records, National Archives, Washington, D.C., File S. 31,709.

[7] *Arkansas Gazette*, 11 November 1834.

[8] Williamson County, Tennessee, Deed Book A-2, p.205.

[9] Gray family file, William E. Woodruff Papers, Arkansas History Commission, Little Rock, Arkansas.

[10] Williamson County, Tennessee, Tax Books 1800-1821, Microfilm of Original Books, Church of Latter Day Saints, Salt Lake City, Utah.

[11] Williamson County, Tennessee, Court of Pleas and Quarter Sessions, 1800-1821, Microfilm, L.D.S.

[12] Ibid., 1819-1820.

[13] Williamson County, Deed Book F, 304.

[14] Woodruff Papers.

[15] Williamson County, Deed Book F, 367.

[16] Woodruff Papers.

[17] Ibid.

[18] Make-up of the migrating party was obtained from Williamson County, Marriage Records 1805-1824, Tax Records 1800-1821, and Court of Pleas and Quarter Sessions Records 1804-1821 (Microfilm, L.D.S.), Federal Census Population Schedules for 1820 Williamson County, Tenn., and for 1830 Pulaski County, Arkansas, Woodruff Papers, and *Biographical and Historical Memoirs of Central Arkansas* (Chicago, Ill: Goodspeed Publishing Co., 1889; reprint ed., Easley: Southern Historical Press, 1978), 613-614, 627.

[19] Williamson County, Tenn.,Tax Records.

[20] Mecklenburg County, North Carolina, Court of Pleas and Quarter Sessions, 1783-1808, Microfilm, L.D.S.

[21] Shared Gray, Application for Revolutionary War Pension, Military Service Records, National Archives, Washington, D.C., File S. 31,707.

[22] Williamson County, Tenn.,Tax Records.

[23] Josiah Shinn in *Pioneers and Makers of Arkansas* (Little Rock, 1908; reprint ed., Baltimore: Genealogical Publishing Company, 1967), 49-50, reported that there was another brother, Joseph Gray, who came to Arkansas Territory with the family migration. No evidence has been found to support the belief that the Joseph Gray who died in Arkansas County, (Arkansas County Court Records, 1815-1816), and whose estate was settled by Wright Daniels in Pulaski County (Arkansas Gazette, 22 September 1821), was related to the Gray family from Williamson County, Tennessee.

[24] Williamson County, Tenn., Court of Pleas and Quarter Sessions.

[25] Federal Census, 1830, Pulaski County.

[26] *Biographical and Historical Memoirs*, 613.

[27] *Arkansas Gazette*, 11 November 1834.

[28] Woodruff Papers.

[29] *Arkansas Gazette*, 4 February 1823.

[30] Ibid., 11 April 1826.

[31] Ibid., 11 November 1823.

[32] Margaret Ross, *Arkansas Gazette: The Early Years 1819-1866* (Little Rock, Ark: Arkansas Gazette Foundation, 1969), 57.

[33] Pulaski County, Arkansas, *Deed Book C*, 160.

[34] Woodruff Papers.

[35] Ibid.

[36] Ibid.

[37] Federal Census, 1830, Pulaski County, Arkansas.

[38] Woodruff Papers.

[39] *Arkansas Gazette*, 15 August 1825.

[40] Federal Census, 1850, Prairie County, Arkansas.

[41] Woodruff Papers.

[42] *Arkansas Gazette*, 15 August 1825.

[43] Ibid., 25 October 1825.

[44] Woodruff Papers.

[45] Ibid.

[46] *Arkansas Gazette*, 4 November 1823.

[47] Ibid., 30 March 1824.

[48] Ibid., 14 January 1823.

[49] Ibid., 28 January 1823.

[50] Fay Hempstead, A *Factorial History of Arkansas: From Earliest Times to the Year 1890* (St. Louis: N. D. Thompson Publishing Co., 1890), 770.

[51] *Arkansas Gazette*, 17 July 1827.

[52] Ibid., 15 February 1825.

[53] Ibid., 10 May 1825.

[54] Ibid., 25 July 1826.

[55] Ibid., 20 March 1827.

[56] Ibid., 12 June 1827.

[57] Clarence Edwin Carter, *The Territorial Papers of the United States, Vol. XX* (Washington, D.C.: U. S. G. P. 0., 1954), 510, 512.

[58] *Arkansas Gazette*, 5 November 1827.

[59] Carter, *Territorial Papers, Vol. XX*, 570, 585.

[60] Ibid., 620-621.

[61] *Arkansas Gazette*, 13 November 1827.

[62] Ibid., 9 December 1828.

[63] Ibid., 3 June 1829.

[64] Ibid. 9 September 1829.

[65] Carter, *Territorial Papers*, Vol. XX, 541.

[66] *Arkansas Gazette*, 31 July 1827.

[67] Ibid., 28 August 1827.

[68] Woodruff Papers.

[69] *Biographical and Historical Memoirs*, 627.

[70] Woodruff Papers.

[71] Ibid.

[72] *Arkansas Gazette*, 18 July 1832.

[73] Woodruff Papers.

[74] Ibid.

[75] *Arkansas Advocate*, 20 April 1831. The *Arkansas Advocate* began publication in Little Rock on 31 March 1830. The paper became the rallying point for the opposition to Woodruff and Sevier.

[76] *Arkansas Gazette*, 8 June 1831.

[77] Hempstead, *Pictorial History of Arkansas*, 841.

[78] Shinn, *Pioneers of Arkansas*, 239.

[79] *Arkansas Gazette*, 26 June 1833.

[80] John Hallum, *Biographical and Pictorial History of Arkansas*, (Albany, N.Y.: Weed, Parsons and Co., 1887), 42.

[81] Woodruff Papers.

[82] William F. Pope, *Early Days in Arkansas* (Little Rock: Fredrick E. Allsopp, 1895; reprint ed., Easley: Southern Historical Press, 1978), 74.

[83] Gray, Revolutionary War Pensions, Files S. 31,707, S. 31,709.

[84] Shinn, *Pioneers of Arkansas*, 209.

[85] Woodruff Papers.

[86] Grant Foreman, *Indian Removal* (Norman: University of Oklahoma Press, 1932), 29.

[87] Woodruff Papers.

[88] Foreman, *Indian Removal*, 75.

[89] *Arkansas Gazette*, 11 September 1833.

[90] Carter, *Territorial Papers*, Vol. XXI, 462-464.

[91] Ross, *Arkansas Gazette: The Early Years*, 106.

[92] *Arkansas Gazette*, 17 July 1833.

[93] Pope, *Early Days in Arkansas*, 73-74.

[94] *Arkansas Advocate*, 24 October 1832.

[95] Ibid., 31 October 1832.

[96] Ibid., 28 November 1832.

[97] *Arkansas Gazette*, 5 December 1832.

[98] Ibid., 28 October 1832.

[99] Woodruff Papers.

[100] *Arkansas Gazette*, 18 February 1834.

[101] Ibid., 19 August 1834.

[102] Woodruff Papers.

[103] *Arkansas Gazette*, 11 November 1834.

[104] Shannon J. Henderson, *Arkansas Gazette Index: 1830-1839* (Russellville: Arkansas Tech University Library, 1978), 155.

[105] *Arkansas Gazette*, 9 December 1834, 15 February 1836, 10 January, and 4 April 1837.

[106] Woodruff Papers.

[107] *Arkansas Gazette*, 2 May 1837.

[108] Ibid., 23 December 1834.

[109] Ibid., 12 December 1837.

[110] Ibid., 16 December 1840.

[111] White County, Arkansas, Deed Book A, pp. 134-141.

[112] Eugene Cypert, "Origin of the Names of White County Townships," Searcy Daily Citizen, 18 August 1924, printed Arkansas Family Historian 1976, p. 186.

[113] Shinn, Pioneers of Arkansas, 50.

[114] Cypert, "Origin Of White County Townships," 186.

[115] Murrell Taylor and Watson Nixon, interviews with author, Jacksonville Historical Society Inc., Jacksonville, Arkansas, 8 September 1983.

"THE QUAINT OLD PLACE CALLED 'TANGLEWOOD'": HANNAH DONNELL KNIGHT'S GARDEN IN LITTLE ROCK.

Harriet Jansma

Only recently have professional historians begun to show the interest in environmental concerns that is reflected in this article on gardening, which provides a wonderful insight into the mind and life of an early resident of Little Rock. Harriet Jansma was working as a legislative aide in 1983 when she discovered the letters of Hannah Donnell Knight in the archives of the "Arkansas Gazette" and began working on this project. She went on the work for the University of Arkansas in Fayetteville and was director of communications when she retired several years ago. She has continued her interest and involvement in Arkansas garden history throughout her career.

> Across from Mr. Worthen, [Georgine Woodruff wrote late in her long life,] John E. Knight lived in a cottage surrounded by forest trees and wild flowers. There were borders of flowers near the house, but the rest of the place was left as Nature had made it, an ideal "Poet's Home," as it was called.[1]

The "Poet," John Elliot Knight, had come to Little Rock in 1843 and had worked for a time for William Woodruff as assistant editor of the *Democrat*, then of the *Gazette and Democrat*, later the *Arkansas Gazette*. In her history, *Arkansas Gazette: The Early Years 1819-1866*, Margaret Ross has summarized the major events of Knight's life: Born in 1816 in Newburyport, Massachusetts, he married Hannah Donnell in September 1843 and moved west soon afterward, arriving in Little Rock on November 3, 1843. Unhappy in his first work there as an overseer of slaves, Knight began to work for Woodruff and soon began also to practice law. After he left the *Gazette* in 1850, Knight maintained a law practice and pension agency, served a brief term as mayor of Little Rock, remained active in community life and politics until about 1855, then lived quietly on Arch between Markham and Second streets until his death in 1901.[2]

Hannah Donnell, who married John Knight at age twenty and came west with him, does not mention their homestead of over half a century in her brief and simply written story, "Hospitality of Early Days,"[3] probably her only published writing, composed after the death of her husband and three years before her own death in 1911. However, twenty-two letters that Hannah Knight wrote between 1843 and 1893 to the family she left behind in Newburyport, and later to her brother Charles in California, tell us a great deal about the life the Knights lived in Little Rock during that half-century.[4] The letters reveal much about ordinary town life in Little Rock and chronicle many a newsworthy event in its history. They are of particular value, however, for the accumulation of comment they contain about life on a Little Rock town homestead, for always – especially – Hannah Knight wrote to her family about the growing plants in her life and about household activities related to her garden.[5]

". . . Left as Nature had made it," Georgine Woodruff described this garden. Hannah Knight's letter to her sister written in early 1851 confirms Miss Woodruff's memory of its landscape style: "Our house is in the midst of a grove of forest trees, and in the sum it is entirely hid by them, the shade makes it very cool and pleasant."[6]

Josie Clendenin Royston, who said that she had often visited Mrs. Knight as a child in the 1870s, wrote a similar description of the property:

> The home of Mr. and Mrs. John E. Knight stood where the Acme Storage Company now stands, on the corner of Markham Street, and was the quaint old place called "Tanglewood" . . . . I wish I could do justice to this little home. The grounds were allowed to grow up in a wild natural growth. Never a sprig of anything was cut. It truly deserved its name, "Tanglewood." [7]

How unusual would such a naturalistic garden have been in the Little Rock of its day? Allan Brown tells us that some of Little Rock's earliest buildings were constructed in the midst of forest and swamp undergrowth. But by the 1840s, only two decades later, extensive formal flower gardens had been planted to complement Roswell Beebe's grand house on Markham Street, and Absalom Fowler's formal walkway was flanked by young magnolias. Just one block east of the Knight property were the formal gardens and topiary cubes of the William B. Wait homestead, pictured and described in an article in the *Pulaski County Historical Review* (Summer 1983).[8]

Albert Pike, another Little Rock poet, and an earlier immigrant to Little Rock from Newburyport, was aware of the fashion for a new naturalism in garden design that accompanied the Romantic Movement in literature. Pike, a strong proponent of the new natural style, rejected the earlier style of square formal beds, "wherein art hath not so far advanced as to seem like nature."[9] The Knight garden, that of another Romantic poet, must have been an extreme example of the new taste for naturalism, for it had advanced so far as to appear to be nature itself![10]

Descriptions of the Knight thicket do not tell the whole story, however. The Knights grew many plants in the 1840s and 1850s that could not have thrived as forest undergrowth. Their large city property allowed them to plant an orchard and a kitchen garden as well as to enjoy the luxury of a tree-shaded cottage in the debilitating heat of Little Rock summers that Hannah Knight sometimes complained of.11 A list of the plants mentioned in the ten pre-Civil War letters, all written by Hannah Knight to her sister Mary Boston in Newburyport, Massachusetts, will reveal the importance of the kitchen garden in the early years of the Knight household:

PLANTS IN KNIGHT GARDEN MENTIONED IN LETTERS OF HANNAH KNIGHT, 1844(?) - 1857[12]

green peas	1844 (?); 1852
ambrosia	1851
mignonette	1851
sypress vine	1851
unnamed flowers from seed	1851;1852; 1857
cucumbers	1852
potatoes	18592
beans	1852
head letuce	1852
roses	1853
goosbery	1854
strawberrys	1854
apples (Greening variety)	1857
peaches	1857
tomatoes	1857
pears	1857
plums	1857
unnamed green house plants	1857

Hannah Knight took pleasure in growing and using the crops of the garden and wrote often about them. She and her sister Mary saved and exchanged seeds wrapped in newspapers, obviously enjoying both the news and the plants. Hannah wrote to Mary in 1851:

> I will try and get you some flower seeds and send in a news paper. I can get some Ambrosia and Migonette seed and some Sypress vine.
> I planted quite a variety of flower seed but the summer has been so dry

that they did not come to anything. [13]

Again she wrote in 1852:

> . . . the last mail brought a newspaper with the flower seeds and I am
> very much obliged for them. I went out yesterday morning early and
> prepared a nice little bed, and planted them. I hope they will come up
> well; it is rather late to plant seeds here, but if we do not have dry
> weather very soon they may do well. We are getting quite a variety of
> vegetables from our garden and I enjoy them very much. We have new
> potatoes, and beans and peas plenty . . . . I am sorry I had no letuce seed
> to send mother. I had but little in the spring that Mrs. Worthen (my
> neighbor) brought from Kentucky. It was the head letuce and very nice.
> I have plenty gone to seed, and shall save it and will send her some in
> the Fall. [14]

and in 1854:

> I planted the goosbery seed you sent and I think they are coming up.
> The dry summer has killed all my finer strawberrys. I have been quite
> distressed about it. I watered them and tryed hard to save them but all
> to no purpose. [15]

The Knights also kept a cow and hens ("so we can have plenty of pudding,"
Hannah told Mary[16]) and butchered hogs and pigs, salted and smoked their meat,
and made sausage. [17]

The Knight garden of the antebellum years is not all necessity, however. By 1857
Hannah wrote to Mary: "We have quite a variety of flowers. I have made a number
of beautiful bouquets from my pit this winter."[18] In May of that same year, after a
devastating late frost, she mentioned "green house plants" that seem to have been
pot-grown ornamentals:

> I had taken all my green house plants out of the pit; and I was too
> unwell that day to be out doors to attend to them. John and Lizzie
> put some of the tenderest ones back or I should have lost all. Of
> course all that were left out were killed. I hope they will spring up from
> the root. [19]

The list of plants mentioned by Mrs. Knight in her letters written after the war
years will reveal how important pit, or green house, gardening became for her, as it
did for many a householder of the late-Victorian era (the Wait garden had a pit).[20]
Although Mrs. Knight did not name specific plants in these early letters, it is clear
that she was growing tender ornamentals as early as 1857.

The Knight household was also quick to embrace the latest method of food preservation, canning. Hannah Knight wrote to Mary, also in 1857:

I put up 40 quarts of peaches in tin cans. They are almost as fresh as when taken from the trees. I put up also a few cans of tomatoes, pears, and plums. It is a great invention. The fruit is so much nicer than preserved.21

Though Nicolas Appert had received a cash prize from the French government in 1809 for inventing a method of food preservation by sterilization, not until 1825 was a tin-plated can patented in the United States, and not until 1847 was a machine-stamped tin can patented.22 Just ten years later, Hannah Knight was enjoying the results of the new process, which made her fruits taste "almost as fresh as when taken from the trees."[23]

In the wartime letters – there are only three, written to Hannah's brothers, Charles and George – Mrs. Knight's attentions are given to her worries about the war and to the death of her mother. With the earliest of the postwar letters, however, Hannah Knight began to write in such detail about the ornamental plants she grew that it seems obvious these plants occupied a central place in her daily life. At the time of the following letter, Hannah had been away from Newburyport for twenty-five years, yet her memory of the plants that grew there was keen:

I should like to have sister Mary send me some roots of Lily of the Valley. I have not seen any since I left home. I have still some Tulips, the Red and Pink that I brought from home. If she can send me any other varieties I shall be much obliged. I have sent some Apple geranium and it is the sweetest of all the Geraniums. I think it will not grow from slips. I raised a good many last winter and sold them at our flower sale this spring.24

The flower sale is that of the Presbyterian Church in Little Rock; the Knights were active members,[25] and the sale was advertised daily in the *Arkansas Gazette* during March of 1868.[26] Hannah Knight mentions another sale in 1875.[27]

No real clues exist about the appearance of the Knight gardens during these later years beyond those of Georgine Woodruff, Josie Clendenin Royston, and Hannah Knight herself: of a house hidden and shaded by the forest trees and undergrowth. But in terms of her behavior, Hannah Knight was a gardener typical of her day in many ways. The Victorian era in gardening was a time when the urban and suburban garden replaced the huge estate garden in importance. Its rise was a result of the growth of the middle classes and of their growth in affluence and awareness. John Highstone, who has written a handbook to aid the twentieth-century gardener who wishes to plant a garden in the Victorian manner, says that the nineteenth-century garden was everyman's: "no longer the exclusive domain of a privileged few, [it] became the delight of the middle classes."[28] The result, as Highstone and other historians of landscape have noted, was often a garden of seclusion and natural beauty, a "created segment of nature." The garden became a place for the owner to be and enjoy nature rather than a vast space to be looked at.

Hannah Knight's garden was a modest one in comparison to the grander gardens of Little Rock, just as her frame cottage was modest in comparison to the young town's grander mansions. She clearly entered her garden and worked there, and she enjoyed what she saw and heard and touched there. In early 1871 she wrote to her brother Charles:

> ... birds are singing in the grove in front of the house. We shall commence gardening this week . . . . My green house flowers are looking beautifully [sic]. The Pond Lily is alive. I am going to get some mud for it.[29]

The next year, in a letter charming in tone, written to her nephew Eddie, she reported on a particular bird:

> I will not forget to tell you that I have a fine mocking bird that I caught in a small cage that I put out in the garden on the top of another that had Lizzie's bird in it. I put cedar berrys in the cage and Lizzie's bird called him, and the cedar berry induced him and watched till he went in and ran and shut the door; he had been round the house for some time, and one of the sweetest singers I ever heard.[30]

Hannah reported on walnuts harvested from a tree she had started from seed[31] and resolved to plant seed of some especially nice plums brought from California and sold in Little Rock.[32] She mailed and received plants more and more during the postwar period, as her fascination with unusual new plants, especially tender greenhouse species, grew:

> I was sorry to loose [sic] my Lemon Geranium that sister Mary Knight gave me, as I had not seen this variety before. If sister Mary's is alive and large enough to take a slip from I should like to have you send me one through the Post Office, just roll it in a piece of cotton and put it in an envelope.[33]

> I have a beautiful lot of plants blooming in my pit. I have lately added some new ones from Robert J. Halidays, Baltimore. Azaleas, variegated geraniums, double white primrose, cyclamens, variegated wire plant, bouvardeas, one dozen new varieties. They came in fine order and

were the cheapest plants I ever bought.[34]

In his chapter on "The Plants of the Garden," Highstone says, "In the Victorian era, imported exotic plants, shrubs, and trees were enormously popular in gardens. Plants never seen before became topics of great conversation . . . ."[35] In this too, as can be seen in the letter just excerpted, Hannah Knight was a woman of her time. She wrote to her brothers about new plants and new varieties, always finding and growing yet another, always full of curiosity and delight over the plants of her pit.

The list of plants mentioned in the letters written between 1868 and 1893 contrasts sharply with that of the early letters, though we have no evidence either in the letters or elsewhere that the garden changed greatly in appearance:

PLANTS IN KNIGHT GARDEN MENTIONED IN LETTERS OF HANNAH KNIGHT, 1868-1893[36]

lily of the valley	1868
tulip (red and pink)	1868
apple geranium	1868
pond lily	1871
lemon geranium	1871
oxalis	1871
orange	1871
cactus	1871
night-blooming cerious	1871
gladiola	1871
lily	1871
oleander	1874; 1893
rose	1875
azalea	1875
variegated geranium	1875
double white primrose	1875
cyclamen	1875
variegated wire plant	1875
bouvardeas	1875
wallnut	1875

Many of these plants would have been grown in containers in the pit or greenhouse and been brought outdoors only for the summer. It should be no surprise that the Knights enlarged the greenhouse in 1847, as Mrs. Knight reported:

I have been quite busy getting my plants in the green house. I have had it all made over new this Fall and have made it some larger so that I can get into it better and it is not so crowded as it was. It is all finished and the plants are all in. It is really a beautiful sight. I have a variety of plants in bloom. I wish you could be here and enjoy it with me.[37]

Hannah Knight's interest in plants did not end in her own greenhouse. She shared with her contemporaries a fascination with tropical plants. To Charles she wrote, in the year of the Great Cotton Exposition in New Orleans:

. . . if you go to New Orleans perhaps we can meet you there; for I want to go, and I think Lizzie will go too – I expect it will be a fine exhibition. I am very anxious to see the Tropical garden I hear they are going to have; it will be different from anything I have ever seen.[38]

And almost a decade later, in the year of the Knights' fiftieth wedding anniversary, Hannah Knight mentioned Chicago's Columbian Exhibition. In that letter, at age seventy-one, she was writing as usual about her active relationship with her plants:

I am busy now as it is time for me to be getting my plants into the little green house. I have repoted [sic] some and still have some to repot. I hope the Oleanders that I sent are doing well. I have some white ones for you but will not send them till Spring.[39]

It is as if she wrote her own epitaph in this continuing report: repotting the plants, wintering them over, preparing to share them with her family in the spring. Hannah Knight lived eighteen more years at her home in Little Rock. She is buried at Mount Holly Cemetery.

NOTES

This article first appeared in the *Pulaski County Historical Review*, 32 (Summer 1984): 22-30.

[1]Georgine Woodruff, "A Pioneer Childhood in Little Rock," *Arkansas Gazette*, 7 November 1931.

[2] Margaret Ross, *Arkansas Gazette: The Early Years 1819-1866* (Little Rock: Arkansas Gazette Foundation, 1969), 273.

[3]Hannah Donnell Knight, "Hospitality of Early Days," *The Arkansas Pioneers*, vol. I:1 (September 1912): 11-12.

[4] Knight Letters, Arkansas Gazette Foundation Library, Little Rock. There are actually twenty-three letters in the group, but one of them was written by Lizzie Knight Pollock,

the daughter of Hannah and John Knight. She was born in Little Rock in 1844, and married James S. Pollock. They lived in a house built in 1871 on the Knight property, as reported in the letter written by Hannah Donnell Knight to her brother Charles on July 5, 1871. Lizzie died in 1901, just six days after her father. The Pollocks are buried in Mount Holly Cemetery.

[5] I am grateful to Margaret Ross of the *Arkansas Gazette* for bringing to my attention these letters and their significant contribution to the history of gardening in Little Rock.

[6] Hannah Donnell Knight to her sister, 17 February 1851. Knight Letters, Arkansas Gazette Foundation Library, Little Rock. The letters are hereafter identified by the name of the recipient and the date of the writing. I have retained Mrs. Knight's irregular spellings but have sometimes added periods for the sake of clarity.

[7] Josie Clendenin Royston, "The Home of Mr. and Mrs. John E. Knight, 'Tanglewood'," in "Historical Sites in Little Rock Before the Civil War," undated typescript, Arkansas History Commission, Little Rock.

[8] C. Allan Brown and William Lake Douglas, *A Garden Heritage: Little Rock: 1819-1865* (Little Rock: The Arkansas Territorial Restoration Foundation, 1983), 5, 8-9, 15-19; and C. Allan Brown, "The Legacy of the City of Roses," *Pulaski County Historical Review*, 31:2 (Summer 1983): 24-27.

[9] Albert Pike, *American Monthly Magazine* (January 1836), quoted by Frederick Allsopp, *Albert Pike: A Biography* (Little Rock: Parke-Harper Co., 1928), 53. See also Allan Brown's discussion of the new movement in *A Garden Heritage*, 10-11.

[10] See also Frederick W. Allsopp, *The Poets and Poetry of Arkansas* (Little Rock: Central Printing Company, 1933), 48-49. Mr. Allsopp says that John E. Knight returned to his home at Second and Arch streets in about 1860 and became a recluse until his death in 1901. It is interesting to ponder whether the Knight cottage, hid entirely from view by its untrimmed landscape, may have helped to shape the public image of its owner.

Knight's "Scribblings," a manuscript book of poems and sketches long in the possession of Mr. Allsopp, is now housed in the Special Collections and Archives, University of Arkansas at Little Rock. The John E. Knight Archive, consisting of legal and personal papers, and including documentation related to the settlement of early land claims in Little Rock, is in the Archives of the Arkansas History Commission, Little Rock.

[11] "This is a bilious climate, we all suffer from it. I wish I could get away from it every summer. The winters are pleasant and that is some compensation." Hannah Knight to her brother Charles, 2 December 1875.

[12] The names of the plants and their spellings are Hannah Knight's.

[13] Hannah Donnell Knight to Mrs. Mary Boston, her sister, 25 August 1851.

[14] Hannah Donnell Knight to her sister Mary, 25 May 1852.

[15] Hannah Donnell Knight to her sister Mary, 14 October 1854.

[16] Hannah Donnell Knight to her sister Mary, 8 February 1857.

[17] Hannah Donnell Knight to her sister Mary, 19 December 1853. In this same letter

Hannah complained that the river was so low that the boats could not reach Little Rock. No raisins and currants were to be had: "I don't know what the folks will do for Christmas. I think the Mince Pies will have to suffer a little. I guess we shall make some without any raisins. I have never tasted a real good one since I left brothers. We can't get cider to put in them and they are not as good without it." The importance of the home garden in the Little Rock of 1853 is obvious.

18 Hannah Donnell Knight to her sister Mary, 8 February 1857.

19 Hannah Donnell Knight to her sister Mary, 2 May 1857. This writer, herself a gardener, finds interesting – and all too human – Mrs. Knight's contrasting descriptions of the winter of 1857, the one written before the killing late frost, the other after it: "The weather is quite mild and pleasant. We have had only a few cold days this winter and only one slight snow." (8 February 1857) "We have had the coldest and most disagreeable winter I have ever known in this state." (2 May 1857).

20 Brown and Douglas, *A Garden Heritage*, 16.

21 Hannah Donnell Knight to her sister Mary, 8 February 1857.

22 Earl Chapin May, "Important Dates by Decades," in *The Canning Clan* (New York: Macmillan Company, 1938), 434-435.

23 It is interesting to note that the earliest commercial canning in the United States was concentrated along the New England coast, where salmon, lobster, and oysters were canned for inland distribution. (Ibid.) Perhaps Hannah Knight learned early about the process from her New England family. She also mentioned canning in glass jars in a later letter (Hannah Donnell Knight to her brother Charles, 2 December 1875).

24 Hannah Donnell Knight to her brother Charles, 25 August 1868.

25 Margaret Ross, "Little Rock in the Mid-1800s, As Revealed in Two Letters," *Arkansas Gazette*, 24 September 1958. ("The Chronicles of Arkansas," no. 11).

26 *Arkansas Gazette*, 7 March 1868, 2.

27 Hannah Donnell Knight to her brother Charles, 2 December 1875.

28 John Highstone, *Victorian Gardens* (San Francisco: Harper and Row, 1982), 2.

29 Hannah Donnell Knight to her brother Charles, 19 February 1871.

30 Hannah Donnell Knight to her nephew Eddie, 4 April 1872. In this letter Mrs. Knight also reports to Eddie that Little Rock has a roller-skating rink.

31 Hannah Donnell Knight to her brother Charles, 2 December 1875.

32 Hannah Donnell Knight to her brother Charles, 21 October 1874. In an earlier letter of the 1870s, that of 5 July 1871, Mrs. Knight regretted the necessity of cutting down two fine orchard trees on the property in order to build a house on that spot for Lizzie and her husband.

33 Hannah Donnell Knight to her brother Charles, 19 February 1871.

34 Hannah Donnell Knight to her brother Charles, 2 December 1875.

35 Highstone, *Victorian Gardens*, 35.

[36] As before, the spellings and names are those used by Mrs. Knight.

[37] Hannah Donnell Knight to her brother Charles, 21 October 1874.

[38] Hannah Donnell Knight to her brother Charles, 11 September 1884.

[39] Hannah Donnell Knight to her brother Charles, 30 October 1893.

THE LITTLE ROCK FREEDMEN'S HOME FARM, 1863-1865

By Carl H. Moneyhon

Carl H. Moneyhon, one of several professional historians who have written articles in the Review, *is a professor at the University of Arkansas at Little Rock. His Arkansas publications include "Portraits of Conflict: A Photographic History of Arkansas in the Civil War", co-authored with Bobby Roberts and published in 1987, and "The Impact of the Civil War and Reconstruction on Arkansas: Persistence in the Midst of Ruin", a major reinterpretation of that period that appeared in 1994. In the piece that follows he provides an account of a little-known aspect of the social history of the Civil War.*

Union armies, which began to occupy Southern territory as early as the autumn of 1861, brought within federal lines thousands of slaves. Congress debated their legal status until 1863, but entry into Union lines made the slaves virtually free, no matter what action Congress might take. Unfortunately, few of the freedmen had the resources necessary to establish their freedom securely. They had little money or property. Most had no education. Many found employment as wage laborers, but their steadily increasing numbers overwhelmed the ability of the communities to which they escaped to provide work. By the middle of the war, thousands lived under terrible conditions in refugee camps across the South. These conditions ultimately forced the federal government to create a program to help the freedmen make the adjustment from slavery to freedom, providing aid in adjusting to free labor and supporting education. The project was without precedent for the national government. One small part of that program, the development of the Little Rock freedmen's Home Farm, helps to illustrate the results of the federal effort and its ultimate successes and failures.[1]

On September 10, 1863, a Union force under General Frederick Steele occupied the city of Little Rock. At Little Rock, as elsewhere, hundreds of slaves sought freedom and protection within the lines of the city. Raids into the surrounding countryside, activity in the Fort Smith vicinity, and Steele's expedition into southwestern Arkansas in the spring of 1864 brought thousands more to the capital city. The refugees gathered in neighborhoods called "Lickskillet" and "Brownsville" by local whites. They threw up log houses. By 1865, one military inspector reported that these communities had not been organized along streets or any discernible pattern but had grown up "as indifferently as mushrooms." [2]

At least initially many of the refugees found ready employment within the city.

The United States Army and other government agencies needed hundreds of workers. Ex-slaves built fortifications, loaded and unloaded boats and trains, worked as teamsters, cooked, and laundered. Early on, one government official estimated that at least a thousand freedmen toiled from "early dawn till early night" in jobs within the city, making it possible for only a few of them to be "dependent on the Government for rations." [3] A teacher with the American Missionary Association wrote from Little Rock in January 1864 that nearly all of the freedmen who had come in from the countryside "find employment and are quite comfortable."[4]

From the beginning, however, some of the refugees could not find work. Generally the aged, the very young, and the ill gathered at the "contraband camp" near the city where they relied upon federal aid for survival. In addition, freedmen's aid societies in the North sent workers to provide support for the freedmen. One early report indicated that there were only one hundred and fifty freedmen in the contraband camp, but they were found to be in a "destitute condition." Teachers from the American Missionary Association visited the camp in December 1863 and found life for the inhabitants was much worse than in the other freedmen's communities within Little Rock. Their clothing was poor, they were crowded into cabins that, although comfortable and with floors, were "overflowing." "Here there is more suffering & destitution," the Reverend D. T. Allen of the AMA informed the association's secretary, and "many are in great need of clothing & shoes."[5] They suffered, according to one military inspector, from the "idea that anything is good enough for a 'nigger,' " which had an "abiding place still in the midst of not a few connected with the freedmen."[6]

Official policy toward the freedmen prior to November 1863 was primarily the responsibility of local commanders, but at that time General Ulysses S. Grant created the position of General Superintendent of Freedmen to establish an integrated program in the Mississippi River Valley. He named John Eaton, Jr. as the first General Superintendent. Eaton in turn named Major William G. Sargent superintendent of freedmen in Arkansas. Sargent arrived at Helena in January 1864. He found conditions there to demand much of his time and, as a result, he did not set up his office at Little Rock until the following March.[7]

The advance of Union forces in the autumn of 1863 and the spring of 1864 worsened conditions in the contraband camps. More and more freedmen came into Union lines, and the jobs available for the freedmen were filled. Reverend Allen informed his association as late as March that he had received few supplies, conditions in the camps were getting worse, and that many of the women and children were particularly needy.[8]

When Sargent finally arrived, he implemented a general program for the freedmen initially created by the Treasury Department in February. Officials assigned to look after freedmen's matters were to encourage those who were able to enter into labor contracts with private citizens, although the conditions for such contracts were regulated. Many were put to work on plantations leased to loyal planters. The Treasury had recognized, however, that many of the freedmen were not ready for integration into the free labor market. To aid in the transition from slavery to freedom, the department proposed creating Home Farms to which freedmen would come initially. They would be registered and then remain there until they could be placed in a job, usually on a leased plantation. In addition, the army could recruit black soldiers from these farms. The Home Farm was designed to be a place of "temporary labor for those who are not otherwise employed."[9]

The plan recognized, however, that many would require further support. The Home Farm was also to be a place where the helpless — specifically the aged, infirm, and orphans — could, in the words of a Treasury official, "be more properly and economically cared for than in such 'contraband camps,' and military posts as are now filled with them, and in which they are fed in idleness and demoralized in many ways disgraceful to us, and ruinous to them." In addition to working on the farm, the inmates of the Home Farm were to receive education and support that would allow them to establish their freedom more firmly.[10]

In addition to implementing the general program for freedmen, Major Sargent created the Little Rock Home Farm on May 5, 1864. He appointed its first permanent superintendent when he named Lieutenant J. J. Williams, 63rd U.S. Colored Infantry, to take charge of operations. From the beginning, the history of the Home Farm reflected both the bad and the good of the government's efforts to help the freedmen throughout the South.[11]

The Home Farm was opened on one of William R. Vaughan's plantations that had been seized by the Treasury Department. Vaughan was one of Pulaski County's wealthiest planters, with land near Little Rock and elsewhere in the county. In 1860 the forty-four-year-old Vaughan reported in the census that he held $50,000 in real and $59,000 in personal property. The tax rolls showed that he owned 1,766 acres in the county and fifty-three slaves. The land taken by the government for the freedmen's farm was four miles south of the city on the south side of the Arkansas River, between the abandoned plantation of James R. Keatts and Fourche De Anne. (It was either under or just east of Adams Field.) Just outside the city, it was easily protected and offered some 500 to 600 acres of arable land for cultivation.[12]

The plantation was not, however, in the best shape for its new role. The military found the plantation to be dilapidated, with all of the buildings either torn down or almost uninhabitable. The fences were down. There were no farm implements or teams remaining on the plantation. Even the wells had been filled in and the cisterns broken apart. Major Sargent reported that because the property had belonged to "traitors to the country" it had "fared badly at the hands of our soldiery."[13] To serve the expected new inhabitants, the army began construction of sixty cabins and a hospital. Most of this work was left to what Sargent called the "lame, the women and the children."[14]

The same people were also put to work in other areas in order to relieve the "burthen and expense to the Government." The inhabitants of the camp chopped wood, which was sold for fuel in the city or was sent to the boat landings to power the government steamboats. The freedmen also improved the plantation, building some 1,320 feet of fence. The government always intended that the camp be self-sustaining, which meant that ultimately it had to be put back into cultivation. Major Sargent complained that by the time the plantation was in shape to work, however, he could find no military officer who could serve as superintendent for agricultural activities. As a result, Sargent leased the land to J. W. Medbury, a Northerner, who employed the freedmen who were on the Home Farm, paying one-third of his profits to the laborers and one-third to the army for use of the land. Sargent reported in July 1864 that Medbury had put some four hundred acres of land into cultivation that spring.[15]

In addition to its agricultural activities, the freedmen's farm became the center of military recruiting. On May 2, 1864, Captain Samuel N. Yearick and Lieutenant Alonzo Garrison, white officers of the 69th United States Colored Infantry, were assigned quarters at the freedmen's farm. By July 1864, they had their first company ready to be mustered into service as a part of the 69th United States Colored Regiment.[16]

The hopes that the Home Farm would be a place where the freedmen would begin an efficient transition from slavery to freedom, and where the helpless could be taken care of was, however, slow to be fulfilled. On May 30, 1864, Private James W. Wheelock was assigned as Acting Hospital Steward for the Home Farm to establish a hospital for the freedmen. Wheelock arrived to find that the medical treatment of the residents of the Farm had been neglected and that it was filled with disease. Not only were there the sick from the Home Farm in need of treatment, but there were additional sick freedmen that the army sent from the city and laborers that plantation lessees returned to the Farm. Wheelock reported in July that the hospital averaged approximately one hundred patients at any one time. While various relief organizations had sent clothing for the freedmen, he had nothing for the sick. In a letter to Major Sargent, Wheelock indicated the inadequacy of medical facilities when he requested 200 cotton shirts, 200 pairs of drawers, 200 sheets, 100 bedspreads, 200 pillows and cases, 100 mosquito bars, 300 handkerchiefs, 100 hospital gowns, and a supply of canned fruit and barrels of brandy for his patients.[17]

In addition, despite the stated intention of the Freedmen's Department to educate the freedmen, no schools were created on the Little Rock Home Farm. Two were put into operation within Little Rock itself, but that was too far away for the residents of the Home Farm to attend. The city schools were housed in freedmen's churches and were free. In the spring of 1864 these schools were under the direction of Reverend Allen and his wife, plus Misses Young, Moffat, and Mary E. Vickory. The teachers were paid by benevolent societies, which also furnished books. The government provided rations and quarters for the teachers.[18]

The basic problem for Sargent's educational effort was that the number of teachers who came to Arkansas to assist the freedmen was never large enough to spread the schools into the rural areas. Even the minimal effort made in the spring of 1864 ceased when the teachers went back north for the summer to avoid "malarious diseases."[19]

The operations of the Home Farm were seriously impaired further during the first year by the near complete failure of the cotton crop. The state superintendent reported, however, that despite the crop failure, other endeavors had made it possible for the freedmen to reimburse the government for all of its expenses, but conditions were not improved. The Farm had been able to just barely achieve its goal of self-sufficiency. The freedmen themselves had come away from the first year's farm effort with no savings that would allow them to go out on their own in the future.[20]

Additional problems were caused in 1864 by a turnover of managers and what appeared to be unfortunate choices of personnel. On June 28, Lieutenant J. Williams, the Farm's initial superintendent, was sent to take charge of the Home Farm at Pine Bluff. Command of the Farm was given to Lieutenant Garrison, who had little interest in the agricultural or social activities of the Farm but considered his primary responsibility to be recruiting men for the 69th U.S. Colored Infantry. In November, Garrison was relieved from duty and replaced by Captain Yearick, who also was concerned with recruitment.[21]

Yearick's administration proved particularly unfortunate. Initially he seemed interested in providing relief for the residents of the Farm. At the end of his first month in command, Yearick reported to Sargent that conditions were "extremely impoverished and depressed." The problem, according to the captain, was that no money was available for any aspect of his effort. He requested Sargent at least to put in place a system of fees so that lessees and others could be charged to help create a fund for the freedmen. "The poor should not be neglected," he complained, "the laborer should be compensated, the prosperous should bear their proportion of expense."[22]

Yearick found the problems overwhelming, however. Little had been done to solve the problems, and conditions worsened. Part of the problem faced by Williams, Garrison, and then Yearick was that the camp constantly increased in size. By July, Major Sargent indicated that at least four hundred freedmen were on the Home Farm at any one time and drawing rations.[23] Many of the freedmen in the camp that summer had come to Little Rock as a result of General Steele's invasion of southwestern Arkansas, although the majority were sent to another Home Farm at Pine Bluff. Additional residents arrived when the Union army decided to abandon its positions in western Arkansas, sending the freedmen from Van Buren and Fort Smith to Little Rock. Those who arrived invariably were destitute and in poor condition.[24]

When Yearick took command he found that little had been done under his predecessor. The influx of freedmen from Fort Smith had not been prepared for, and the Farm did not have the facilities for a sizable increase in inhabitants. More cabins were constructed, but one inspector reported that they were of inferior quality. The hospital that was under construction the previous summer did not appear to have been completed. The combination of poor conditions in the camp and the poverty of the refugees meant that a large number of the freedmen became sick. The result was tragic. The inspector of the Farm at the end of 1864 reported that "an undue portion" of the freedmen had died.[25]

Apparently Yearick despaired of his effort at helping the poor, and began to help himself. Complaints to headquarters led to Yearick's removal and return to his unit on January 12, 1865. His successor, Lieutenant James H. Rains of the 126th Illinois Infantry, arrived to find the Home Farm desolate. There were 400 persons in the camp, and no preparations had been made for any farming activity. There were no farm implements and only one "very poor" mule team. The fences that had been repaired the previous summer were down. Even worse, after inspecting the books, Rains found that the Farm was in debt to various persons for $500 and there was no money to pay.[26]

A cloud of suspicion surrounded the activities of Yearick, and Rains faced a barrage of inquiries from headquarters for information about what had taken place and whether or not there had been some sort of malfeasance. Complaints had been received that Yearick had misappropriated a note from a black lessee for $745. Missionaries had protested that the captain had a woman living with him at headquarters and that he had moved his clerk from the office to give her a place to live. Rains gracefully concluded that Yearick was "inexperienced" and "totally ignorant of managing business."[27] But Rains summed up the activities of the Farm during its first year of operation when he concluded that the people assigned to help the freedmen had done little to aid them. "Trade, traffic and pecuniary interests," he wrote, "to all appearances had occupied the time and attention of those whom you had supposed to be interested in the welfare of the Freed people."[28]

Under Lieutenant Rains for the first time the Home Farm was thoroughly organized so that its potential for assisting the freedmen in their transition to freedom began to be realized. That did not mean, however, that Rains did not face continuing problems. Almost as soon as he took over, Rains' efforts suffered a serious setback when his assistants were ordered to abandon their work at the Farm and return to their regiments. Rains was frustrated in all of his efforts at obtaining replacements and was forced to carry out on his own the myriad duties necessary to the operation of the Farm.[29]

Rains, however, did not let the problems overcome him. In the face of adversity, he immediately set about rebuilding the camp. The hospital was finally finished — a frame building, 30 feet x 60 feet, capable of holding thirty patients. He also had the healthy residents of the Farm plant part of the plantation in vegetables. Beginning with twenty acres, he hoped to expand the land in cultivation to forty acres devoted to oats, corn and cotton.[30] He had no teams to work the fields, so the superintendent requested animals from the quartermaster. He persisted and ultimately secured these critical animals and forage for them from the commanding general with the intervention of Sargent.[31]

In addition, Rains and Sargent also, for the first time, allowed freedmen themselves to lease land on the Home Farm to cultivate for themselves rather than to farm in squads. By the end of the spring, 400 acres were actually leased to freedmen rather than to white lessees. This marked a real break from the labor system practiced on plantations. The freedmen took responsibility for all major decisions on the land that was leased, allowing the tenant the freedom most considered a real mark of their liberation. The success of the initial lessees was considered essential in encouraging others to move out on their own.[32]

One of the most positive moves that Rains accomplished was to open a school on the Home Farm, with the support of Chaplain Joel Grant, who Sargent had named Superintendent of Freedmen's Education in January 1865. Rains assigned Mr. and Mrs. H. M. Barstow, two teachers sent South by the North West

Freedmen's Aid Commission, to the Farm. Barstow devoted his time to regular classroom work, while his wife spent her time on the "industrial and domestic interests" of the camp's needy. They began with 113 enrolled students in January. Within three months the two teachers were working with 135.[33]

The reports of the Barstows indicate something about the massive problems faced by those who worked with the freedmen. The Barstows taught school for six hours each day, devoted another hour each day to moral and religious instruction, then averaged another nine hours each day in mission work and visiting the sick. They found their scholars anxious to learn, but they did not have the books and supplies necessary for their beginning students. The school was cold because the room was too open. Still, in the face of it all, Barstow concluded at the end of his first month at the Home Farm, "Good is being accomplished." [34]

The Home Farm was becoming a model operation. It appeared to be achieving at least some of the goals set for it earlier in its history. Freedmen came to the Farm and had an opportunity both to work for themselves and to go to school. Barstow's conclusion regarding the educational effort seemed appropriate to the entire experiment. After a year of delay, then a spring of success and growing hope, however, the potential for the Home Farm experiment was never realized. The approaching end of the Civil War doomed the entire project.

For the army, the war's end brought a conclusion to the "freedmen's problem." While many activities carried out by the army were transferred in the spring of 1865 to the Freedmen's Bureau, the effort at creating a controlled environment within which many freedmen could make their first step toward freedom ended. The Farm was closed. Those who had leased land were allowed to continue farming until they harvested crops, then they were thrown off the land. William R. Vaughan got his land back, and the freedmen were abandoned to their fate. As with the effort among the freedmen throughout the South, the government's effort had been flawed, had been too little, had been too late, and, when the war ended, was essentially abandoned. The Home Farm idea represented an important experiment. In Pulaski

County it reflected an important movement in the transition from slavery to freedom. Ultimately, however, the history of the Little Rock Home Farm provided an example of the problems involved in that process throughout the South.

NOTES

This article was first published in the *Pulaski County Historical Review*, 42 (Summer 1994): 26-35.

[1] A discussion of the overall wartime policies of the federal government may be found in Louis S. Gerteis, *From Contraband to Freedman: Federal Policy toward Southern Blacks, 1861-1865* (Westport, Conn.: Greenwood Press, 1973). An excellent collection of documents relating the development of federal programs is Ira Berlin, ed., *Freedom: A Documentary History of Emancipation, 1861-1867* published by Cambridge University Press in several volumes over the last ten years.

[2] *Report of The General Superintendent of Freedmen, Department of the Tennessee and State of Arkansas for 1865* (Memphis, Tenn.: Published by Permission, 1865), 68.

[3] Joseph Warren, comp., *Extracts from Reports of Superintendents of Freedmen* (Vicksburg, Miss.: Freedmen Press Print, 1864), 16.

[4] D. T. Alien to C. H. Fowler, January 1, 1864, American Missionary Association Papers, Amisted Collection, Tulane University.

[5] Ibid.

[6] Warren, comp., *Extracts from Reports of Superintendents of Freedmen*, 17.

[7] *Report of the General Superintendent of Freedmen, Department of the Tennessee and State of Arkansas for 1864*, 5, 6.

[8] D. T. Alien to George Whipple, March 1, 1864, American Missionary Association Papers, Amisted Collection, Tulane University.

[9] *Report of the General Superintendent of Freedmen, Department of the Tennessee and State of Arkansas for 1864*, 13-14; William P. Mellen, *Report Relative to Leasing Abandoned Plantations and the Affairs of the Freed People in the First Special Agency* (Washington, D.C.: McGill & Witherow, 1864), 5, 9, 14.

[10] *Report of the General Superintendent of Freedmen, Department of the Tennessee and State of Arkansas for 1864*, 13-14; Mellen, *Report Relative to Leasing Abandoned Plantations and the Affairs of the Freed People in the First Special Agency* 8, 9, 24.

[11] Report of Major W. G. Sargent, July 1, 1864, Letters Received, Department of Arkansas, 7th Army Corps, and 4th Military District, RG393, National Archives; D. T. Alien to C. H. Fowler, January 1, 1864, American Missionary Association Papers, Amisted Collection, Tulane University; Special Order No. 22, May 2, 1864, Letters Received, Arkansas Field Office Records (Little Rock), Bureau of Refugees, Freedmen and Abandoned Lands (hereinafter cited as BRFAL), RG105, NA.

[12] Report of the Superintendent of Freedmen, State of Arkansas, July 1, 1864, in Letters Received, Department of Arkansas, 7th Army Corps, and 4th Military District, RG393, NA; Assignment of Abandoned Lands, April 13, 1865, Letters Received, Arkansas Field Office Records (Little Rock), BRFAL, RG105, NA; 1860 Census, manuscript returns for Pulaski County; Pulaski County Tax Rolls, 1860, AHC; *Arkansas Gazette*, July 27, 1877 (obituary).

[13] Report of the Superintendent of Freedmen, State of Arkansas, July 1, 1864, Letters Received, Department of Arkansas, 7th Army Corps, and 4th Military District, RG393, NA.

[14]Ibid.

[15]Ibid.

[16]Ibid.; Special Order No. 22, May 2, 1864, Special Orders and Special Order No. 41, April 26, 1864, Letters Received, Arkansas Field Office Records (Little Rock), BRFAL, RG105, NA.

[17] Special Order 116, May 28, 1864, Letters Received, Arkansas Field Office Records (Little Rock), BRFAL, RG105, NA; J. W. Wheelock to W. G. Sargent, July 16, 1864, Letters Received, Arkansas Field Office Records (Little Rock), BRFAL, RG105, NA.

[18]Report of the Superintendent of Freedmen, State of Arkansas, July 1, 1864, Letters Received, Department of Arkansas, 7th Army Corps, and 4th Military District, RG393, NA.

[19]Ibid.

[20]*Report of the General Superintendent of Freedmen, Department of the Tennessee and State of Arkansas for 1864,* 69-70.

[21]Special Order No. 26, June 28, 1864, Special Order No. 33, November 1, 1864, Special Orders. Arkansas Field Office Records (Little Rock), BRFAL, RG105, NA.

[22]S. W. Yearick to Sargent, November 25, 1864, Letters Received, Arkansas Field Office Records (Little Rock), BRFAL, RG105, NA.

[23]Report of the Superintendent of Freedmen, State of Arkansas, July 1, 1864, Letters Received, Department of Arkansas, 7th Army Corps, and 4th Military District, RG393, NA.

[24] *Report of the General Superintendent of Freedmen, Department of the Tennessee and State of Arkansas for 1864,* 71.

[25]Ibid.

[26]J. H. Rains to W. G. Sargent, March 31, 1865, Reports and Miscellaneous Papers, J. H. Rains to W. G. Sargent, February 18, 1865, Letters Received, Arkansas Field Office Records (Little Rock), BRFAL, RG105, NA.

[27]J. H. Rains to W. G. Sargent, March 31, 1865, Reports and Miscellaneous Papers, Arkansas Field Office Records (Little Rock), BRFAL, RG105, NA.

[28] J. H. Rains to W. G. Sargent, March 31, 1865, Retained Copies of Reports, Reports Received, and Misc. Papers, Arkansas, BRFAL, RG105, NA.

[29]Ibid.

[30]J. H. Rains to W. G. Sargent, March 31, 1865, Reports, Arkansas Field Office Records (Little Rock), BRFAL, RG105, NA.

[31]J. H. Rains to W. G. Sargent, February 18,1865, Letters Received, Arkansas Field Office Reports (Little Rock), BRFAL, RG105, NA.

[32]Quarterly Report of W. G. Sargent, March 31, 1865, Retained Copies of Reports, Reports Received, and Misc. Papers, Arkansas, BRFAL, RG105, NA.

[33]Joel Grant to W. G. Sargent, February 28, 1865, School Reports, Field Office Records (Little Rock) BRFAL, RG105, NA.

[34]Report for Period Ending February 1, 1865, Report of March 29, 1865, Home Farm School, School Reports, Arkansas Field Office Records (Little Rock), BRFAL, RG105, NA.

Little Rock Did Herself Proud: A History of the 1911 United Confederate Veterans Reunion

By Michael David Polston

Michael David Polston was a history teacher in Cabot when he published this article in 1981, encouraged to do so by the F. Hampton Roy Awards that were first given that year. He continued to teach until 2005 when he became Staff Historian at the Encyclopedia of Arkansas History and Culture, a project of the Butler Center for Arkansas Studies at the Central Arkansas Library System.

"Tired but happy," is how one Gazette reporter described Little Rock on May 19, 1911.[1] The reason for such a description was that the Arkansas celebration of all time, the twenty-first National United Confederate Veterans Reunion, had just ended in Little Rock. No other Arkansas city has ever been host to such a celebration. For three days in May, Little Rock was host to one of the largest gatherings of Confederate veterans ever held. The capital city with a population of 45,941 quickly became a sea of 140,000 people including some 12,000 veterans of the "Lost Cause."[2]

The concept of a Confederate Reunion evolved years before the Little Rock meeting. The United Confederate Veterans organization, sponsors of the reunion, was founded in 1889 at New Orleans, Louisiana. It arose from the many state veterans organizations formed shortly after the end of the War Between the States. Through the efforts of Colonel J. F. Shipp and others, these state camps were joined together to form the now famous UCV. The organization grew rapidly until there were more than fifteen hundred camps throughout the United States.[3] The annual reunion was a major part of the group's activities. The first national gathering was held in 1894 in Chattanooga, Tennessee, with subsequent meetings in other southern cities. In 1910, Little Rock was chosen by the veterans as the site of their twenty-first annual reunion.

Little Rock prepared itself well for the reunion. No less than forty-eight committees were formed to take care of every conceivable necessity.[4] Lodging, eating, entertainment and numerous other committees were formed, all under the direction of Judge W. M. Kavanaugh, chairman of the Executive Committee. A major concern of this committee centered on how to feed and house the then projected fifty thousand sightseers.[5] It was no simple task to prepare a city of less than fifty thousand to entertain such a large group of visitors.

Hotels were the chief means of lodging in the city. It was estimated that five thousand hotel rooms were available varying in price from fifty cents to five dollars.[6] These five thousand beds would not be nearly enough. To solve this shortage, other arrangements were made throughout the city. One of the chief alternate sites for lodging was the city schools. Nine schools, with a lodging capacity of about four thousand, were furnished with cots at a rate of a dollar a day.[7] These makeshift hotels were scheduled to open on May 15. Arrangements for another thirty-five thousand beds were made in private residences in Little Rock and surrounding communities.[8] The success of the Lodging Committee is shown by the fact that almost nine thousand available beds were not used.[9] Housing was also provided for special groups. Arrangements were made to board women teachers in the Blind and Deaf School. A special bachelor barracks named Camp Kavanaugh was provided opposite the Rock Island Station. These special barracks were provided with beds, showers, and rest rooms to accommodate five thousand men.[10]

To avoid the rush of Reunion week, it was suggested that all visitors to the city make prior reservations by contacting the Hotel Committee. But to help simplify matters for those who had not pre-registered and for those who had, a booth was established at each railroad station to register guests and provide information. It was suggested that upon arriving by train the first step should be to visit one of these registration booths. Upon approaching one of these centers, a card file, arranged by the number in a party, would be searched. The lodger then would be given a card listing information on prices and directions to a hotel that could fill his needs.[11]

To help control extortion by unscrupulous restaurant and hotel owners who intended to increase prices during the three-day reunion, the Lodging Committee hoped to sign a contract with each business. This contract required set prices for services rendered. All businesses signing this agreement would display a copyrighted, yellow sign so there could be no doubt as to which establishments were approved by the committee.[12] These yellow signs were constructed of cardboard and labeled "Official Restaurant Endorsed by Reunion Committee." These words encircled a camp scene forming a crude seal.[13] Prices were to be displayed on walls in plain view or on a restaurant's menu.[14] The system seemed to have worked well, for very few complaints were registered. A representative of the Lodging Committee stated that there were "not one hundred instances of real overcharging during the entire four days of the Reunion."[15] Major W. W. Screws of the Montgomery, Alabama, *Advertiser* concluded, "there was no extortion at Little Rock."[16]

The procurement of meals was another major concern. As with hotels, all restaurants supported by the Reunion Committee were required to sign a contract setting their prices. Meals were provided throughout the reunion at an average price of thirty-five to forty cents.[17] There seemed to be sufficient eating establishments, for it was reported that no one had to wait an unreasonable amount of time to be served.[18] In addition to the restaurants numerous cafes were temporarily opened throughout the city. The Women Teachers Association of Little Rock served meals at the high school and the Kramer School.[19] Many women of religious groups and charitable organizations also served meals.[20] It seems safe to say that no one went hungry for want of a place to purchase a meal.

Special efforts were taken to provide for the guests of honor.[21] No expense was spared for the old soldiers. All veterans were free to stay where they chose, but most stayed free of charge in the official camp of the veterans named Camp Shaver. The camp took its name from the much-admired, "Fighting" Robert Glenn Shaver, colonel of the famed 7th Arkansas Infantry. It was also Shaver's honor to be in command of the camp for the duration of the reunion.

The City Park (now MacArthur Park) had been chosen as the site for the veterans' camp. It was an excellent choice because the historic federal arsenal was located on the park grounds and was an important part of Arkansas Civil War history. Only fifty years before, the arsenal had been surrendered to secessionist forces just prior to the secession of Arkansas and the outbreak of war.

Ironically, lodging for the old Confederates was provided and constructed by the federal government. A bill to supply tents was introduced by Senator Clarke and had passed unanimously.[22] On May 3 a squad of forty men from Little Rock's Fort Logan Roots began to erect the first of four carloads of government supplied tents numbering some 1,333.[23] The tent would be as it had been years before, the hotel room of the Confederate soldier. Each tent could hold four to eight men and was furnished with all the necessities, including cots, blankets, sheets, pillows, towels, wash bowls, water pitchers, and water. [24] Six tents were pitched in front of the armory to house the registration officials and the officers in command of the camp.[25] In front of these tents was a flagpole upon which flew a newly made Confederate flag.

Camp Shaver was organized so as to make it simple to locate an old friend or comrade. Much like a military camp, the veterans' temporary homes were laid out by state, division and corps.[26] Thus, all Texas veterans were housed together and so on down the line. To further simplify matters each veteran was assigned a numbered tag that corresponded with his tent number.[27]

To properly feed the Confederate veterans, four mess tents were constructed within the camp.[28] On the average these mess tents contained over one thousand square feet of floor space and were equipped with tables to serve some two thousand hungry guests at a time.[29] The best equipment available was provided for these temporary kitchens — eight double ranges, six sixty-gallon coffee urns, four large boilers and broilers with steam warmers, and an eighteen-by-twenty-foot ice chest, to name just a few. Some twenty-five cooks, sixty waiters, and twenty kitchen employees were hired to cater to every want and need of the old veterans.[30]

To complete the camp a number of benches were constructed throughout the compound on which the old soldiers could rest and reminisce. A large bandstand was also provided behind the armory, and a single refreshment stand operated by Levi and Pletz was provided for the enjoyment of the campers and their visitors.[31] For sanitation purposes four lavatories were connected to the camp, and two rest rooms were located in the old armory.[32] The camp was a luxurious resort when compared to the camps of the war days.

To keep order within Camp Shaver and the city, the Public Safety Committee organized a group called the Reunion Guards. The Guards were identified by a badge and like the police could make arrests. Other groups including the Arkansas militia, railroad detectives, and law enforcement officers from other towns were also used to control the tremendous influx of visitors.[33]

The Reunion Committee took great pains to make the Little Rock affair more elaborate than all previous meetings. Decoration of the city began the first week in May, and in a very short time over a hundred city streets were bedecked with red, white and blue.[34] Citizens were requested to clean up their property and decorate their own yards if they desired. "Keep our front as clean as possible," was the call of the Yell County Democrat.[35]

The most decorated area of the city was along the route of the great parade. This path, named Confederate Way, ran for some fifteen blocks from the Free Bridge to Camp Shaver via Main and Tenth streets.[36] Along these streets were constructed sixty, plaster-of-Paris columns. Standing twelve feet tall and three feet square at the base, each of these ionic columns was crowned with a white globe with red and white lights.[37] The columns were connected with thousands of electric "garlands" of lights. Each pole served as a support for a shield displaying a picture of a Confederate general and surrounded by Confederate and United States flags. In addition to the aesthetic value of these columns, the decorated poles served as a guide to Camp Shaver.[38]

The most spectacular decoration of the entire city was in the general meeting hall next to City Hall. Pillars stood throughout the auditorium draped with Confederate flags, each dedicated in honor of some Confederate hero.[39] The most dramatic decoration was the ceiling itself, which was covered with what was described as the "largest" Confederate flag ever produced.[40]

When finished the decoration of the city was second to none. Colonel John Hickman, Adjutant General of the Army of Tennessee Department, said he had attended all previous reunions and had "never visited any city more elaborately decorated in Confederate colors."[41]

By May 16, the opening day of the reunion, Little Rock was well prepared to accept the expected visitors. People began to arrive in the capital city well before the festivities were to begin. By May 15, eight thousand visitors had already reached Little Rock, and Camp Shaver was said to be "overflowing."[42] The next day the number had risen to forty-six thousand including eleven thousand veterans.[43] In describing the numbers the *Daily TexArkanian* reported that a, "night visitor . . . will be wrapped in blankets and stood up in the corner for the period of sleep."[44] By the last day of the reunion the number in the city had rocketed to over 106,000.[45]

Most people journeyed to Arkansas by train, the most efficient means of travel of the day. Several railroads connected Little Rock with the rest of the United States, and all went out of their way to bring people to the reunion. Improvements were made, travel programs were printed, and new tracks, baggage and waiting rooms were constructed.[46] All railroads added extra trains to carry the influx of visitors. The Iron Mountain ran thirteen extras with other railroads following suit.[47] Newport, Booneville, Des Arc, Forrest City, Fordyce, Hot Springs, Memphis (Tennessee), Ruston (Louisiana), and numerous other cities in and out of state were connected with the "City of Roses."

The official opening of the twenty-first National United Confederate Veteran reunion took place on the morning of May 16. The day was to begin at 8:30 a.m.[48] Many veterans arose hours before the initial meeting, however, in order to do a little sight-seeing and visiting. Some citizens of Little Rock became concerned thinking the veterans had no place to go and were just wandering the streets. The Lodging and Eating Committee reported that they could not keep the veterans in bed after 4:00 a.m.[49] By six o'clock the Camp Shaver mess halls opened for breakfast and served until about 9:00 a.m.[50] After breakfast the old soldiers were supposed to make their way to the auditorium next to City Hall. However, only a small number, 2,331, of the veterans actually attended the meetings.[51] These veterans sat on the lower floor according to states, each of which was identified by a small blue pennant.[52]

Promptly at 8:30 a.m. the twenty-first UCV Reunion opened with a prayer followed by music from twelve bands and the United Confederate Choir singing such catchy tunes as "We Are Old Time Confederates."[53] When all had settled, the meeting was called to order with the rap of a gavel.[54] The morning session was taken up primarily with welcomes from various dignitaries. With General James Smith presiding, the various speakers made their eloquent remarks. Mayor Charles E. Taylor and Governor George W. Donaghey were two of the more notable welcomers. Mayor Taylor made particular reference to the eagerness of the Grand Army of the Republic to welcome the old Confederates. The Union Veterans had designed a banner depicting a pair of clasped hands bearing the words, "The GAR Welcomes the UCV."[55] The Governor followed with a general welcome on behalf of all the citizens of the state of Arkansas.

After the numerous welcome speeches General Smith introduced the Commander-in-Chief of the UCV, General George W. Gordon, who addressed the veterans.[56] The final business of the morning was a special welcome sent to the veterans by President William Howard Taft. In a short letter President Taft expressed "the hope that they will have a pleasant and successful Reunion."[57] The message was well received, and the next day the old Confederates sent a reply of thanks. Near noon the morning session broke for lunch. For those who journeyed back to Camp Shaver a free meal was provided from 12:00 to 2:30. During one of these noon meals the roof of one of the mess tents caught fire. The old veterans hardly noticed and continued their meal. When a Negro worker extinguished the blaze with a bucket of water an old soldier calmly stated, "that is the quickest cloudburst I ever saw in my life."[58]

The afternoon session included the annual oration by Dr. R. C. Cave of St. Louis and the reading of poems by Mrs. Virginia Frazier Boyly.[59] With these items of business completed, the first day of official meetings ended, but the celebration had only begun.

After the evening meal a variety of entertaining activities awaited the old soldiers. Various clubs and organizations opened their doors. The Quapaw Club hosted an afternoon reception for the maids and sponsors, and the Scottish Rite Consistory held an Historical Evening followed by a dance.[60] One could also have gone to a drama at the Capitol Theater, or visited Forest or West End Parks, gone to the penny arcade, or to a snake show, an oriental show, or even to the Little Russian Prince show. If these were not enough there were horizontal bar, acrobat, and double trapeze acts along with a hot air balloon.[61] After a long day and night of activities the old soldiers settled down to a well-deserved night's rest.

The second day of the reunion opened as the first. The soldiers once again gathered at the auditorium meeting hall. The most notable event of the morning session was the appointment of a Sergeant at Arms to clear the hall of the many visitors. The visitors had become so unruly that only the official delegates were allowed to attend the afternoon session.[62]

The afternoon session opened with a special memorial service for General William Lewis Cabell.[63] Business then continued with the approval of a reply to President Taft, re-election of General Gordon, election of other officers, and the selection of the site for the next year's reunion. Macon, Georgia, was chosen over several other cities that had made bids to host the twenty-second meeting.[64] With the business meetings of the twenty-first reunion concluded, all that remained was the long-awaited parade of old veterans.

As the night before, the night of May 17 was loaded with things to do. Open houses and receptions were held at many of the social clubs of Little Rock, and at 8:00 p.m. the Maid and Sponsors Ball was held at the auditorium rink.[65] With these and other activities over, all bedded down for the night anxiously awaiting and dreading the inevitable end of the great reunion.

The morning of May 18 began as the ones that preceded it. But it was to be a special day for the veterans involved for it would be the last time that many of the old soldiers would see each other. Many of the faces of 1911 would not be present in Macon, for death and old age would take its toll. But for this day all would be proud and happy and think not of the future but only of the present. The parade was as carefully planned as the other aspects of the reunion had been. Considering that the youngest veteran to participate was seventy-two years old, the parade had to be tailor-made for the veterans.[66] The month of May had been chosen because of the relatively cool temperatures. Initially a short procession had been planned, but the prospect of the congestion caused by some fifteen thousand participants forced the reunion committee to opt for a longer route.[67] For the protection of the veterans several medical facilities were established along the parade route. Hospital tents were located on Conway Street, Ninth Street, and Main Street with two additional ones on the northeast corner of Markham and Broadway.[68] These first aid stations were sufficiently supplied and staffed by a qualified doctor and nurse.[69] For further protection ambulances followed each division in the parade.[70] In this way accidents and illnesses could be handled promptly.

The parade began to form early in the morning on Markham Street at the intersection of State Street and each cross street between State and Main.[71] Visitors packed the sidewalks along the route, and sightseers were visible in "each nook." The stands constructed along the route were full, people stood on roofs, children sat on parents' shoulders, and some people climbed poles to get a better view.[72] The largest crowd of the week formed on the streets of Little Rock to witness the climax of the reunion.

With a bugle fanfare from the Newton Bugle Corps the parade began promptly at 10:00 a.m. In the lead walked James B. Dickinson carrying a large silk Confederate flag. Then came General Smith and his staff, the mounted police, and the members of the organization committees, followed by the first of several bands. These bands were very impressive. Representing Arkansas, Texas, Mississippi, Oklahoma, Kentucky, and Tennessee, they totaled more than 350 members and "marched through the streets of Little Rock producing, such a spectacle as was never seen before." [73] As they marched all played different tunes simultaneously with all ending in "Dixie." Following the first band was General Van Zant and staff followed by the maids and the reunion queen, Kathleen Barkman, in her decorated float pulled by four gray horses. Another band marched behind them and just to its rear was the attraction all had waited for, the first of four divisions of veterans. The honor to march first fell to the Virginia Division. Led by the Robert E. Lee Camp Number One, the gray-clad veterans of the Old Dominion proudly accepted the waves and cheers of the thousands of admirers. The Virginians were followed by the first ambulance and then another band. Then marched the Tennessee Division followed by another band and then the most popular division of all, the Trans-Mississippi. This division was a special favorite for it contained veterans from the host state. The Forrest Cavalry Corps was the last of the four divisions of veterans. The rear of the parade was brought up by the Sons of Confederate Veterans, the Governor and staff, and finally another band. It took almost two hours for the entire procession to pass one point.[74]

There was much to see in the parade. One group of veterans carried a hornet's nest and a banner bearing the word "SHILOH."[75] Another group carried a proud banner bearing "The Immortal Six Hundred," and another performed a rifle drill. [76] Many times the old veterans broke ranks to shake hands with old friends or to get a drink of water from the many water barrels located along the parade route.[77] Some veterans had to be helped along by lady escorts, and some who were too feeble to march viewed the parade from a special grandstand constructed in front of the Old State House. One humorous incident occurred when the flag bearer of one group broke ranks to rest in the shade. When his comrades continued, he ran to catch up causing a roar of laughter from the crowd.[78] In another incident a drunk man, not a veteran, was dared to bite off the head of a bird. Not shunning the dare he promptly did the bird in.[79]

As each group passed General Gordon's Headquarters at the Marion Hotel, the veterans made a special salute in honor of the ill general. The procession then continued down Markham, turned right on Main to Tenth, then left on Tenth to the City Park. All along the route thousands of admirers shouted words of encouragement and applauded the old soldiers. From Tenth the parade entered City Park and passed in front of the Knapp Fountain where a children's choir greeted each old flag by singing "The Bonnie Blue Flag."[80] Before the procession could countermarch the route, twelve of the old veterans dropped out not able to continue.[81] As the procession countermarched down Tenth then Main and back to Markham, the twenty-first reunion quickly came to a close. For the spectators the reunion had ended, and many made a mad rush for the train stations causing one of the few problems of the week's festivities. But for the old veterans the reunion would not end until later that night.

At eight o'clock the last of the many balls was held at the auditorium. This grandest of all, the Veterans' Ball, was the last official activity of the reunion. Some 5800 people attended the dance, the highlight of which was a precision drill by the Memphis Southern Cross Drill Corps. The ball lasted for about four hours and ended with a touching rendition of "Home Sweet Home."[82] With the singing of this old tune the twenty-first reunion concluded. All that remained was the parting of friends and the trip home.

The reunion was judged a complete success. Numerous words of praise were bestowed upon the "City of Roses." "No city has ever excelled Little Rock in hospitality," said one participant. John Bratcher of the Sterling Price Camp of Waldron, Arkansas, stated, "this Reunion is said to be the best of all."[83] It may not have been the best, but it was the largest up to that time. The railroad figures revealed that over 106,000 people had used their facilities during the preceding week, more than twice the number expected. One man summed up all the praise in five words, "Little Rock did herself proud."[84]

Along with the praise came the inevitable criticism, most of which was trivial. A Colonel Hickman complained that women appeared in the parade "astraddle" their horses. This upset the old veteran for such behavior was against the UCV law and unbecoming to a lady. He expressed a hope that it would not be repeated.[85] In a letter to the editor, Sallie Belcher complained that not enough attention was paid to the mothers of the Confederacy. Perhaps the most trivial and most humorous complaints came from the old veterans at Camp Shaver. The criticism ran from toothpicks or rocking chairs all the way to the complaint that no strawberry ice cream was served.[86] Such complaints were hardly of a serious nature.

Within a few days all had returned to normal in the capital city. Little Rock was no longer the crowded, decorated city visited by people from all over the United States. Camp Shaver was disassembled, decorations were removed, and committees were dissolved. All that remained of the celebration were the memories of a happy and successful reunion. A successful reunion that has not and should not be forgotten.[87]

NOTES

This article first appeared in the *Pulaski County Historical Review*, (Summer 1981): 22-32.

1 *Arkansas Gazette*, 19 May 1911, p. 4.

[2]Dallas T. Herndon, *Annals of Arkansas*, 4 vols. (Hopkinsville, Ky., and Little Rock: The Historical Record Association, 1947), 2:524; *Arkansas Gazette*, 19 May 1911, p. l.

[3]Dallas T. Herndon, *The Centennial History of Arkansas*, 3 vols. (Chicago and Little Rock: The S. J. Clarke Publishing Co., 1922), 1:965; Francis T. Miller, The Photographic History of the Civil War, 10 vols. (New York: Thomas Yoseloff, 1912), 10:296.

4 "Rock Island Line," *United Confederate Veterans Reunion Little Rock, Arkansas, May 16-17-18, 1911*, p. 6. A complete listing of these committees can be seen in "Cotton Belt Route," *UCV Reunion*, p. 16. Both these sources are available at the Arkansas History Commission.

5 "Frisco Lines," *UCV Reunion*, no page numbers.

6 *Confederate Veteran* 19 (May 1911): 19; "Missouri Pacific Iron Mountian," *UCV Reunion*, May 16, 17, 18, 1911, p.10.

[7]*Confederate Veteran* 19 (May 1911): 193.

8 *Fayetteville Daily*, 16 (May 1911): 1.

9 *Confederate Veteran* 19 (May 1911): 193.

10 *White River Journal*, 9 March 1911, p. 1.

[11]*Arkansas Gazette*, 6 May 1911, p. 1. A group of young men called the Reunion Scouts were used as aids at the reception booths. *Arkansas Democrat*, 15 May 1911, p. 12.

12 "Missouri Pacific Iron Mountain," *UCV Reunion*, p. 10; *Confederate Veteran* 19 (May 1911):190.

13 *White River Journal*, 23 March 1911, p. 1. Though no evidence exists, hotels and other businesses probably were supplied with a similar sign, restaurant being dropped and hotel added.

14 "Missouri Pacific Iron Mountain," *UCV Reunion*, p. 10.

15 *Confederate Veteran* 19 (June 1911): 275.

16 *Ibid.*, 19 (June 1911), 277. One restaurant was said to have charged forty cents for two eggs. When reported the restaurant was closed. *Fayetteville Daily*, 16 May 1911, p.1.

17 *Fayetteville Daily*, 19 May 1911, p. 3.

[18] *Confederate Veteran* 19 (June 1911): 275.

[19] *Ibid.*, 19 (May 1911):197.

[20] "Frisco Lines," *UCV Reunion*, p. 5.

[21] The *Marked Tree Gazette* stated, "Everything possible for the old soldiers and the visitors." *Marked Tree Gazette*, 26 May 1911, p. 1.

[22] *White River Journal*, 9 February 1911, p. 1.

[23] *Arkansas Gazette*, 3 May 1911, p. 11; James Eison, "The Arsenal in Little Rock," *Pulaski County Historical Review* 16 (June 1968): 21.

[24] *Arkansas Gazette,* 3 May 1911, p. 11.

[25] *Ibid.*, 7 May 1911, p. 1.

[26] Frisco Line, *UCV Reunion*, p. 4.

[27] "Missouri Pacific Iron Mountain," *UCV Reunion*, p. 12.

[28] "Rock Island Lines," *UCV Reunion*, p. 5.

[29] *Arkansas Gazette*, 5 May 1911, p. 1.

[30] *Ibid.*, 3 May 1911, p. 11 and 5 May 1911, p. 1.

[31] *Ibid.*, 3 May 1911, p. 11 and 5 May 1911, p. 1.

[32] *Ibid.*, 5 May 1911, p. 16.

[33] *Confederate Veteran* 19 (May 1911): 193.

[34] *White River Journal*, 9 February 1911, p. 1. The decorations can clearly be seen in the numerous photos taken. A series of sixteen photos can be seen at the Arkansas History Commission.

[35] *Arkansas Gazette*, 4 May 1911, p. 1.

[36] "Frisco Line," *UCV Reunion*, p. 3; *Arkansas Gazette*, 3 May 1911, p. 11.

[37] *Confederate Veteran* 19 (June 1911): 277; *Arkansas Gazette*, 3 May 1911, p. 11.

[38] *Confederate Veteran* 19 (June 1911): 277.

[39] Ibid.

[40] "Frisco Lines," *UCV Reunion*, p. 4.

[41] *Confederate Veteran* 19 (June 1911): 276.

[42] *Daily TexArkanian*, 15 May 1911, p. 1; *Arkansas Gazette*, 15 May 1911, p. 1.

[43] *Arkansas Gazette*, 16 May 1911, p. 1. There is some conflict of sources concerning the number of veterans in attendance. *Lonoke Democrat* of May 25, 1911 stated 16,000. *Pulaski County Historical Review* of June 1968 page 21 stated 14,978. An exact number could be made by a time consuming count of the official registration lists at the Arkansas History Commission. *Registration List of the United Confederate Veterans Reunion 1911 Little Rock, Arkansas,* 2 rolls of microfilm 170 feet.

[44] *Daily TexArkanian*, 15 May 1911, p. 1.

[45] *Arkansas Gazette*, 19 May 1911, p. 5.

[46] *Ibid.*, 4 May 1911, p. 10.

[47] *Ibid.*, 3 May 1911, p. 5.

[48] *Ibid.*, 4 May 1911, p. 5 When four veterans were found sleeping on the grounds of the Old State House, they were offered housing but refused saying it had been a long time since they had slept under the stars. *Confederate Veteran* 19 (June 1911): 276.

[49] *Confederate Veteran* 19 (June 1911): 276.

[50] *Arkansas Gazette*, 5 May 1911, p. 1.

[51] *Arkansas Democrat*, 17 May 1911, p. 1.

[52] *Arkansas Gazette*, 5 May 1911, p. 1.

[53] *Lonoke Democrat*, 25 May 1911, p. 1; *White River Journal*, 4 May 1911, p, 1.

[54] Nathanael Greene was a Rhode Island general whose military reputation was second only to George Washington. For a full biography on Greene see Mark Boatner III, *Encyclopedia of the American Revolution*, (New York: David McKay Company, Inc., 1966), pp. 453-456.

[55] *Confederate Veteran* 19 (May 1911): 190; "Missouri Pacific," *UCV Reunion*, p. 15.

[56] 'Frisco Line,' *UCV Reunion*, p. 5; *Arkansas Gazette*, 10 May 1911, p. 1. General Gordon was the fifth man to hold this office following John B. Gordon, S. D. Lee, Clement Evans, and W. L. Cabell. Miller, *Photographic History*, 10: 300. At the outbreak of war Gordon enlisted as a drill master in the 11th Tennessee, fought at Stones River, Chickamauga, Missionary Ridge, Atlanta, and Franklin, and became a Brigadier General August 15, 1864. After the war he studied law and was elected representative from Tennessee. Mark Boatner, *The Civil War Dictionary*, (New York: David McKay Company, Inc., 1959), p. 348.

[57] *Arkansas Democrat*, 17 May 1911, p. 1.

[58] *Ibid.*; *Fayetteville Daily*, 19 May 1911, p. 3. The following is a sample of the foods served to the old soldiers: 16,000 loaves of bread, 8,000 pounds of steak, 3,000 pounds of roast beef, 110 cases of eggs, and 1,700 pounds of coffee. See *Pulaski County Historical Review* (June 1968), p. 21. A Mr. Ike Well provided at least one meal for some of the veterans in the form of a cask of kraut. *Arkansas Democrat*, 20 May 1911, p. 1.

[59] *Confederate Veteran* 18 (May 1911): 190; "Missouri Pacific," *UCV Reunion*, p. 15. One of her poems, "Greetings to Our Heroes at Little Rock Reunion" can be seen on the cover of *Confederate Veteran* 19 (June 1911). Mr. Cave had previously spoken at the dedication of the soldiers and sailor monument in Richmond, 1894. *Confederate Veteran* 19 (April 1911): 148.

[60] *Confederate Veteran* 19 (May 1911); 190; "Missouri Pacific," *UCV Reunion*, p. 15.

[61] "Frisco Line," UCV Reunion, p. 5; *Arkansas Gazette*, 10 May 1911, p.1.

[62] *Arkansas Democrat*, 17 May 1911, p. 1.

[63] For a biography of Cabell see Clement A. Evans, *Confederate Military History*, 12 vols. (Atlanta, 1899), 10: 392-394. Also a complete obituary and photograph of

General Cabell can be seen in *Confederate Veteran* 19 (April 1911): 148.

[64] *Arkansas Democrat*, 17 May 1911, p. 1; *Fayetteville Daily*, 19 May 1911, p. 3.

[65] *Confederate Veteran* 19 (May 1911): 190; "Missouri Pacific," *UCV Reunion*, p. 15.

[66] *Lonoke Democrat*, 25 May 1911, p. 3.

[67] "Frisco Line," *UCV Reunion*, p. 6; *Arkansas Gazette*, 4 May 1911, p. 11. The average May temperature in Little Rock was 87° to 90° daytime and 68° to 71° night. *Arkansas Democrat*, 19 May 1911, p. 9.

[68] *Arkansas Gazette*, 7 May 1911, p. 1.

[69] *White River Journal*, 13 April 1911, p. 1.

[70] *Confederate Veteran* 19 (May 1911): 193. No deaths occurred during the parade but three occurred before. W. L. Galloway of Tennessee fell from the second story of a school; W. M. Kivers of Georgia and W. F. Smith of Texas died of heart attacks. *Daily TexArkanian*, 17 May 1911, p. 1. One veteran died in Shreveport, Louisiana, on his way to Little Rock. *Daily TexArkanian*, 16 May 1911, p. 4.

[71] *Confederate Veteran* 19 (June 1911): 277. For a complete order of the parade see *Pocahontas Star Herald*, 12 May 1911, p. 3.

[72] *Arkansas Democrat*, 18 May 1911, p. 1; *Arkansas Gazette*, 19 May 1911, p. 12.

[73] *Confederate Veteran* 19 (June 1911): 277.

[74] *Arkansas Gazette*, 19 May 1911, p. 1. Obviously referring to the battle fought in Tennessee April 6-7, 1862.

[75] *Arkansas Gazette*, 19 May 1911, p. 1.

[76] *Arkansas Democrat*, 18 May 1911, p. 9. These six hundred were captured Confederate officers held at Morris Island, South Carolina, under fire by Union guns. This was a reprisal for similar treatment of Union prisoners at Charleston. For a history of Arkansas men among these six hundred see: Robert Logan, "Arkansas Confederates Among the Immortal Six Hundred," *Arkansas Historical Quarterly* 16 (Spring 1957): 91-95.

[77] Eison, "Arsenal," *Pulaski County Historical Review*, p. 21.

[78] *Arkansas Gazette*, 19 May 1911, p. 12.

[79] Eison, "Arsenal," *Pulaski County Historical Review*, p. 21.

[80] *Arkansas Gazette*, 19 May 1911, p. 12. Several old battle flags were carried in the parade. A flag of a Missouri regiment, Pindall Sharpshooter was carried. Dallas T. Herndon, *The Arkansas Handbook 1941-1942* (Little Rock: Arkansas History Commission, 1942), p. 116. Several flags now in the possession of the Arkansas Commemorative Commission (HQ at the Old State House) were probably carried in the parade.

[81] *Arkansas Democrat*, 18 May 1911, p. 9.

[82] *Arkansas Gazette*, 19 May 1911, p. 12.

[83] *Confederate Veteran* 19 (June 1911): 267.

[84] *Ibid.*

85 *Ibid.* In contrast Judge Basham of Omer Weaver Camp of Alabama requested women to ride with him in the parade. In return for this favor he was willing to waive the riding habits. His request was denied in letter stating "I never speak of that . . . only at low breath." Arkansas Gazette, 4 May 1911, p. 11.

86 *Arkansas Democrat,* 20 May 1911, p. 1.

87 A few interesting sidelights to the reunion are in order. Arkansas's first night and day bank was created during the reunion. *Arkansas Gazette,* 21 May 1911, p. 12. Of special interest was the making of a movie of the parade by the Industrial Moving Picture Company of Chicago. Unfortunately no copy of this 3000 feet film is known to exist. *Ibid.,* 19 May 1911, p. 13. A series of still photographs were taken and offered for sale by Jungkind Photo Supply Company of Little Rock, thirty-two different views for one dollar or eight for twenty-five cents. *Confederate Veteran* 19 (October 1911): 503. Sixteen of these views can be seen at the Arkansas History Commission.

IMAGES OF PULASKI COUNTY

Pinnacle Mountain, known to the colonial French as Mamelle, overlooks the Arkansas River a few miles above Little Rock. To explorer and biologist Thomas Nuttall, who traveled up the river in 1819, "it presented the appearance of a vast pyramid, hiding its summit in the clouds." It has been a favorite hiking spot for the citizens of Pulaski County for two centuries and is today a state park, although the area around it is more built up now than it was when this picture was taken, perhaps in the mid-Twentieth Century.

Exploring the Arkansas River up from its mouth at the Mississippi River in 1722, the Frenchman Bénard La Harpe reached "a bluff of mountainous rock, which forms three very steep peaks" and named it Frenchman's Rock. Now called Big Rock, it is part of North Little Rock.

UALR Archives and Special Collections

Exactly when Little Rock got its name is not known, but an 1819 document refers to "a place called Little Rock Bluff" and a town that had been surveyed and divided into blocks and lots that was to be "called and known by the name of 'Little Rock'." In June 1821 the territorial capital was moved from Arkansas Post to Little Rock. The original size and look of the rock itself is also unknown, in part because the city made part of it the southern terminus of a bridge.

UALR Archives and Special Collections

This picture shows the present Arkansas State Capitol not too long before it was open for business in 1911.

Library of Congress

Little Rock's Markham St. looking east from Main St. toward Scott St., as it appeared during the Federal occupation of the city during the Civil War. Whether the run-down condition of the wooden building at the far right is related to wartime conditions is not clear, but the brick buildings at the left, especially the Anthony House hotel at the far left, suggest the prosperity that the capital city had achieved by 1860.

UALR Archives and Special Collections

When U.S. Army Captain James Totten was forced to surrender Little Rock Arsenal to Arkansas Governor Henry Rector after the fighting began at Ft. Sumter, Harper's Magazine described the event and illustrated the story with this drawing. The article noted that the cannon shown were "the famous Bragg Battery which did such good service at the Battle of Buena Vista" in the War with Mexico. The central structure is the Tower Building, a brick storehouse for munitions built in 1840. Not shown is the distinctive tower, either left out or on the other side. The Tower Building was later used to house officers and was the birthplace of General Douglas MacArthur. Today it houses the MacArthur Museum of Arkansas History.

Library of Congress

The United Confederate Veterans held their annual reunion in Little Rock in 1911, drawing 140,000 people to the city, including 12,000 veterans. It brought more people to the capital city than any other event down to the night in 1992 when Bill Clinton was elected President of the United States.

UALR Archives and Special Collections

This scene of the wharf in Little Rock at the foot of Commerce St. illustrates the role that steamboats played in the economy of Pulaski County from the 1820s well into the 20th century. In the distance is the Baring Cross Bridge. Built about 1873, it was the first bridge across the Arkansas

River, and today a modernized version carries Union Pacific railroad cars.

UALR Archives and Special Collection

The Mosaic Templars was incorporated in Little Rock in 1883 by two former slaves who used the organization to sell insurance to African-Americans. It flourished into the 1930s and at one time had had a membership of perhaps 100,000. The building shown here was built by the Templars at 9th and Broadway to serve as its corporate headquarters. It was completed in 1913, destroyed by a fire in 2005, and is being rebuilt with the expectation of opening in 2008 as the Mosaic Templars Cultural Center.

Located on West Ninth St. in Little Rock, the center of the city's African-American culture, Taborian Hall housed shops on its first floor and the Dreamland Ballroom on its third floor. From the late 1930s until the late 1960s, Dreamland was the venue for performances by some of the top bands and musical artists of the time, among them Louis Armstrong, Ella Fitzgerald and Ray Charles. Local bands such as C. Dewees Hodges and his Philander Smith Collegians, shown here in a performance probably in 1947, were regular attractions.

Ninth Street Resource Committee, Arkansas Museum of Science and History/Museum of Discovery

North Little Rock, known as Argenta when this photo was taken around 1900, was less grand than its sister city across the river, but it did have this water sprinkler to keep down dust on the dirt roads that were standard in both cities at the time. It also had nattily dressed citizens like the bicyclist at the left.

UALR Archives and Special Collections

The Pulaski County Courthouse is recognized as one of the most architecturally significant of the more than 700 county courthouses in the United States.

Construction began on a capitol building in 1833, when Arkansas was still a territory and was completed in 1842, six years after it became a state in 1836. The unfinished building was in use in 1837 when an argument over a bill led to a knife fight in which the speaker of the house killed one of his colleagues. The building continued in service until 1911 when the state built its existing capitol. It is now The Old State House Museum.

Library of Congress

Camp Pike, pictured here was built on the northern edge of North Little Rock in 1917 to train soldiers for World War I. During World War II, it was greatly expanded and renamed Camp Robinson. Today Camp Robinson is the headquarters of the Arkansas National Guard.

Library of Congress

The Old Mill, located in the Lakewood area of North Little Rock was created in 1933 by sculpter Dionicio Rodriquez. In addition to stone, he used faux bois, reinforced concrete designed to simulate wood, creating a structure and site realistic and beautiful enough to serve as the backdrop to the opening credits of the movie Gone With the Wind.

Worth Horton and the Butler Center for Arkansas Studies

Printed for automobile users in 1920, this map shows the dimensions of both Little Rock and North Little Rock at that time.

Arkansas History Commission

During the Flood of 1927, Mississippi River water inundated much of eastern Arkansas. The Arkansas River also overflowed its banks, creating scenes like this one in North Little Rock.

UALR Archives and Special Collections

The eastern portion of Pulaski County is flat and fertile and had produced cotton for more than a century when this picture was taken in the 1930s by New Deal   photographer, Ben Shahn. During that one hundred years, tech-niques for harvesting the crop had not changed very much.

Library of Congress

Western Pulaski County is typical of north-ern and western Arkansas, more suitable for small farms than plantation or corporate agriculture. This farm was located on Kanis Road in Little Rock, a part of the city recently developed into expensive residential neighborhoods.

UALR Archives and Special Collections

After being denied entrance to Central High School at the beginning of the fall 1957 semester by troops of the Arkansas National Guard called out by Governor Orval Faubus, nine black students were escorted to classes by soldiers of the U.S. 101st Airborne Division sent to Arkansas by President Dwight Eisenhower. Incidents associated with these events made Little Rock a symbol of racial segre-gation in the nation and around the world.

UALR Archives and Special Collections

This photo shows Murray Lock and Dam under construction in the Arkansas River at Little Rock. The wall-like structure at the back is a coffer-dam built so that a section of the river could be drained while the work was going on. Completed in 1969, Murray is one of seventeen similar structures that form the McClellan-Kerr Arkansas River Navigation System that makes possible water commerce from the Mississippi River to the vicinity of Tulsa, Oklahoma, and has also turned the Arkansas River into a recreational facility.

U.S. Army Corps of Engineers

This picture, taken in the late 1930s, shows the Hinderliter Grog Shop, built in the late 1820s. Now the oldest building in Little Rock, it is completely restored and part of the Historic Arkansas Museum.

Courtesy of the Historical Arkansas Museum

"Putting on Their Red Shirts and Bringing Down the Engine": A History of the Little Rock Volunteer Fire Department

By Linda Ruth Pine

Linda Ruth Pine was a student in the Public History Program at the University of Arkansas at Little Rock when she wrote the story of the volunteer firemen of Little Rock. She is now Head of Archives and Special Collections in the Ottenheimer Library at UALR.

In American history the volunteer fire company traditionally has been a group of concerned citizens who organized themselves to protect their establishments from fire. Fire protection was considered the responsibility of the private citizen rather than the prerogative of municipal government. For more than fifty years, fire protection in Little Rock was provided by volunteer businessmen and shopkeepers.

These fire companies were self-governing, drawing up constitutions under which to operate and electing their own officers. While membership in the volunteer fire company was not an easy job, given the arduous task and methods of fighting fires in the nineteenth century and the discipline maintained by the company, it was a brotherhood of men. The fire house became a place for social intercourse and fraternal membership. The volunteer fire organizations in Little Rock possessed many traditions in common with volunteer fire companies around the country. Although fire companies in Little Rock experienced an uncertain beginning, they developed into an efficient force like their counterparts elsewhere. This essay traces the development of the Little Rock Volunteer Companies from 1839 to 1892. During that period the fire companies in Little Rock underwent a transformation from businessmen, "putting on their red shirts and bringing down the engine"[1] to salaried professionals who were employed by the city.

In 1827 Hiram Abiff Whittington, a Boston-bred young man, settled in Little Rock. He mentioned in a letter that year that there were ". . . about sixty buildings, six brick, eight frame and the balance log cabins..." in the town.[2] There were highly combustible materials in towns like Little Rock that could cause a fire. Pitch, paint, gunpowder, turpentine, coal oil, candles, lamps, and lanterns could easily ignite given the right conditions. Open fires could produce sparks, and unclean flues or chimneys could cause fires.

Although the overwhelming number of buildings in the town were made of wood, no record of any fires exists before 1830. In March 1830, a fire occurred in the business section of the small settlement of Little Rock. The wind, a constant threat and the source of danger when fire did occur, was not strong. Also rain had fallen for the previous day and a half. As a result the fire was quickly extinguished by the citizens.

The first of many editorials by *Arkansas Gazette* editor William E. Woodruff appeared concerning what became of one of his favorite topics: the establishment of a fire department or some type of fire protection for the town of Little Rock. "In a town as large as ours," Woodruff wrote, "there is not a single fire bucket, much less an engine and hooks and ladders, within its limits. Is it not high time that a proper fire apparatus should be provided for our town . . . ." [3]

While the Act of Incorporation of Little Rock in 1831 gave the Common Council the authority to purchase fire engines and organize fire companies, it was several years before the Council authorized the mayor to contract for a fire engine.[4] However, the town lacked the necessary funds to purchase one, having only $834.14 available in the treasury. [5] Therefore, in 1838, the Council requested an appropriation from the Arkansas General Assembly to purchase an engine. The request was referred to the Ways and Means Committee, which ruled that any action by the legislature was inappropriate.[6]

Both the purchase of an engine and the establishment of a fire company became a priority by 1839. In January 1839, the mayor was authorized to negotiate a five thousand dollar loan from the State Bank of Arkansas for the purchase of a fire engine.[7] The Council also commissioned a man who was going to the East to purchase an engine and apparatus for the town.[8] The mayor notified the town, through advertisements in the newspapers, that he would enroll the names of all those interested in becoming a part of the "Fire Engine Company" of the city.[9] An engine company ordinance was adopted by the Council in February, which listed the provisions and rules and regulations of the company.

Each person who enrolled in the company had to serve for at least two years, and no fireman could resign from the company without permission. Each member of the company was required to keep two fire buckets in his home. The company was empowered to enforce rules and regulations concerning attendance at drills and fires and to elect its officers. The captains of the company had the power to raze or demolish buildings to prevent fire from spreading and the power to command any firefighter or citizen at a fire.[10] In organizing the new company, the Council did not exempt the firemen from military duty, poll tax, or jury duty, which were traditional forms of reward for firemen in many communities in America. The *Arkansas Times and Advocate* stated that the omission of such traditional exemptions ". . . gives to the firemen no compensation for his time and exertions . . . ."[11] The newspaper writer believed that an exemption from the poll tax, for example, would provide an incentive for citizens to join the company and was the only way ". . . to get a well-drilled and efficient company." [12]

The fire engine, along with hose and hose cart, which had been ordered months before, finally arrived on September 16, 1839. With the purchase of the engine and the establishment of a fire company, it became quickly apparent that the maximum number of men, thirty, permitted under the ordinance of the city, was barely able to work the engine, much less fight the fire.[13] Until the invention of the steam engine and pump in the 1850s, the water from engines was pumped by manpower. Although not much is known about this first fire engine in Little Rock, most engines in that period weighed four to five thousand pounds. The firemen were expected to pull the engine to the fire and then pump the brakes on both sides of the engine to produce enough pressure for a stream of water to shoot from the hose. The brakes consisted of bars running the length of each side, and it took seven to twelve men on each side to pump the engine. It was tiring work, and the men could only pump for about ten minutes, so companies employed shifts.[14]

For this reason and probably due to a lack of organization, this early fire company had difficulties in the early years of its existence. Several fires occurred in 1840 and 1841, one of which caused $25,000 damage.[15] The *Arkansas Gazette* complained after a fire in December 1841 that, although the citizens were willing to help, there was no authority to direct either the citizens' or the fire company's efforts. The newspaper concluded that there was ". . . a want of proper organization and order. . ." on the part of the fire company.[16]

In early February 1842, a select committee reported to the Council on the status of the engine and engine house. The committee reported that:

> The building in which the Engine and Hose are kept, was originally put up in the most slight and unsubstantial manner, and suffered severely in the tornado which passed over this City, in May 1840. It now stands, apparently ready to fall with the first high wind.[17]

The condition of the fire engine was no better. The hose was rotting, the copper valves were corroding, and the engine was full of sand.[18] The committee recommended that an engineer be hired by the city to care for the engine and engine house, but the Council never acted on the recommendation.

By 1846, the fire company was no longer in existence or was so unorganized as to be completely ineffectual. However, following an appeal by the *Gazette* a group of citizens met in February to reorganize the company.[19] Those attending the meeting elected William E. Woodruff, president, and Lemmel H. Goodrich, vice president. Colonel Thomas D. Merrick, David W. Galloway, and Dr. R.L. Dodge were elected captain, secretary, and treasurer, respectively. Other members were appointed to committees in charge of obtaining subscriptions from the citizenry to purchase apparatus, writing a constitution, and drawing up the by-laws.[20]

In January 1847, a constitution and by-laws were amended and adopted by the Little Rock Fire Company. Among other things, the constitution clearly placed control of the engine and company under the captain. Men applying for membership were voted on by the membership for admittance. There was a maximum of fifty members allowed in the company, and no one could be under twenty-one. Each new member was required to pay fifty cents dues. There were rules concerning conduct and attendance at practice drills and parades. Monetary fines were instituted to ensure that firemen performed their duties faithfully. These fines ranged from ten cents for missing a meeting to fifty cents for missing a drill or failing to answer roll call after a fire to one dollar for disobedience to the captain. Elections were also provided for and were to be held the first Monday of each January.[21]

As a result of this reorganization the fire company was better organized, and the company was able to perform more efficiently at fires. Houses still burned down, but often this was because the building was too far away for the engine to reach before the building burned or because the fire was too far from a cistern or the river, which were the chief sources of water. It was not until the early 1850s that the fire company realized that there needed to be an additional company.

In the first two months of 1854 a record number of fires occurred and, on February 7, 1854, the Little Rock Fire Company petitioned the Council to organize a hook and ladder company. The company also asked the Council to appoint a chief for the two companies. The company emphasized ". . . the necessity or propriety of the appt. by your Honorable Body of some suitable person or Chief Engineer of the whole Fire Department and which shall be under his absolute control."[22] Colonel Thomas D. Merrick was unanimously elected Chief of the Little Rock Fire Department,[23] and an ordinance was later adopted concerning his duties.[24]

Before the Defiance Hook and Ladder Company could be organized, the worst fire in the city's history occurred on February 21, 1854. A quarter-block of buildings in the business section was destroyed. All but one of the city's newspaper offices were burned. The *Gazette* published one last issue three days after the fire and then suspended publication until May.[25]

A number of actions occurred at a public meeting that followed the disastrous fire. According to the *Arkansas Whig*, nearly one hundred of the town's citizens enlisted in a night police that was organized to prevent looting and to guard against possible fires. The Defiance Hook and Ladder Company was also formally organized during this meeting.[26] The establishment of the hook and ladder company provided additional protection to the city; between 1854 and the beginning of the Civil War there were only eight fires reported.

The 1860s and 1870s marked a golden period for the volunteer fire companies in Little Rock. In 1860 the Little Rock Fire Company was renamed the Pulaski Fire Company, when a second engine company, the Torrent Fire Brigade, was organized. By the end of the Civil War, the Little Rock Fire Department had developed into an efficient fire fighting force working well together under its chief engineer. At one fire in January 1866, the Hook and Ladder Company arrived first at the scene. The company, under the direction of the chief engineer, used its ladders and buckets to keep the fire under control until the engines arrived.[27] The department's improved effectiveness elicited praise for the firemen. The greatest compliment came in August 1866, however, when the *Gazette* after a fire, stated that ". . . with electric speed (a characteristic element of the Little Rock Fire Department) this dangerous and demoralizing visitor was soon combatted with the energy and determination inherent in a good and moral community."[28]

In 1867 a third engine company was organized, when the City Council purchased the city's first steam fire engine, wheel hose carriage, and one thousand feet of hose. The engine was christened "Pat Cleburne" after Arkansas' Civil War general, and the new engine company was called the Pat Cleburne Steam Fire Engine Company. The engine weighed five thousand pounds, was bright red, and could be pulled by hand or horse.[29]

Because the new engine was a steam-pumped engine rather than a hand-pumped engine, the Council enacted an ordinance to employ an engineer who could take care of the new fire engine. The salary for the engineer was one hundred dollars per month. The engineer's major responsibility was to keep the steam engine in perfect working condition, and he was accountable for any damage done to the engine. He was stationed at the engine house and had to remain on duty at all times. Like many other city officers, the engineer had to post a bond of one thousand dollars.[30]

For the first time, in 1869, the *Arkansas Gazette* printed a list of the officers and members of the four companies. There were a chief engineer, four assistants, and a secretary of the department. Each company had from five to seven officers. Defiance Hook and Ladder Company had thirty-six members and five officers, and the Torrent Fire Brigade had twenty-nine members and eight officers. The smallest company was the Pulaski Fire Company with twenty-eight members and seven officers. The Pat Cleburne Steam Fire Engine Company was the largest with forty-six members and six officers.[31]

This group of almost two hundred businessmen, craftsmen, and shopkeepers celebrated the founding of the fire department each May. In 1903, Isaac Pareira, a long-time foreman of the Torrent Fire Brigade, recalled that:

> May Day was the greatest holiday of the year, and especially for the firemen. Hundreds of beautiful girls would visit the place where the engines and hooks and ladders were kept, and literally cover them with flowers. After the parade we would take these flowers to the graves of dead firemen. One of our favorite stopping places was at the hospitable residence of Dr. Peyton . . . . We were always treated to plenty of cold spring water and refreshments were often served.[32]

The first parade reported in the *Gazette* was in 1860. The companies formed the procession at the engine house at Scott and Mulberry streets. The mayor led the parade followed by the marshals, a brass band, the aldermen, and the fire companies. The parade stopped at Dr. C. Peyton's for refreshments.[33]

In 1867 the *Gazette* again reported on the parade and described the uniforms of the different companies. The Pulaski Fire Company members wore grey shirts trimmed in red. The Defiance Hook and Ladder Company wore plain red shirts, black pants, and fire hats. The Torrent Company wore Garibaldi jackets trimmed in deep blue, black pants, and hats. The Pat Clebume Company had the most elegant uniform, which was black pants and hats, red shirts with green collars and cuffs, and a large shield on the breast embroidered with the name and number of the company. All the engines and trucks were decorated with flowers and evergreens.[34] The firemen were invited to the house of a friend for a luncheon, and, according to the *Daily Conservative*, "The sparkling champagne, together with native wit, elicited some happy hits, and jokes and repartee, with numerous toasts, which enlivened the occasion."[35] A ball was held that evening at the Anthony House, which lasted until three o'clock.[36]

By 1869 the decorations on the engines had become more elaborate. Kiosks and pagodas decorated with flowers and evergreens were often put atop the engine or truck with children riding inside. The girls were usually dressed in white; the boys were often in the company uniform or blue satin. Banners reading "Honor to the Brave," "Union is Strength," "Public Good Our Aim," and "We Raze to Save," were on the truck or engine. There were pleas for more water, with banners proclaiming, "Give us a little more water," and "We can do nothing without water." The hose carriage of the Torrent was drawn by members, and the ropes of the hose carriages were wrapped in red and white ribbons. Lantern boys often accompanied the members of the parade.[37]

The most extravagant display was in the 1870 parade. The Defiance Hook and Ladder truck was drawn by eight horses led by black grooms dressed in scarlet trousers, turbans, and white shirts. The truck was decorated with flowers and evergreens and bore on its top a young fireman standing with a pike in his hand among burning debris and planks.[38]

By the mid-1870s the companies began competing with their engines during the parade festivities. In 1874 a newly purchased rubber hose was tested. Three hundred feet of hose each was assigned to the Torrent and Pulaski Companies. The Gazette reported that the Torrent Company ". . . had a solid stream playing through an inch nozzle . . . a distance of 175 feet . . ." in less than a minute of pumping the brakes. The Pulaski next tried the hose, and it took them eight minutes to get water through the hose but it was thrown a distance of 225 feet.[39] The *Little Rock Daily Republican* noted that ". . . the nozzlemen occasionally varied their work by playing the hose upon the spectators." [40]

Sometimes competition between members of the companies and their engines extended beyond trials of the engine and hose. Brawls and fights occasionally occurred. In August 1871, the *Gazette* reported that, "... quite a number of firemen became engaged in a quarrel about who threw first water, which resulted in a general fight, resulting in several knockdowns, broken noses and bruised faces."[41] While the Torrent Company was given credit for throwing first water, the captain of the Pulaski Company claimed that the honor belonged to his company.[42] The competition to throw first water encouraged firemen to arrive at a fire and locate a source of water as quickly as possible. As a result of the fight, the chief engineer called a meeting of the department, and the companies resolved to settle their differences by means other than force.[43]

While the companies argued among themselves, they were very protective of their status as members of the Little Rock Fire Department. In 1871 an attempt by a group of mechanics to form a fire company failed when the chief of the Fire Department opposed its organization.[44]

When the Washington Fire Company (Colored) tried in 1877 to form a company for the sixth ward of the city, the Fire Department again strongly opposed the organization of such a company. The City Council originally approved the formation of the company and the purchase of an old, hand-operated fire engine.[45] Fifty-six members of the department signed a resolution that detailed their opposition to the plan. The members maintained that ". . . it is our exclusive privilege to suggest and recommend all things effecting this city so far as fire matters are concerned."[46] As a result of the pressure of the department, the City Council rescinded its previous vote to purchase an engine and to recognize the Washington Fire Company (Colored).[47] There were no other efforts by groups to form volunteer fire companies until 1888, although there were several hose companies organized during the 1880s.

During the 1880s several changes occurred in the Little Rock Fire Department. While most of the members continued to be volunteers, the need for full-time salaried professional employees, who could handle and care for the equipment, became apparent. Despite the fact that the department was increasingly a salaried one, the members were overwhelmingly businessmen who had occupations other than firefighting.

In 1881 the officers of the department consisted of the chief engineer, three assistants, and the treasurer. Their occupations included those of furniture dealer, confectioner, chief clerk, and saloonkeeper.[48] The Pat Cleburne Company had five officers whose occupations included a china and glass dealer, the chief of police, a policeman, the owner of a hardware store, and a carpenter.[49]

The Defiance Hook and Ladder Company had fewer officers and their occupations were bookkeeper, clerk, and a wine and liquor dealer.[50] The Pulaski Company had seven officers. The president of the company was an attorney and the foreman was a pressman. The occupations of the other officers included a barber, a bookkeeper, and a bowling alley owner.[51] The officers of the Torrent Company had occupations that included an attorney, jeweler and engraver, clerk, cabinetmaker, and tinsmith.[52] During the years that followed, the occupations of the officers of the companies included butchers, druggists, contractors, tailors, coppersmiths, and letter carriers.[53] These were the members of the fire companies who stopped whatever they were doing at the sound of the alarm bell and rushed to the scene of the fire.

One of the areas in which these businessmen had requested assistance from the City Council for many years was in the purchase of horses to expedite the engine's arrival at fires. In 1881, the Council debated the feasibility of purchasing horses for use by the department. After the development of the horse-drawn engines in the late 1860s, a fee was paid to anyone who used his horse to haul the engines to fires. The fee was usually five dollars for hauling a hose carriage, and ten to twenty dollars for hauling an engine.[54] Citizens were also paid for hauling the engine to be washed or repaired. Horses were purchased for the Pulaski Company in 1881, and by the mid-1880s all the engine companies had horses, although some of them were provided by the individual members of the fire companies.[55]

From 1885 to 1892 the Little Rock Fire Department became increasingly a salaried department. Beginning in 1881, the issue of a salaried fire department was debated, but no action was taken. Instead of making the entire department salaried, the Council gradually created salaried positions within the department. The office of tillerman for the Defiance Hook and Ladder Company, with a salary of fifty dollars a month, was established in 1885.[56] Additional salaried positions in the department included the drivers of hose carts and the driver of the Hook and Ladder truck, with salaries of sixty-five and seventy dollars a month, respectively.[57]

The most important salaried position was the chief engineer whose salaried position was created in 1888 when the Council adopted another ordinance for the regulation of the fire department. The chief engineer, although salaried, continued to be elected by the delegates of the fire companies, with the approval of the Council. The salary was $125 per month. The chief engineer was required to visit each of the engine houses daily and to report to the Council on matters affecting the department, such as the causes of fire that had occurred, the expenses of the department, and the status of the engines and other apparatus.[58]

In 1888 the Union Fire Company, No. 5 was organized,[59] and the fire department, after nearly fifty years of existence, was given the right of way when the fire alarm sounded. Vehicles were to move to the lane opposite the one in which the fire engines were progressing, and there were fines for those who violated this provision or who rolled over the hose while the firemen were fighting a fire.[60]

All the last ordinances enacted concerning the Little Rock Fire Department were related to the salaried members of the department rather than with the volunteers. Officers and employees of the department were required to provide themselves with the uniform that was worn by the St. Louis Fire Department in 1891, which became the official uniform of the Little Rock Fire Department.[61] Also beginning in 1891, the city physician was required to furnish free medical service to the employees of the Fire and Police Departments.[62]

The era of volunteer fire companies in the city came to a close February 8, 1892, when an ordinance creating a paid fire department was read the first, second, and third times. The volunteer fire companies held meetings to select some of their members for the paid department. The Pulaski Fire Company recommended three men as paid firemen at fifty dollars per month each, and two men as call men at fifteen dollars per month each.[63] On February 11, 1892, these and other firefighters were sworn in as regular salaried employees of the Little Rock Fire Department. The colorful names of the Pat Cleburne Steam Fire Engine Company, the Pulaski Fire Company, the Union Fire Company, and the Torrent Fire Brigade became the prosaic names of Engine Companies 1, 2, 3, and 4 respectively, and the Defiance Hook and Ladder Company, No. 1 became Hook and Ladder Company, No. 1.

Thus ended the fifty-three year history of the volunteer fire companies in Little Rock. From a small village of 1500 persons in 1840, the city had grown to a population of 25,000 when the department became salaried. In 1840 the town did not have the ability to support a fire company, and municipal government expected the citizens to support such institutions as fire departments. The development of fire companies in Little Rock reflected the development of volunteer companies around America in the nineteenth century.

While the primary function of the companies was to fight fires, the companies were also social clubs which provided fraternal membership like other organizations during the nineteenth century. The work was arduous and difficult, and sometimes dangerous, but the men who were members of the Little Rock Volunteer Fire Department walked proudly in the May parades and knew they were performing a service for themselves and the community.

NOTES

This article was first published in the *Pulaski County Historical Review*, 33 (Spring 1985): 2-12.

[1] *Arkansas Gazette*, February 3, 1854, 2:1.

[2] Margaret Ross, "Letters of Hiram Abiff Whittington: An Arkansas Pioneer from Massachusetts, 1827-1834," Pulaski County Historical Society, Bulletin Series Number 3, December 1956, p. 1.

[3] *Arkansas Gazette*, March 23, 1830, 3:1.

[4] *Arkansas Gazette*, July 29, 1834, 3:1; Act of Incorporation, City of Little Rock, Section 9.

[5] *Arkansas Gazette*, July 29, 1834, 3:1.

[6] *Journal of the Arkansas State House of Representatives*, 1837-1838, p. 403,408.

[7] *Proceedings of the Council of Little Rock*, January 29, 1839, Record Book A, Council Minutes, p. 108.

[8] *Arkansas Gazette*, February 20, 1839, 2:1.

[9] *Proceedings of the Council of Little Rock*, February 20, 1839, Record Book A, Council Minutes, p. 138.

[10] *Ordinances of the City of Little Rock*, A.D. May, 1848, (Little Rock, Arkansas: Gazette Printing Office, 1848), pp. 57-60.

[11] *Arkansas Times and Advocate*, March 4, 1839, 2:2.

[12] Ibid.

[13] *Arkansas Gazette*, September 25, 1839, 2:1,

[14] Earnest P. Ernest, *The Volunteer Fire Company: Past and Present* (New York, New York: Stein and Day, 1979), p. 33.

[15] *Arkansas Gazette*, April 29, 1840, 2:1.

[16] *Arkansas Gazette*, December 8, 1841, 2:1.

[17] *Proceedings of the Council of Little Rock*, February 1, 1842, Record Book A, Council Minutes, p. 376.

[18] Ibid., pp. 376-377.

[19] *Arkansas Gazette,* February 23, 1846, 2:2.

[20] *Arkansas Gazette*, March 2, 1846, 2:3.

[21] *Constitution and By-Laws of the Little Rock Fire Company*, (Little Rock, Arkansas: Democrat Office, Print, 1847), UALR Archives and Special Collections, UALR Library, University of Arkansas at Little Rock, Pamphlet 110, pp. 3-5, 7-8.

[22] *Proceedings of the Council of Little Rock*, February 7, 1854, Record Book B, Council Minutes, p. 53-54.

[23] Ibid., p. 54.

[24] *Proceedings of the Council of Little Rock*, March 7, 1854, Record Book B, Council Minutes, p. 56.

[25] *Arkansas Gazette*, February 24, 1854, 2:4.

[26] *Arkansas Whig*, March 2, 1854, 2:1.

[27] *Arkansas Gazette*, January 27, 1866, 1:6.

[28] *Arkansas Gazette*, August 4, 1866, 2:4.

[29] *Arkansas Gazette*, April 16, 1867, 3:3.

[30] *Proceedings of the Council of Little Rock*, April 16, 1867, Record Book C, Council Minutes, p. 199.

[31] *Arkansas Gazette*, July 18, 1869, 4:1.

[32] *Arkansas Gazette*, August 16, 1903, Section I, 10:3.

[33] *Arkansas Gazette*, May 26, 1860, 2:2.

[34] *Arkansas Gazette*, May 7, 1867, 2:1.

[35] *Daily Conservative*, May 3, 1867, 3:1.

[36] Ibid.

[37] *Arkansas Gazette*, May 5, 1869, 3:1.

[38] *Arkansas Gazette*, May 4, 1870, 4:1.

[39] *Arkansas Gazette*, June 6, 1874, 4:4.

[40] *Little Rock Daily Republican*, June 5, 1874, 4:3.

[41] Arkansas Gazette, August 12, 1871, 4:2.

[42] *Morning Republican*, August 12, 1871, 4:3.

[43] *Arkansas Gazette*, August 17, 1871, 4:3.

[44] *Arkansas Gazette*, August 17, 1871, 4:3.

[45] *Proceedings of the Council of Little Rock*, January 30, 1877, Record Book F, Council Minutes, p. 346.

[46] *Proceedings of the Council of Little Rock*, February 20, 1877, Record Book F, Council Minutes, p. 361.

[47] *Proceedings of the Council of Little Rock*, February 27, 1877, Record Book F, Council Minutes, p. 370.

[48] *Combined Directory of Little Rock, Hot Springs, Pine Bluff, Eureka Springs, and Fort Smith*, (no publ. listed, 1881, pp. 18, 86,110,165,179.

[49] Ibid., pp. 18, 34, 47, 62, 77, 80.

[50] Ibid., pp. 18, 51, 110, 152.

[51] Ibid., pp. 18, 46, 64, 72, 100, 120.

[52] Ibid., pp. 18, 47, 71, 135, 155, 186.

[53] *Sholes' Little Rock, Hot Springs, Pine Bluff, and Fort Smith City Directories* (Augusta, Georgia: A. E. Sholes, 1883-1884), pp. 32, 198, 322, 381; *Gazette City Directory for 1887* (Little Rock, Arkansas: Gazette Printing Company, 1887), pp. 312, 117, 162; and *Dow's City Directory of Little Rock for 1886*, (Memphis, Tennessee: Fred P. Dow, Publisher, 1886), pp. 11, 20.

[54] *Proceedings of the Council of Little Rock*, November 29, 1881, Record Book H, Council Minutes, p. 379 and *Arkansas Gazette*, September 17, 1875, 4:3.

[55] *Arkansas Gazette*, January 28, 1881, 1:6.

[56] *Council of Little Rock, Ordinance Book 2*, Ordinance Number 89, pp. 366-367.

[57] *Council of Little Rock, Ordinance Book 3*, Ordinance Number 256, p. 123.

[58] *Council of Little Rock, Ordinance Book 2*, Ordinance Number 129, pp. 537-545.

[59] *Council of Little Rock, Ordinance Book 2*, Ordinance Number 154, p. 579.

[60] *Council of Little Rock, Ordinance Book 2*, Ordinance Number 124, p. 531.

[61] *Council of Little Rock, Ordinance Book 3*, Ordinance Number 380, p. 269.

62 *Proceedings of the Council of Little Rock*, November 16, 1891, Record Book K, Council Minutes, p. 688.

63 *Arkansas Democrat*, February 11, 1892, 8:1.

THE HISTORY OF MARCHE, ARKANSAS

By Julia G. Besancon-Alford

Little Rock and North Little Rock are the major population centers of Pulaski County, and the mass of its population have been white and black people born in the United States, most of them in the South. There have always been towns outside of the cities, however, some of which, such as modern-day Jacksonville and Maumelle, have thrived, and there have also been immigrants, many of them from Germany. Marche, first settled by Polish immigrants, is now within the metropolitan boundary of Little Rock, but it has its own very distinctive history.

INTRODUCTION

Marche (pronounced "Mar-shay") is a community located in the north central section of Pulaski County, Arkansas. Since its last naming in 1878 by the Polish colony that settled there, Marche's domain has been redefined many times, and today its area is considerably smaller.[1] The remnants of old Marche proper are located ten miles northwest of Little Rock and two miles north of the Arkansas River. It may be visited by driving northwest on Interstate 40, turning off at the Morgan Exit, traveling east on the old Conway Highway (365) to the Marche road sign, then turning south to drive to the Missouri Pacific (formerly Little Rock and Fort Smith, a branch of the Cairo and Fulton) railroad tracks where Marche's original center of commerce was located. This area consisted of a depot, dry goods stores, blacksmith and livery stables. Most of old Marche consisted of farms scattered over the countryside, most ranging from forty to eighty acres in size. Today, all that remains of the original town is an abandoned store and two houses. Another section of old Marche, known as West Marche, is located on the opposite side of I-40 in and near the incorporated town of Maumelle. This is the sector in which the Maumelle Ordnance Works Plant existed during World War II. Old Marche's cultural and spiritual center remains in its original location just north of State Highway 365 on Jasna Gora Road (translated "Blue Hill"). The Jasna Gora site consists of the Immaculate Heart of Mary Catholic Church, rectory, school buildings, sisters' home, and a two-part cemetery divided by a road.[2]

Since 1878, when the Polish colony settled there, Marche has been referred to as Arkansas's "Little Poland." Until recent years this community exhibited a unique ethnicity. Several generations of Polish descent practiced old-world customs and traditions and spoke and worshipped in the language of their ancestral home — Poland. Today, only a few descendants of the original 300 Polish families live in the area, and most of the old-world influence has disappeared.[3]

Ironically, the name given this Polish community, "Marche," is not Polish, but French, meaning "market" or "market place." This name was probably selected by the colony's founder, Count Timothy von Choinski (pronounced Ko-in-skee), a linguist who spoke seven languages and knew French to be the language of European courts. One plausible reason this name was selected is that for several years prior to the Polish colony's arrival, Marche's site had been platted as a diversified market and manufacturing town and was to be named after its originator, the former circuit judge, Liberty Bartlett. Judge Bartlett's ambitious plans to found "Bartlett Springs" failed, and the property title reverted to its former owner, the Little Rock and Fort Smith Railroad Company, which renamed it "Warren Station" and created a rustic recreation area to stimulate interest and land sales in the area. The company had hoped to create markets and services for its line and did so in 1878 with the arrival of the Polish colony.[4]

The reason for renaming "Warren Station" "Marche" was to end the confusion between it and that of another city in Bradley County also named "Warren." A complaint lodged by a party in Bradley County, and a subsequent rebuttal from a Little Rock Post Office official, appeared in the Arkansas Gazette in 1882 in which public notice was served that it took some mail as long as six weeks to be delivered to the correct destination. Until Marche's post office was established in 1890 by order of President Grover Cleveland, mail was addressed and received at Marche's railroad depot, which still bore the name "Warren Station." Railroad maps continued to identify Marche as "Warren" as late as 1890.[5]

PULASKI COUNTY'S SECOND POLISH COUNT

A century after the Polish patriot and American Revolutionary War hero, Count Kasimir K. Pulaski, led 300 dragoons and light infantry into battle for American independence, another Polish count and patriot, Timothy von Choinski, led 300 independence-seeking Polish refugees to Pulaski County, Arkansas.

Poland had not existed as an independent country since the 1700s and had been partitioned by Russia, Germany, and Austria. After the Polish revolt of 1863, the Polish language was forbidden in public places, and many of the patriots and nobles were executed or exiled to Siberia. Many of those escaping the civil, political, and economic oppression of their foreign governors emigrated to the United States.[6]

A large number of the disfranchised Poles settled in the Great Lakes region in the large industrial cities of Chicago, Detroit, and Milwaukee. Because most of them were peasant farmers who could neither speak nor read English and knew little about American culture, they were employed in jobs requiring long hours for low wages, such as in slaughterhouses, stockyards, and coal mines. Their poor living conditions, coupled with the severe winters, caused ill health and discontent among the Poles.[7]

After several trips south, looking for a milder climate and a healthier environment for himself and his family, Count Choinski decided at the age of fifty-two to found a colony of Poles in the Southwest United States. Those answering his call were mainly from the provinces of Posen (Poznan), Galicia, and Silesia, and most had been farmers in the old country.[8]

Unlike the majority of his followers, Count Choinski was a member of the Polish nobility and a descendant of Cossacks. He was born in Gniezo in the province of Poznan in western Poland January 24, 1825, the son of Count Frank von Choinski and Countess Frances Racsinski Choinski. The Choinski status and wealth permitted Timothy a superior education at two German universities where he studied languages and mathematics. He fluently spoke French, German, Russian, Greek, Latin, and Hebrew, as well as his native Polish. During his youth he had participated in at least one of the Polish revolts against the foreign conquerors. After completing three degrees, he became a professor of German at a German university.[9]

Upon his arrival in the United States with his family in 1873, he quickly learned English and applied for certification as a professor of German. The Milwaukee Board of School Commissioners granted him this certification June 21, 1874. By September 1, 1874, he had signed a teaching contract with the Jefferson Public School of Milwaukee for an annual salary of $1,000. Eventually, he assumed the position of Professor of German at the prestigious Englemann Academy of Milwaukee.[10]

Count Choinski's wife, the Countess Loccadia Barbara Dembinska Choinski, was also of royal birth and a native of Poznan, Poland. She was born December 6, 1829, the daughter of a Polish earl, Mattias Dembinski, and his wife and cousin, Katharine Dembinski. The Dembinskis were a family of musicians. Loccadia's father and brother, Boleslaw (pronounced Boleswof), wrote music for organ as well as songs and cantatas. Upon Boleslaw's death in 1914, his daughter inherited a library of compositions in Poland. Loccadia was an accomplished musician also, playing the piano, organ, violin, harp, and trumpet. On October 4, 1848, Loccadia Barbara Dembinski and Timothy von Choinski were married in Poznan. The Choinskis had twelve children, nine of whom survived childhood, immigrated with them to the

United States in 1872, and also followed them to Pulaski County, Arkansas, in 1878.[11] The Choinski children were first educated at home and later at various European and American academies and universities. Each brought contributions to the development of their adopted homeland.[12]

Had it not been for his own failing health and the depressing conditions in which most Poles lived, Count Choinski would have remained in the secure and comfortable middle class position of professor of German in Milwaukee. However, he was grieved by the dismal and seemingly hopeless condition in which the majority of his fellow Poles had to live in the industrialized northern cities. Until his death on April 9, 1890, he lived in Marche — a place he hoped would provide a better and brighter future for his family and the colony he founded. After his wife's death on August 24, 1900, his body was transferred from the Marche cemetery to Pine Bluff, Arkansas, and placed alongside his wife's at Pine Bluff's Bellwood Cemetery.[13]

EDITORS, RAILROADS, AND THE POLISH COLONY

The establishment of the Polish Colony in Pulaski County began with a letter to the editor of the *Arkansas Gazette*, written by Count Timothy von Choinski from his home in Milwaukee, Wisconsin, March 12, 1877, and published in the *Gazette* March 16, 1877:

POLISH IMMIGRANTS - Fifty Thousand Acres of Land in One Tract Wanted for Five Hundred Actual Settlers.

The following letter was received at this office on the 15th, and we publish it in order that it may reach the eyes of persons having lands to dispose of, and in order that, if possible, some inducements can be found to draw to our state the colony mentioned in the letter:

Milwaukee, Wis., March 12, 1877

Editor Gazette: Polish inhabitants of America, being almost without exception farmers from birth and living dispersed as laborers in cities and towns, after my advice, and compelled by the dull times, made up their minds to settle again as farmers in any suitable state, and authorized me to select and buy a corresponding tract of land. There are till now about 500 families, who resolved to take part in this settlement, but their number is still increasing, and I dare say that thousands will follow as soon as I shall have found a convenient place. I directed my eyes chiefly to the western part of Arkansas and eastern part of Texas, but being unacquainted with proprietors of larger tracts of land I hope you will not deny what may turn to a benefit to your state, viz: to summon in your newspaper all those gentlemen to apply to me, the undersigned, with statements of the lands for sale. The people's wants are: at least 50,000 acres in one body, wood land with good soil; both sides of a river or rivulet; with a view to locating a future town and for manufacturing purposes; not far from a railway, low prices; good terms. I am convinced you will help the poor men, and insert a corresponding advertisement of this letter three or four times in your paper. Other newspapers please copy.

Respectfully, T. Choinski, 666 Broadway, Milwaukee, Wis.[14]

Colonel W. D. Slack, Land Commissioner for the Little Rock and Fort Smith Railway, answered the letter. Soon afterward, Count Choinski on one of his many trips south came to Little Rock to inspect the available land and discuss the terms. On May 22, 1877, he returned to Little Rock accompanied by twenty-two Polish colonists. Captain George W. Johnston, a railroad official, took the party on a tour of the company's land holdings. The colonists first expressed a preference for Conway or Pope Counties but finally decided to buy lands in Pulaski and Faulkner Counties.[15]

We know one of Count Choinski's visits was made to Pulaski County in June of 1877. The city editor of the *Gazette* commented in his local news column Wednesday, June 27, 1877, that, "Yesterday we saw a little Polish miss of twelve years who could speak her native language, English, and German fluently." In all probability the editor referred to one of Count Choinski's daughters, who like her parents was an accomplished linguist.[16]

It was first reported that the Poles had purchased 70,000 acres, but later and more reliable statements showed the tract to be considerably smaller. About 11,000 acres were purchased from the Little Rock and Fort Smith Railroad Company, and approximately the same amount in an adjacent location from the St. Louis, Iron Mountain and Southern.[17]

It was good business sense to advertise land sales directly or indirectly in the newspapers, so all railroad land sales were reported accordingly. One such account appeared in the *Arkansas Gazette* Wednesday, August 8, 1877:

We have learned through the local agent of the land department of the Fort Smith Railway that Dr. Chowinski [sic], who was here recently searching for lands on which to settle a colony of Poles, has created a great furore [sic] in the Northwest about Arkansas, and that there will be a very heavy immigration of these industrious and hardy people to this part of our state this fall. They are indeed, already arriving in small parties; but about October the heavy immigration will set in. Then will our forest wale [sic] to the stroke of the woodsman's ax.[18]

Apparently, newspapers were in competition for the news of immigrant settlers in their respective areas, because August 29, 1877, two days before twenty-six Polish families arrived in Little Rock (September 1, 1877), the *Gazette* bragged about their land purchase and impending arrival:

For the information of our Arkadelphia cotemporary [sic] we will state that the Polish Colony have [sic] purchased lands in Pulaski and Faulkner Counties, buying we believe, from the Little Rock and Fort Smith, and Cairo and Fulton Railway companies.[19]

On September 26, a special train left Chicago, carrying 330 people, members of 169 Polish families. They arrived at the depot opposite Little Rock two days later and were immediately sent on to Warren Station. Another 100 families were scheduled to leave Chicago a few days later. Commenting on the arrival of the Polish settlers, an editorial in the *Arkansas Gazette* stated:

... in a short time the country in the vicinity of Warren Station will be filled with a working and vigorous population. The members of the colony are fine looking people, of whom the state may be proud. This is the biggest thing that has yet happened in the immigration line in Arkansas, and the end is not yet, for we are informed that on Sunday 100 more families will leave Chicago to join the Arkansas colony. We say to them thrice welcome.[20]

MARCHE'S DISMAL BEGINNINGS

It was a long and weary trip for the Polish colonists who brought only minimal personal baggage with them. The railroad companies did everything possible to encourage this venture, providing free transportation on a special, nonstop passenger train to Arkansas. However, the travelers were not happy with the arrangement because they were not permitted to get off the train at any stops along the route to Little Rock. The railway company did provide a little assistance. On the day after their arrival, the company sent wagons to Warren to be used for hauling lumber and other supplies. Each family selected and purchased its homesite, usually about eighty acres, and families joined together to help each other build simple cabins. For the colony's founder, Count Choinski, the venture meant investing his life savings and assuming much of the burden of feeding the people during the first hectic days.[21]

What the Poles found upon their arrival dismayed many. Understanding there was a town-site on part of the land, some of the colonists thought they would find houses they could immediately occupy, but Warren did not measure up to their expectations. Instead, they found not even a depot but only a landing platform, an open-air dancing pavilion, a couple of concession shacks, and an abandoned sawmill — the remains of the Warren recreation area. Some thought crops of potatoes and corn had already been planted for them to harvest, but what awaited them was a vast wilderness that had to be cleared before it could be farmed. Having grown up in Poland as farming peasants, they probably had not realized they would now be tilling virgin land and that making a home and planting crops would require great personal strength and sacrifice.

Disappointed to learn they would have to make their own Utopia, many of the immigrants who could pay their railroad fare returned north on the same train that had brought them. Others went to North Little Rock (Argenta and Baring Cross), where they found lodgings and jobs with the railroads' construction crews or in the repair shops and engine round-house. Those who left clearly felt that they had been deliberately misled and that the colony's promoters had intentionally misrepresented the situation. This does not seem likely, since twenty-three of their number had inspected the site before the land was purchased. It is more plausible that they had not understood that their agents had spoken more of the colony's potentialities than of its current condition.

Some seventy-five to one hundred families decided to stay and build the colony according to the original plan. They boarded up the open sides of the pavilion to make a temporary shelter, where they slept on piles of hay covered with blankets. Since the weather was still pleasant and the pavilion was crowded, some camped out in the woods for a short time.

As soon as one rough-hewed log cabin was built another one was begun, leaving the finishing touches of windows and doors to be accomplished at leisure. By the middle of October 1877 quite a few houses were occupied, and the colonists swarmed into Little Rock to buy cooking utensils, stoves, and other household items from the Fones Brothers Hardware Store, then located at Second and Main streets. By late 1881 a few business buildings were erected. One of the most enduring business establishments was a dry goods store owned by Mr. Malachowsky. This structure is the only original business building still in existence in old Marche proper.[22]

As an agricultural community, the colony was a success. Here the people could have the freedom they had been denied in their native land, and for many years they clung to the old Polish customs, living very much as they would have lived in Poland under happier political circumstances. For many years it was a bilingual community, as both English and Polish were spoken and taught in the school. Their faith had seen them through revolutions, hardships, deprivations, immigration, and change. It was their faith that led them to establish a church and erect a house to accommodate it in the fall of 1878.

Despite their rough and rugged beginnings in Arkansas, the Poles determinedly struggled to carve out a prosperous life at Marche, one full of hard work and spiritual and cultural richness brought from their homeland of Poland. They doggedly fought against endemic malaria and other warm climate diseases that they had not experienced before. The mortality rate was high among infants, and many mothers grieved their children's early demise. Nevertheless, until the turn of the twentieth century, Polish immigrants continued to find their way to Marche to make their homes among the colony. Marche became the largest Polish settlement in the state, known far and wide for its old-world traditions, delightful Polish food, wholehearted celebrations, hard work ethics, and generous hospitality.[23]

OLD WORLD CHARM IN MARCHE

The Poles of Marche were industrious people who enjoyed a joyous and lively celebration to break the monotony of hard work. Two of these social customs occurred in connection with church activities. During these occasions the Poles played as hard as they had worked.

One of the most popular occasions in Marche was a wedding. The marriage ceremonies were elaborate and colorful. The reception and festivities following the ceremony began in the afternoon and featured traditional Polish foods, music, and dances. The music was provided solely with a violin and cello. As the night progressed, musicians were less formal in their manner of playing. The violinist did not rest his chin on his instrument but sawed away on it on his lap or in any other position comfortable for him. The cello had two strings, and its master never fingered the strings but sawed first on one and then on the other, twice on one, three times on the other. These festivities continued until late at night or early the next morning.

The bride, dressed in Polish costume, was required to dance with everyone present: men, women, and children. It was a trying ordeal for her, but she was the center of attention, and when the festivities were over she was presented with a handsome purse as a wedding gift, sometimes as much as $400.

The method of obtaining the purse was as novel as the other features of the ceremony. A stack of dinner plates was placed at a table, and each man present was required to break a plate by throwing a silver dollar at it. The dollar went to the "jack pot." If the thrower missed the plate, he was required to throw again. Both dollars went to the "jack pot." If he missed a dozen times he was taxed accordingly. If the plate was broken by the first dollar, that was the extent of his contribution. The ability to break the plate usually depended upon his state of inebriation.

The best description of an early bridal gown was that on a bride doll owned by Father Charles Hertel, one of Marche's parish priests. The dress was very elaborate and the young woman's rank was signified by the number of her petticoats, two to five in number, of white material with embroidered edges. The outer skirt was of a heavy silk material, almost completely hidden by a brocaded apron. The blouse was of sheer white with laced edges and puffed sleeves, but it was partially hidden by a heavily embroidered and fringed silk shawl, which was worn over the shoulders and crossed in front. The hair was tied with a long and broad red ribbon, which tied in the back in an immense bow and then hung down almost to the hem of the skirt. Her crowning glory, however, was her wreath. It was fully two inches wide, made of flowers, and worn very low on her head, almost on a level with the eyebrows.

Another occasion that was much celebrated was the welcome of a bishop for the dedication of a new church building. When the bishop arrived by train, he was met by a colorfully decorated horse-drawn carriage bedecked in red ribbons and followed by the congregation of the church on foot as in a parade to the church a few miles away.[24]

JASNA GORA – SPIRITUAL AND CULTURAL CENTER

Most of the Poles immigrating to Pulaski County were devout Roman Catholics. Not long after the colony arrived, representatives from Morrilton's Catholic Mission of the Order of the Holy Ghost Fathers came to organize a church at Marche. The mission in Morrilton had been a dismal failure since the German colonists who had settled there had met with much sickness, malaria, and epidemics. Many of the Germans left Morrilton seeking a climate more like their homeland. The Holy Ghost Fathers, therefore, were anxious to acquaint the Poles with the local maladies and help them adjust to their challenging new environment in the hope that they would stay.[25]

The hardships of creating a home and farm out of virgin land were immense, and the Fathers knew the Poles would require a source of spiritual leadership and strength. They immediately set about making plans to obtain land for a church site, but a dispute arose between the Fathers and Count Choinski over the selection of a suitable one. The Holy Ghost Fathers wanted it located in the heart of Marche near the railroad depot, but Count Choinski prevailed, and eighty acres located a couple of miles away on a hilltop was purchased for one dollar and deeded to the Holy Ghost Fathers by Jos Strup [sic] (The Very Reverend Joseph Strub) on August 18, 1882.[26]

The first parish priest was a member of the Morrilton order, the young Father Anthony Jaworski, a native of Poland. During the seven years he pastored the Marche church, 1878 to August 1885, he shared their hardships, poverty, and determination to survive. For this reason he is still remembered lovingly by the community. Many of the Poles who were poorly educated feared priests who were well educated, but Father Jaworski was particularly sensitive to his parishioners' needs, both spiritual and financial, and was able to overcome their fears.[27]

The Marche congregation met for the first time in 1878. Their church was dedicated by Bishop Edward Fitzgerald on May 23, 1880. The first church building, a small, wood frame structure, was named "Kosciol Najswietszej Marji Panny na Jasnej Gorze, Arkansas," translated, "The Church of the Most Blessed Mary on Bright Mountain, Arkansas." Therefore, it was named after "Our Lady of Czestochowa," a famous Polish shrine that the Poles held near and dear to their hearts and forever in their memory. The name Jasna Gora is poetically translated "Bright Sky Blue Mountain," but the local English-speaking residents refer to it as "Blue Hill."[28]

Very soon after the founding of the parish, a small school was built. Most boys in these early days went to school only until they were prepared for First Confession and First Holy Communion, and even many of the girls had to leave the classroom early to work on the farm or to find employment in the city to help support the family.

In 1896, after being in use for sixteen years and having been damaged by high winds, the first church building was torn down and a larger church was built on the hillside of Jasna Gora. Father Hippolitus Orlowski, who served from 1894 to 1897, supervised the building of the second structure, which was named "The Holy Hearts of Mary Church" and was dedicated by Bishop Fitzgerald on May 26, 1896.[29]

Even though many of the priests sent to the Marche church were Poles, the congregation had a difficult time retaining a priest. Some of the reasons for this pertained to the financial hardships of the parishioners, others to personality conflicts. The Poles were determined to control the future of their church as well as their own lives.[30]

The church land and buildings remained in the possession of the Holy Ghost Fathers until 1908 when it was transferred to the Right Reverend John B. Morris, D.D., Bishop of Little Rock. A rectory was built in 1906 and a school house in 1923, followed by a sisters' home in 1925 which was destroyed by fire in 1950.

In 1924 a large, three-room, frame school was built that served until 1959. Benedictine Sisters from St. Scholastica Convent operated the school. Sister Cecelia Wenzel first taught half a day in English and half a day in Polish. Sisters Bernardine and Seraphine taught for over forty years at the school.[31]

A fire destroyed the second church building on November 7, 1931. Father Charles Hertel (pastor from 1907 to 1949) supervised the building of a third church and a matching two-story rectory of buff brick in 1933 at a cost of $18,010.40 and $7,684.93 respectively. Bishop John B. Morris dedicated this church May 3, 1933. Designed by Ginnochio Architects, these structures stand today a short distance down the hill from the original church site and cemetery.[32] Father Hertel, a Pole from Silesia, arrived in Arkansas in 1905 and completed his education at Subiaco the same year. Two years later he was ordained and became the pastor at the Marche church. During his tenure at Marche he witnessed four tornadoes; the fourth one damaged the church grounds by downing trees, but the church, rectory, and school were untouched by the storm. Due to ill health, this popular pastor retired in September of 1949 and died at Subiaco February 1, 1950.

Monsignor Thomas J. Prendergast, a native of Fort Smith, Arkansas, served as pastor of Immaculate Heart of Mary Catholic Church from September 1, 1956, to July 1, 1970. During Monsignor Prendergast's tenure a second school and a parish hall were built on Jasna Gora at a cost of $100,000. These were dedicated by the Little Rock Bishop, the Most Reverend Albert L. Fletcher, on November 27, 1960. The following year a new road and water supply improvements were made to the Marche parish plant. Father Prendergast celebrated his Silver Jubilee at Marche. He also served as the executive editor of the Catholic publication, *The Guardian*, from September 17, 1935, to May 1959, and was appointed State Chaplain of C.D.A. Monsignor Prendergast retired in 1974 due to ill health, died May 24, 1978, and was buried in the cemetery of his beloved Marche church.[33]

At the time of this writing, the pastor of Immaculate Heart of Mary Catholic Church is the Reverend Albert Schneider.

NOTES

This articles was first printed in the *Pulaski County Historical Review*,41 (Winter 1993):78-90.

[1] It is bordered to its north by Faulkner County (created in 1873), to its west by Maumelle (new town), to its south by Crystal Hill (formerly known as Chrystal Rock), to its east and north by the Arkansas National Guard's Camp Joseph T. Robinson (formerly known as Camp Zebulon Pike), and to its south and east by the Oak Grove community. Since Marche is not an incorporated city, its entity is that of a western sector of the city of North Little Rock. Its land survey and legal description is that of Congressional Township 3 North, Range 13 West, plus a former connecting portion located in the western half of Township 3 North, Range 12 West of the State of Arkansas midline survey. It is shared by two of Pulaski County's political subdivisions: Pyeatt(e)Township (created in 1823) and Worthen Township (created out of Pyeatt(e) in 1886). Marche's original boundaries overlap both townships and several smaller communities, therefore, for the purpose of this paper Marche shall be referred to as both a domain and a community. Russell Pierce Baker, "Pyeatt and Worthen Townships' Creation Dates," *Townships of Arkansas Counties* (Little Rock, Ark.: Arkansas History Commission); Russell Pierce Baker, "Marche Post Office, 1875 to 1930, Section 26, T3N, 13W" *From Memdag to Norsk: A Historical Directory of Arkansas Post Offices 1832-1971* (Hot Springs, Ark.: Arkansas Genealogical Society, 1988), 141; Ernie Deane, "Marche," *Arkansas Place Names*, 1st ed. (Branson, Mo.: 1986), 111; "Pyeatte and Worthen Townships," *General Highways and Transportation Maps of Arkansas* (Little Rock, Ark.: Arkansas State Highways Department, 1936), 33; "Marche," *The Roads of Arkansas* (atlas) (Fredericksburg, Tx.: Shearer, 1990), 76.

[2] Ibid.

[3] Lewis Gillespie, "Little Poland in Arkansas," *Arkansas Democrat*, April 27, 1947, Sunday magazine sec., p. 1.

[4] Helen Schnable Majewski, interview with author, October 2 and 30, 1992, Pine Bluff, Ark. (She is a descendant of Count and Countess Choinski, founders of Marche.) Choinski Papers (a collection of documents, letters, clippings, and photographs dating from 1829 in the possession of Helen S. Majewski); Tape recordings of Helen Choinski; "Choinski and Marche," *Arkansas Gazette*, February 6, 1938, Sunday magazine sec., p. 1. clippings.

[5] Letter to editor from H. C. Hale, Postmaster, *Arkansas Gazette*, January 21, 1882, p. 4.; Letter to editor from M. C. Wilson, Chief Clerk Mail Services, *Arkansas Gazette*, January 24, 1882, p. 4; Andrew M. Modelski, Map showing Warren Station on the Santa Fe and Connections Route of 1888, Little Rock and Fort Smith Railroad line, *Railroad Maps of North America, The First Hundred Years* (Washington, D.C.: Library of Congress, 1984), 104-105.

[6] Margaret Ross, "Chronicles of Arkansas, Plans for Polish Community at Marche Began with Letter to Editor of Gazette," *Arkansas Gazette*, February 19, 1967, p. 6E.

[7] Letter to Mrs. Bernie Babcock from Ruth Choinski Schnable, December 28, 1937, with reply December 29, 1937, concerning "corrections to story about Marche," Choinski Papers.

[8] "Lub W. Redakeij Gazety Polski" quoted, *Kurjer Nowojorki,* (Polish language newspaper), Chicago, Illinois, nd., Choinski Papers.

[9] Bernie Babcock, "First Settlers of Marche," *Arkansas Gazette,* February 6, 1938, magazine sec., p. 1.

[10] Helen von Choinski Schnable, "Notes of Recollections, February 6, 1938," Choinski Papers; Tape Recordings of Helen Choinski, granddaughter of Count and Countess Choinski (ca. 1960s), Mrs. Helen Schnable Majewski, Pine Bluff, Arkansas.

[11] Helen von Choinski, "Commonplace Book," "Genealogy," nd., Choinski Papers.

[12] Lewis Gillespie, "Little Poland in Arkansas," *Arkansas Democrat,* April 27, 1947, Sunday magazine, p.1. One of the sons, Charles Choinski, served Pulaski County in the General Assembly in 1883 and was a successful businessman and farmer. *Goodspeed's Biographical and Historical Memoirs of Pulaski County, Arkansas,* (reprint, Easley, S.C.: Southern Historical Press, 1978), 378; *Historical Report of the Secretary of State* (Kelly Bryant, 1968) 347.

[13] Gillespie, "Little Poland in Arkansas."

[14] T. Choinski, "Letter to the Editor," *Arkansas Gazette,* March 16, 1877, p. 4.

[15] "Polish Settlement of Marche Founded by Refugees in 1870," *Arkansas Gazette,* July 13, 1941, sec. I, p. 12.

[16] "Colony Buys Land in Pulaski County," *Arkansas Gazette,* June 27, 1877, p. 4.

[17] H. C. Costello, Assistant Land Commissioner, Little Rock and Fort Smith Railway Company, Letter to Count T. Choinski, Esq., Cleveland, Ohio, August 12, 1877, Choinski Papers; "Large Number of Poles Expected in Arkansas," *Arkansas Gazette,* August 8, 1877, p. 2.

[18] "Conway," *Arkansas Gazette,* August 8, 1877, p. 2.

[19] "Poles in Arkansas, 11,000 Acres Purchased at Warren Station," *Arkansas Gazette,* August 29, 1877, p. 4. Original Land Tract Entries for Pulaski County, Arkansas, Microfilm Roll 14 of Book 43, Arkansas History Commission.

[20] Editorial Response to Letter from T. Choinski, *Arkansas Gazette,* September 29, 1877.

[21] *Arkansas Gazette,* September 29, 1877, p. 4.

[22] L. E. Hebb, "Pioneer Settlers of Marche Still Retain Customs of Native Poland," *Arkansas Democrat,* June 21,1936; Miscellaneous letters written by Ruth Schnable Cameron, Choinski Papers; "Poles from Warren Station Buying Goods in Little Rock," *Arkansas Gazette,* October 13, 1877, p. 4.

23 Jan Sarna, "Marche, Arkansas, A Personal Reminiscence of Mrs. Anne Stozek Sarna," *Arkansas Historical Quarterly*, 36 (Spring 1977): 31-49; Jan Sarna, telephone interview with author, November 7, 1991; Original Land Tract Entries of Pulaski County, Arkansas.

24 Mrs. Louis "Tiny" Zakrzewski Weed, interview with author, October 23, 1991, on "remembrances of socials and box suppers at Marche and Stanislaus J. and Victoria Zakrzewaki, her deceased parents." Elizabeth Pruss, interview with author, October 23, 1991. L. E. Hebb, draft of undated article for *Arkansas Democrat,* ca. 1936, located in Federal Writers' Project File, Arkansas History Commission. Maureen Sullivan, interview with author, December 3, 1991.

25 Jonathan James Wolfe, "Beginning Life in the New Land," *Arkansas Historical Quarterly* 25 (Winter 1966): 362; "Immaculate Heart of Mary Parish History," Catholic Diocese of Little Rock, 1956.

26 *Immaculate Heart of Mary Catholic Church Centennial* (1878-1978) (Booklet), edited by Rev. Edward J. McCormick, Pastor, North Little Rock, Ark.; William Piechocki, Steward and Parish Manager, Immaculate Heart of Mary Catholic Church of Marche, interview with author, October 28, 1991.

27 "Catholicity in Arkansas, Immaculate Heart of Mary Church," *Guardian*, December 20, 1924.

28 Fr. Ladislas Siekaniec, O.F.M., Ph.D., "The Poles of Arkansas," *The Polish American* (Chicago, Ill.), April 10, 1971, Easter ed., p. 10; "Polish Settlement, History of Diocese," Guardian, April 22, 1911.

29 Patrick Zollner, Arkansas Historic Preservation Program, telephone interview with author, January 15, 1992, regarding listing of Immaculate Heart of Mary Catholic Church on the National Historic Register.

30 Letters from members of Immaculate Heart of Mary Catholic Church to their Bishop, the Reverend Edward Fitzgerald, Archives, Catholic Diocese of Little Rock.

31 Theresa Kaplon, interview with author, November 3, 1991; Patrice Yelenich, Elementary School Teacher of Immaculate Heart of Mary Catholic Church, interview with author, October 28,1991.

32 P. V. Burton Cromwell, *Religious Structures of Marche, Arkansas*, Architectural Drawings Nos. 1 through 10, St. Mary's Emaculate [sic] Conception Church, University of Arkansas at Little Rock Archives and Special Collections, Ottenheimer Library, File ArD270. Ginocchio Architectural Drawings of Immaculate Heart of Mary Catholic Church, UALR Archives and Special Collections.

33 Lewis Gillespie, "The Church of the Holy Hearts of Mary Catholic Church of Marche," *Arkansas Democrat*, April 27, 1947, p. 4; "Tornado Tears Through Marche," *Arkansas Gazette,* May 5,1908, pp. 1-2. Western Union Telegram from A. L. Fletcher to Rev. John M. Morris concerning Church and Rectory fire, November 8, 1931, Archives, Catholic Diocese of Little Rock.

FLOODS, FLATCARS, AND FLOOZIES: CREATING THE CITY OF NORTH LITTLE ROCK, ARKANSAS

By Timothy G. Nutt

Timothy G. Nutt had just graduated from the University of Central Arkansas in 1992 when he wrote this classic article on the origins of North Little Rock as a city separate from Little Rock across the Arkansas River. He went on to do graduate work at the University of Oklahoma School of Library and Information Science and later worked at the Butler Center and served as editor of the "Pulaski County History Review". He is now Manuscripts and Rare Books Librarian at the University of Arkansas Libraries, Special Collections.

More than the Arkansas River separates the cities of Little Rock and North Little Rock, Arkansas. With a population of 61,741 people, North Little Rock today enjoys a relatively peaceful coexistence with its sister city to the south. This has not always been the case. Before incorporation as a separate city in 1904, the north shore endured several tortured decades of contentious history. From 1845 to 1866 four separate attempts were made to create a viable town on the shore "opposite Little Rock." Eventually, a coterie of determined north shore leaders employed stealth, cunning, political acumen, and no small amount of subterfuge to create an independent city of North Little Rock.

DeCantillon has the distinction of being the first failed attempt at an Arkansas River north shore settlement. Little Rock was established on the south shore in 1821 and, although there were people living on the opposite bank (mainly because it was a converging point for roads between Memphis, St. Louis, and what became Indian Territory), it would be another twenty years before a concerted and serious effort was made to settle the opposite bank.[1] These early efforts to establish a settlement failed mainly because the river flooded frequently. Despite the unpredictability of the river, Richard D'Cantillon [DeContillon] Collins, a military disbursing agent for Indian removal, and four partners placed an advertisement in the *Arkansas Gazette* on July 25, 1838, announcing: "Persons desirous of settling near Little Rock are respectfully informed that the undersigned have laid out a town . . . on the north bank of the Arkansas River."[2]

Though several lots were sold, the proposed town never got off the ground. The failure was partly due to the 1840 flood that washed away portions of the fledgling settlement. Also contributing to the failure was the tenuous financial situation of the Arkansas State Bank that financed the development.[3] Regardless, the first attempt at a city opposite Little Rock was a bust. The land would remain devoid of any organized settlement until the 1860s.

The United States in the 1850s experienced a boom in railroad construction. Though many railroads were planned for Arkansas, only one was built. The Memphis and Little Rock Railway (M. & L. R.) connected the capital city to the eastern bank of the Mississippi River, although the terminus was actually located on the north side of the Arkansas River. In addition, the government roads linking Indian Territory, St. Louis, and Memphis intersected with the railroad terminus. Around this area evolved a settlement that came to be known as "Huntersville."[4] Hypotheses abound as to the origin of the name. One states that the settlement was so named because of an abundance of wildlife; however, the generally accepted theory is that the settlement was named in honor of an early settler, William Hunter. Although there may have been talk of incorporating the settlement, no petition was filed and the land was never platted.[5] During the Civil War the United States government took control of the captured Confederate railways, but the Military Railroad Office returned the M. & L. R. line to its owners in 1865, and United States Government buildings on the north shore were auctioned off. The settlement population dwindled with the exodus of troops and government officials. The railroad tracks had been virtually destroyed during the course of the Civil War, and the M. & L. R. owners replaced and, in some cases, rebuilt the line, subsequently deciding to relocate the depot a half mile to the north.[6] Later, the Little Rock and Fort Smith Railroad and the Cairo and Fulton Line built their depots in the same general area. However, the M. & L. R.'s terminus was then located on the plantation of the late Thomas W. Newton, Sr.

The new location of the M. & L. R.'s depot was the deciding factor in the creation of yet another community in 1866, but before this William E. Woodruff, former publisher of the Arkansas Gazette, would try to form the town of "Quapaw" from the remnants of Huntersville plus a few hundred additional acres. Nothing substantive came of this venture.[7] The heirs of Thomas W. Newton decided to survey the estate and have it platted into lots and blocks. The new settlement, with a small population, was christened "Argenta." The name was selected because of the periodic efforts to mine silver (argenta in Latin) on the north bank — a practice that continued well into the twentieth century. The recently moved M. & L. R. terminus occupied the southeast corner of the new town, while the Little Rock and Fort Smith Railroad purchased eleven complete city blocks in the northwest section for the sum of $7000.[8] The Cairo and Fulton began actual operations in 1870, using the facilities of the other two rail companies. Woodruff Avenue, the eastern boundary of the newly platted town, was named in honor of William E. Woodruff, who only nine months earlier had attempted to establish "Quapaw" with lands immediately east of Argenta. The western boundary was named in honor of the founding family and called Newton Avenue.

Argenta had a population of several hundred people by 1871, and with the increasing population became a boomtown. As the *Gazette* reported, ". . . buildings are rapidly going up, boarding houses, groceries, saloons and blacksmith shops opened, and a general air of go-aheadiveness and enterprise pervades that little berg [sic]."[9] All the while, the railroad companies were busily expanding and completing the renovation of the tracks. The Cairo and Fulton merged with the St. Louis and Iron Mountain Railroad in the early months of 1873 and began construction of the first bridge across the Arkansas River. However, the bridge would not connect the town of Argenta to Little Rock. Instead, the railroad company chose a site west of the town; there they built a railroad station and named it Baring Cross.[10]

There were some disadvantages associated with the expansion of the railroads on the north side of the river. With incoming trains came hobos and vagabonds. Lawlessness fed on itself since there was no way to control the offenders. Argenta did not have "a justice of the peace or other officer for the administration of justice." The *Arkansas Gazette* in an editorial suggested a solution to the problem: incorporation.[11] Property owners in Argenta agreed with the editor that "life might be more endurable, if, with the prestige of town authority, they united to stamp out the ills with which they were surrounded,"[12] and so they pushed for a petition of incorporation. However, other citizens countered that the settlement was too small and incorporation would lead to an unfair tax burden on a few citizens. The anti-incorporation group squashed the idea and subsequently defeated petitions for incorporation in 1878, 1879, and 1881.

In 1889, another petition for incorporation for Argenta was filed in the Pulaski County Court. It again met with opposition, but instead of withdrawing the request the decision on incorporation was delayed. In January of 1890, the petition was re-evaluated and "an order was issued granting the prayer of the petitioners." This resulted when a majority of the opposition withdrew their protests. Though there were still Argentans who were against incorporation, rumors of a possible annexation by Little Rock changed their minds.[13] The north-side citizens, confident that they had outsmarted the capital city, waited for the final word for incorporation. However, it never came. As soon as Pulaski County Judge William F. Hill issued the order for incorporation, the political leaders of

Little Rock struck back. The leaders, headed by Little Rock Mayor William G. Whipple, requested that Hill withdraw the order. Judge Hill immediately complied, and this outraged the citizens of Argenta.[14] They could not understand how the leaders who "owned not a foot of ground in Argenta" could exert so much influence on the affairs of the town. In addition, they asked why the city fathers of Little Rock would care that Argenta wanted to incorporate.[15] Many people had their ideas. The business leaders of Argenta blamed the business elites of Little Rock. In a booklet published in 1907 the north shore leaders wrote:

> The masters of Little Rock — the great public service corporations — foresaw two cities of equal rank regulating their progress. Certain as the future, a separate city of first class would rise across the river and values would rise with the increasing population and trade. They would be forced to make heavy expenditures. . . . Driven to desperation by the probability of competition in their respective lines, if Argenta established her independence, this corrupting combine spent the public money and its own, like drunken sailors, to encompass the defeat of the People. Corporations dare not fight the public interest, so they buy up the grafters elected by the People. The grafters fight the battles of the corporations in the name of the People and the People pay for it.[16]

The financial situation of Little Rock contributed to the effort to stop the incorporation. In 1890 the capital city had a large debt totaling about $250,000. This debt was a legacy of city administrations during Reconstruction when expensive efforts were made to modernize the town.[17] Argenta, with its burgeoning railroad industry, offered revenue opportunities for Little Rock. Argenta would, as an added bonus to the Democratic Party, bolster the strength of that party in the city. At the time, the city of Little Rock contained a large number of Republicans.[18] Though Republican Mayor Whipple did not support this contention; there was little he could do to stop the Democrat-controlled city council.

To stem the tide of protest and address Argenta's complaints, Judge William F. Hill conducted a hearing in February, less than a week after the withdrawal, with the prominent attorney Uriah M. Rose representing Argenta and Mayor Whipple representing Little Rock. Rose argued that the proper procedure for incorporation had been followed and no formal protest against the incorporation had been filed. In addition, the settlement's incorporation was of no concern to anyone but the citizens themselves. Rose, therefore, stated that "it was the duty of the Court Judge to grant the order." Mayor Whipple countered Rose stating that incorporation would be detrimental to Argenta; annexation would be most beneficial to the settlement as they would receive city services such as municipal water service, street lighting fixtures, and police protection. This suggestion of possible annexation would come to fruition later in the month. Judge Hill, in his decision, stated that he considered Argenta a part of Little Rock and he "did not think it best to permit incorporation." Rose vowed to appeal.[19]

On February 12, 1890, the Little Rock City Council convened. At the meeting city attorney William Terry gave his opinion on the right of Little Rock to annex Argenta. He stated that the boundaries of the city extended to the middle of the Arkansas River; therefore, the territory across the river was contiguous. An ordinance was then introduced based on his opinion. Ordinance 234 submitted the question of annexation to Little Rock voters only. Argenta was not allowed to participate in the election due to a law left over from Reconstruction that permitted a municipal corporation to annex without the consent of the residents living in the contiguous territory. The election was set for April 1, 1890.[20]

Between the city council meeting and the election date, Whipple had to sway the population of his own city. The residents of southern Little Rock vowed to defeat the annexation. Because of the municipal debt, the city was unable to provide these citizens with gas, water, or other public utilities, and they were opposed to providing services to Argenta before they were available to all parts of Little Rock proper. To counter the protest vote, Whipple promised an annexation of all the territory surrounding Little Rock. Whipple claimed that the revenues would be so increased by the new population that public utilities could be dramatically improved.[21] In effect, Whipple had provided the south Little Rock residents with an ultimatum: vote for the annexation of Argenta or do without gas and water. This strategy resulted in a victory, 1,667 for annexation and 473 against. Mayor Whipple immediately requested that the county court direct the annexation. Protests and complaints against the election's outcome poured in from Argenta from both individuals and businesses, but on May 15 County Judge Hill denied and dismissed all protests and approved the annexation.[22] As the judge signed the annexation papers, appeals were already being filed.

The first appeal was that of Joseph Wysong Vestal. Vestal, whose extensive lands on the north shore were devoted entirely to agriculture, believed that his acreage should not be included in the annexation. The decision of the county court, which included Vestal's lands in the annexation, was sustained by the circuit court.[23] The appeal eventually reached the Arkansas Supreme Court where it was decided on March 14, 1891. The main thrust of the appeal was the contiguous territory opinion that was used in the annexation, but the plaintiff, Vestal, also intended to use the argument that agricultural lands were not beneficial to the city. Uriah M. Rose, representing Vestal, stated to the Court:

> Argenta is not contiguous to Little Rock. Being a navigable stream, the Arkansas River, together with its bed and the banks between high and low water mark, belongs to the State.[24]

The Little Rock attorneys John W. Blackwood and John E. Williams responded by saying that the river bed did not prevent a territory from being considered contiguous. Besides, they continued, it was immaterial who owned the river bed because it could be annexed along with the territory.[25] On the question of agricultural lands, Rose stated that it was unreasonable to annex unplatted agricultural lands not needed for city purposes just for the purpose of increasing the city's revenue. Mayor Whipple, in response, declared that the lands were adapted to city purposes and uses. In addressing the contiguous territory issue, the Court ruled that just because the city is on one side of the river and the territory is on the opposite side is not a disqualification for contiguity. It further stated:

> The river is included in the land annexed, and is therefore not a break in contiguity nor an insuperable barrier to a complete amalgamation of the communities upon its opposite banks. That intervening rivers do not prevent such amalgamation . . . and the Supreme Court of Ohio in construing a provision in the same terms . . . held that a city might annex territory on the opposite bank of a large river.[26]

On the question of Vestal's land the Court held that his farm and land were not needed for city use. The Little Rock City Council met and passed an amended resolution for annexation, deleting Vestal's acreage, and filed it in circuit court on May 25.[27] Argenta citizens immediately sued stating that the city council had no right to amend the ordinance by adopting a resolution. The suit was decided in the state Supreme Court in March of 1892. The Court dismissed the suit mainly because the question arose out of a Supreme Court decision and it was not open to litigation.[28] Little Rock immediately incorporated Argenta into the "City of Roses."

It was now up to the Little Rock City Council to decide how Argenta would participate in the city government. It was generally agreed that Argenta would be divided into wards, but "the general opinion in the streets was in favor of making Argenta a distinct ward of itself."[29] But the city council procrastinated, taking no action until a revolt seemed to be brewing in the newly annexed territory. At the December 19, 1892, city council meeting, a plea from Argenta was presented to allow the area to withdraw from the city. It was immediately tabled with no discussion,[30] but it jolted the council into action. At the January 28, 1893, council meeting, Little Rock was redistricted into eight wards — all the territory north of the Arkansas River comprising the eighth. The ward participated in its first municipal election in April of the same year, and as a result, William Chesley Faucette and Frank M. Oliver were elected aldermen.[31]

Faucette was born in northern Mississippi in 1865. The family moved to Arkansas in 1880 and the younger Faucette, along with his brother, James Peter, came to Argenta in 1883. Both became locomotive firemen with the Little Rock and Fort Smith Railroad Company. While Little Rock aldermen, W. C. Faucette and Oliver worked hard to secure public utility improvement within Argenta. In 1896 when the two resigned from the council, they claimed it was because the eighth ward received substandard services, including having only a second-hand hose wagon at the fire station and police patrols on the north side only when there were no pressing matters in Little Rock. Plus, the "Argenta Anarchists," as the two aldermen were known, were frequently voted down fourteen to two.[32] The two, however, remained active in capital city politics.

In 1896, the town of Baring Cross was incorporated. The community had been growing along with Argenta as the Iron Mountain Railroad expanded. In 1898, Baring Cross annexed more territory.[33] The growing town west of Argenta heated up the still simmering desire for northside independence. With the lingering resentment toward Little Rock for preventing incorporation still fresh on Argenta citizens' minds, a secret plan was devised to separate the two areas. In mid-1901, after the Thirty-third General Assembly had adjourned, W. C. Faucette, his brother J. P., businessman Justin Matthews, and several others formed a secret organization that swore to make Argenta a separate municipality. Under the guise of creating a separate school district, papers were filed to incorporate a city bordering Argenta.[34] The area, located north and west of Argenta, was contained between Newton Avenue and the Little Rock and Fort Smith Railroad depot. The southern boundary of the proposed city was the northern boundary of the eighth ward. In July 1901, the incorporation of "North Little Rock" was approved. Frank O. Cook was elected the city's first mayor.[35]

As 1902 came to an end, the secessionist organization prepared for the approaching Thirty-fourth General Assembly, set to convene on January 12, 1903. Five of the state's most prominent lawyers, led by former state senator James P. Clarke, drafted a bill to allow Argenta to break away from Little Rock. Of course, the true purpose of the bill had to remain secret, otherwise Little Rock leaders would derail it. To ensure secrecy only two legislators were truly knowledgeable about the bill's purpose: Representative John E. Martineau of Pulaski

County, and Senator David L. King, representing the Second District, which included Randolph, Lawrence, and Sharp Counties.[36] Martineau was a friend of the Faucette brothers and a former teacher at Argenta. The organization had "implicit confidence" in him.[37] King was considered an enemy of "trusts and monopolies"[38] and was chosen by the organization to introduce the separation bill, innocuously known as the Hoxie-Walnut Ridge Bill, a reference to the two small Lawrence County towns separated only by a railroad track. To make the bill seem legitimate and of no concern to Little Rock, a lobbyist from Walnut Ridge was employed by the Faucettes to attend to the legislation.[39]

On February 4, 1903, Senator King introduced Senate Bill 142, entitled "A Bill for an Act to Amend the Laws in Relation to Municipal Corporations." The bill was read a second time and placed on the Senate's calendar.[40] On February 17, it was read a third time and passed with no debate; the vote was twenty-eight for, zero against, and seven not voting.[41] The bill then went to the House of Representatives where passage was just as easily obtained, eighty-four to one, the one nay being from Representative William Greene of Ouachita County.[42] The Hoxie-Walnut Ridge Bill was sent to Governor Jeff Davis, who signed it into law on March 16, 1903. The new law, Act 86 of 1903, read:

> Any municipal corporation, or any part thereof, may be annexed and made a part of any other municipal corporation located within one mile of the municipal corporation to which the same is to be annexed, in whole   or in part, but before such annexation shall be made and declared, the council or board of aldermen of either   the corporation to which said territory is to be annexed, or that which is to be annexed in whole or in part, shall order an election, after giving thirty days notice thereof . . . [and] petitions asking for said election have been filed with such board or council, signed by a majority of the qualified electors in said territory to be annexed.[43]

The Argenta conspirators were elated, but they waited until the General Assembly adjourned at the end of April before implementing the new law to prevent Little Rock from taking preventive action. In early May, though, the petitions required by the new law began to circulate throughout Argenta and North Little Rock. W. C. Faucette stated that there were close to one thousand qualified voters in the eighth ward and North Little Rock, and it was his hope that the petition would carry the names of nearly every one. The organization wanted the separation from Little Rock and the annexation to North Little Rock to be a "unanimous affair."[44] On May 4, the North Little Rock City Council met and announced the election date for the proposed annexation to be July 21, 1903, in compliance with the law's thirty days notice clause. Only North Little Rock and the eighth ward would be allowed to vote on the proposal. This time Little Rock would be excluded from voting just as Argenta had been in the annexation vote of 1890; the new law stated that only the "qualified electors resident in the corporation, or the part thereof which is to be annexed, as well as those resident in the corporation to which said territory is to be annexed shall be allowed to vote."[45]

Little Rock was shocked to discover that there was a strong possibility that her eighth ward could be taken. State Attorney General George W. Murphy echoed the sentiment of the Little Rock city officials when he declared: "The act is sweeping in its provisions. What the entire world knows as 'Little Rock' may soon consist of three separate municipalities." Little Rock Mayor Warren E. Lenon called for a mass meeting of the citizens of the entire city, including Argenta, to work out a method to prevent the separation. Former Mayor William G. Whipple, under whose administration Argenta was made the city's eighth ward, offered his services in any way deemed necessary.[46] Little Rock city officials then prepared the fight to keep Argenta. The city filed for an injunction in chancery court requesting that the election be canceled, contending that the Hoxie-Walnut Ridge Law was unconstitutional on the basis that the power to change boundaries could not be delegated, and, therefore, the state legislature did not have the authority to direct such a change. John W. Blackwood, representing Argenta and North Little Rock sarcastically responded that the legislature had absolute power to change the Little Rock boundaries and the newly passed law was reasonable and just, especially since Argenta was forcibly annexed in 1890. Blackwood also charged that Little Rock did not have enough facts to constitute a case. Chancery Judge Jesse C. Hart agreed and dismissed the case. The attorney representing Little Rock immediately appealed to the Arkansas Supreme Court.[47] The Court refused to cancel the election or rule on the constitutionality of the Hoxie-Walnut Ridge Law, but it did issue an injunction prohibiting election officials from counting the votes. The injunction was subsequently amended and allowed the officials to count and reveal the numbers, but the ballots were then to be placed in a vault until the Court ruled on the separation case.[48]

There were two polling places set up for the election. In Argenta, the voters gathered in a livery stable, while North Little Rock citizens cast their votes in the back of a grocery store. Little Rock city police officers, in uniform and plainclothes, patrolled the Argenta polling place since it was for the time being still part of the city. The police, however, were not needed; "it was one of the quietest elections ever held in the eighth ward. The saloons were open, as usual, all day, but there was not a drunken man seen on the street."[49] The election made quite an impression on Little Rock citizens. The Arkansas Gazette, which usually relegated local news to the back pages, headlined the results with "For Divorce 475; 44 Votes Against." Argenta cast 455 votes, with 67 in North Little Rock.[50] These two rejoiced over the results. Little Rock was disappointed, and all three anxiously awaited the Supreme Court hearing. Both sides braced themselves for the Court decision.

Little Rock, though, tried to find a solution to the annexation debate up until ten days before the Supreme Court decided, or so said the leaders of the secessionist movement. W. C. Faucette, in a 1906 letter, claimed, as did other Argenta leaders in a 1907 publication, that Little Rock officials employed a woman of dubious morals to compromise the integrity of the secessionists. In late January 1903, a "scarlet woman from Chicago," reminiscent of the "Delilahs and Jezebels of ancient times,"[51] supposedly arrived in Little Rock. The woman, according to the publication, was "swaddled in costly plumage, drove fine horses . . . [and] was not averse to a rendezvous." Faucette believed the woman to be there in "a desperate effort to strike a slanderous blow" to the secessionist movement. The plot, if actually attempted, failed, but before the woman left on the "ill wind that had blown her southward [she had tried to] weave her voluptuous sorceries by spread[ing] the amplitude of her scented lingerie."[52]

On February 6, 1904, at 10:30 a.m., the Arkansas Supreme Court rendered its decision concerning the separation of Little Rock's eighth ward from the city. Both sides had been amply represented during the Court proceedings, and both cited an extraordinary number of legal precedents to support their claims. City Attorney Ashley Cockrill, W. L. and W. J. Terry, and Morris M. Cohn represented Little Rock, while Argenta and North Little Rock were represented by James P. Clarke, Uriah M. Rose, George B. Rose, and John W. Blackwood. The Little Rock attorneys immediately attacked the spine of the secessionists' defense, Act 86 of the 1903 Arkansas Legislature — the Hoxie-Walnut Ridge Law. They charged that the act in question was null and void because its passage was obtained fraudulently.[53] The attorneys cited two portions of the Arkansas Constitution as supporting evidence. In Section 5, Article 22, the constitution stated: "Every bill shall be read at length on three different days in each house, unless the rules be suspended by two-thirds of the house, when the same may be read a second or third time on the same day."[54] The bill was read on its introduction day thus violating the article. Also, Article 5, Section 23, was violated since the title of the bill did not accurately describe its true intention. The constitution article governing accuracy in proposed bills stated: "No law shall be revived, amended, or the provisions thereof extended or conferred by reference to its title only." [55] Cockrill and the other attorneys continued by saying that the act was unconstitutional because in addition to being obtained fraudulently, it sought to take city property without due process of law. The legislature had exceeded its authority by altering boundaries of a municipality, when the power to do this was specifically given to a county. In other words, the authority to annex was not transferable. Therefore, the North Little Rock ordinance calling for an election for the purpose of annexing territory was void due to unreasonableness.[56] The attorneys for Argenta and North Little Rock responded by saying the motives and purposes of a law were not open to question. Clarke and the others then negated every charge made by the Little Rock attorneys.

After hearing both sides, Associate Justice James E. Riddick, representing the majority opinion, rendered the Court's decision, overruling every argument made by the counsel for Little Rock. On the point argued by Little Rock's attorneys that the act was enacted fraudulently, Riddick said: "In the first place, we will say that the language of the act seems to us plainly to authorize the annexation of a part of one city to another town or city when they are so situated in respect to each other as to bring them within the scope of the statute."[57] He continued, stating that it was not up to the Supreme Court to supervise legislation or keep it within the bounds of propriety. The Court also was not obligated to delve into the minds of the legislators to ascertain the purpose or means of passing the act in question. Therefore, the appellants' (Little Rock) contention that the act was fraudulent was a moot point.[58] Riddick then rejected Little Rock's charge that North Little Rock was not authorized under the act to take private property without due process by saying that the act did not pertain to property, only to territory, and even though Little Rock would still be responsible for Argenta's debt incurred while a part of the city, the act was still valid.

On the point of boundary changes, Judge Riddick said a change in boundaries was a legislative power and not a local concern, and it was perfectly legal for the Arkansas General Assembly to pass an act that allowed North Little Rock to call an election proposing an annexation. In conclusion, Riddick stated:

> We have discussed those [questions] which seemed to present the most
> difficulty, and think that it is unnecessary to prolong the discussion of
> the validity of this statute further. We will only add that, feeling some
> doubt of the expediency of cutting off a large portion of the city of Little
> Rock and annexing it to the town of North Little Rock, we have given
> careful attention to the whole argument, and after full consideration
> thereof feel compelled to hold that the statute in question is a valid law,

and that the courts have no power to forbid its enforcement.

We are therefore of the opinion that the judgment of the chancery court refusing the injunction to restrain further proceedings under the act was right, and should be affirmed.

It is so ordered.[59]

In a dissenting opinion, Chief Justice H. G. Bunn, along with an associate justice, interpreted the act as being a delegation of powers.[60]

There would be a fifteen-day grace period before North Little Rock could officially take control of Argenta, time for Little Rock City Attorney Ashley Cockrill to file a motion for reconsideration. Although Argenta was still legally Little Rock's eighth ward until February 26, for all practical purposes the divorce was complete. However, North Little Rock wasted no time in acting on the decision. For five weeks prior to the February 6 judgment, the North Little Rock City Council met every Saturday at 10:00 a.m. awaiting the decision, since the Supreme Court only rendered its opinion of cases on that day. Ten minutes after the decision was read and North Little Rock was victorious, the city council of that city adopted a resolution declaring the official results of the annexation election held on July 21, 1903.[61]

The judgment, of course, elated the citizens of North Little Rock and Argenta for "the shackles were struck from the feet of the people."[62] The decision was a heavy blow to Little Rock. Besides losing more than 7,000 people to the minuscule city of North Little Rock, which had a population close to 2,000, the capital city would lose the revenue generated by the north-side businesses, including the railroads. The *North Little Rock News-Sentinel* proclaimed the Court's decision on the same day in an "extra" edition, scooping the two Little Rock papers. The *News-Sentinel* practically shouted the good news with a banner headline: "Argenta at Last Secures Her Freedom . . . After Thirteen Years of Obedience to the Will of Little Rock, the Supreme Court Decides That Argenta is Entitled to Home Rule . . . The Motto of the Great State of Arkansas (Regnant Populi) Never Applied Better Than in This Case . . . Vive La Argenta!"[63]

On February 22, 1904, the city councils of Little Rock and North Little Rock met concurrently. Both councils enacted identical ordinances that settled property and financial questions resulting from the separation. Little Rock agreed to relinquish its north-side fire station and lot, while leasing the electric lights and gas mains to the new city. Little Rock then agreed to "refrain from prosecuting any further litigation to prevent, hinder or delay the final consummation of the annexation of the Eighth Ward by the town of North Little Rock."

North Little Rock, in exchange, allowed the capital city to retain the 1903 taxes that had been collected in Argenta. Finally, the North Little Rock ordinance provided for the annexation of Argenta.[64] Neither mayor signed the ordinances at the meetings. Instead, the council reconvened the next day, February 23, Little Rock at 1:00 p.m. and North Little Rock at 2:50. At these times, Little Rock Mayor W. E. Lenon and North Little Rock Mayor William M. Mara, signed their respective ordinances. Both mayors agreed to make the exchange of Argenta at 7:00 p.m. that night in the middle of the Free Bridge across the Arkansas River.

At the appointed time, "with no blaring of trumpets or celebration of any kind"[65] North Little Rock, represented by its mayor, assumed control over one of Little Rock's wards. After the exchange had taken place, both sides went home. There were no reported festivities on the north side, and as the Gazette reported the next morning that "one could never have told that the ward had been separated from a city of which it was one-eighth and annexed to a town than which it was eight or ten times larger [sic]."[66]

The February decision allowed the enlarged city of North Little Rock to qualify as a first-class city, and in April of 1904 the first election within the combined areas was held. William C. Faucette, who had been one of the key players in the separation, was elected mayor. In his inaugural address, Faucette reminded the citizens that the city now stood on the threshold of the future. To the newly elected city council, he stated that they were expected to represent the citizens and the citizens should not be disappointed.[67] With formalities completed, the council began to govern. One of the first ordinances passed in 1904 was the annexation of Baring Cross. However, this time both sides agreed upon the annexation.

Argenta became a separate city thirty-eight years after it was first founded. Through those years it had seen itself go from a settlement to a proposed town to a ward of a larger city. At last, though, in 1904 it emerged as its own city; its boundaries had changed and it had had to wage a bitter fight, but it had emerged, nonetheless. Today, the cities of North Little Rock and Little Rock are separate and just as "politics determined the choice of Little Rock as the capital in 1821, politics brought about the divorce."[68]

NOTES

[1] David Yancey Thomas, ed., *Arkansas and Its People: A History, 1541-1930*, 4 vols. (New York: The American Historical Society, Inc., 1930), II: 811; Walter M. Adams, North Little Rock: *The Unique City — A History* (Little Rock: August House, 1986), 32.

[2] *Arkansas Gazette*, 26 July 1838.

[3] Adams, 32.

[4] *Arkansas Gazette*, 14 April 1871.

[5] Adams, 39.

[6] Ibid., 47; *Arkansas Gazette*, 14 April 1871.

[7] Adams, 39.

[8] Ibid., 48.

[9] *Arkansas Gazette*, 22 March 1871.

[10] Adams, 55, 56.

[11] *Arkansas Gazette*, 25 November 1880.

[12] *The Secession of Argenta* (Argenta, Ark.: The Argenta Business League, 1907), 10.

[13] *Arkansas Gazette*, 28 January 1800.

[14] Adams, 73.

[15] *Arkansas Gazette*, 6 February 1890.

[16] *The Secession of Argenta*, 8.

[17] *Arkansas Gazette*, 21 June 1889.

[18] *Arkansas Gazette*, 3 May 1903.

[19] *Arkansas Gazette*, 9 February 1890.

[20] Little Rock City Council Minutes, 12 February 1890; Arkansas Gazette, 3 May 1903; *The Secession of Argenta*, 11.

[21] *The Secession of Argenta*, 12,

[22] Adams, 74.

[23] Ibid., 74. According to a biographical sketch located in the Vestal Nursery Records at the University of Central Arkansas Archives and Special Collections, Conway. Arkansas, Vestal arrived in Arkansas in 1880, when he relocated his nursery business to the banks of the Arkansas River. The nursery was one of the largest in the United States.

[24] *Arkansas Reports* (Little Rock: State of Arkansas, 1891), vol.54, 321.

[25] Ibid., 322.

[26] Ibid., 325.

[27] Adams, 74.

[28] *Arkansas Reports* (Little Rock: State of Arkansas, 1892), vol. 55, 614.

[29] Adams, 75.

[30] *Arkansas Gazette*, 21 February 1892.

[31] Adams, 76.

[32] *The Secession of Argenta*, 22.

[33] Adams, 86.

[34] *Arkansas Gazette*, 3 May 1903.

[35] Adams, 86.

[36] Helen Dianne Best, "North Little Rock Progressivism," *Pulaski County Historical Review*, XXI (December 1973): 90.

[37] Fay Williams, *Arkansans of the Years*, 4 vols. (Little Rock: C. C. Allard and Associates, 1952), III: 59.

[38] *Arkansas Democrat*, 3 December 1903.

[39] Williams, 56.

[40] *Journal of the Senate of Arkansas* (Little Rock: State of Arkansas, 1903), 87.

[41] Ibid., 118.

[42] *Journal of the House of Representatives of Arkansas* (Little Rock: State of Arkansas, 1903), 299.

[43] *Acts of Arkansas, 1903* (Little Rock: State of Arkansas, 1903), 148.

[44] *Arkansas Gazette*, 3 May 1903.

[45] 1903 Acts, 149.

[46] *Arkansas Gazette*, 3 May 1903.

[47] *Arkansas Gazette*, 17 July 1903.

[48] Adams, 90; *Arkansas Gazette*, 22 July 1903.

[49] *Arkansas Gazette*, 22 July 1903.

[50] Ibid.

[51] *The Secession of Arkansas*, 28.

[52] Ibid., 28; William C. Faucette, Argenta, Arkansas, to T. R. MacMechem, Eureka Springs, Arkansas, 15 July 1906, Faucette Brothers Papers, University of Central Arkansas Archives and Special Collections, Conway, Arkansas.

[53] Arkansas Reports (Little Rock: State of Arkansas, 1905), vol. 72, 198.

[54] *Arkansas Constitution* (1874), art. 5, sec. 22.

[55] Ibid., ART. 5, SEC. 23.

[56] *Arkansas Reports*, vol. 72 (1905), 200.

[57] Ibid., 201.

[58] Ibid.

[59] Ibid., 210.

[60] *Arkansas Gazette*, 7 February 1904.

[61] Ibid.

[62] *The Secession of Argenta*, 29.

[63] *North Little Rock News-Sentinel*, 6 February 1904.

[64] *Arkansas Gazette*, 23 February 1904.

[65] *Arkansas Gazette*, 24 February 1904.

[66] Ibid.

[67] Adams, 96.

[68] Thomas, 811.

STREETCARS AND SOCIETY

By Mrs. W. Dan Cotton

Elle Gordon Cotton (Mrs. Wiley Daniel Cotton) was the director of the Little Rock Mental Health Center. She was also a member of the Aesthetic Club, a women's organization devoted to cultural and intellectual activity, where she first gave a version of this charming and informative article.

Before public transportation began in Little Rock, most people walked. One might ride in from the countryside on a horse, or a horse could pull a wagon if a family had prospered enough to own a wagon. Only the rich had carriages. Now steel tracks were to be laid down the middle of the street, and little cars were to be pulled over these tracks by a horse or mule, mules mostly. This would take big money to build, but low fares were to be charged so that everyone could afford to ride. Plans began in 1870, just five years after the War Between the States ended. Arkansas was very poor like the rest of the South, but Little Rock was among the very first cities in the whole nation to begin public transportation. Several groups of Little Rock financiers were interested in the project, each wanting to get started first. It took a franchise granted by the City Council to operate down designated blocks of designated streets. It took money to build a solid bed on which to lay the steel tracks. Cars had to be purchased to roll on the tracks. Then the animals to pull the cars had to be purchased and fed every day. But it took little personnel — one man per car and one man to feed and tend the animals. One newspaper account states that Mr. Pfeifer objected to any tracks on East Markham. The merchants on this street said it would obstruct other traffic on their narrow street. The City Council discussed, and the financiers tried to get money, but nothing got done until October of 1876. Then two groups got their franchise: one included Thomas Fletcher, Logan H. Roots, and John M. Harrell; the other was John Cross and Charles Divers. Cross and Divers started building immediately. The first mile of track was laid straight out Main Street to Glenwood Park at Seventeenth and Main, the beginning of the old South Main line.

Before six months had passed, the mile was completed, and the company had in operation four "bob tail" cars drawn by mules and horses. Six months later the company built an extension down Markham Street from Main to the Union Depot. Inside of two years four miles had been built. After that, extensions were made east on Markham to the oil mill, west on Ninth Street to Capitol Hill, and east on Ninth to the Arsenal (now MacArthur Park). At first the track to the depot had to detour at Cross Street, go north to Water Street, and then to the depot; the hill down Markham was too steep.

In July 1884, a franchise was given to Tom Darraugh, Theo Hartman, George Reichart, C. F. Penzel, and J. Neimeyer. They could lay tracks on Rector Street, Eighth Street east of Main, all of Rock Street, Louisiana from Third to Fifth, and on Broadway. The company eventually installed four routes, and one of the routes went by the home of each of the above named incorporators. Mr. Darraugh lived at Tenth and McGowan, Mr. Hartman at Seventh and Ferry streets, Mr. Penzel at Seventh and Sherman streets, and Mr. Reichart at Sixth and Ferry streets. Mr. Neimeyer lived at Sixth and Cumberland, just two blocks from the business section.

Life in Little Rock began changing, the city began growing again. We were over the war and its immediate aftermath. All America was growing, and soon trains would cross the continent. People from little towns wanted transportation to the cities to shop; salesmen (called drummers because they drummed up business) went to little towns to sell. People increasingly were in and out of the train depots, and most people in Arkansas were overjoyed to have the horse-drawn cars to get them to and from downtown Little Rock or to the homes of relatives to visit. Such transportation began to make it possible to live farther from downtown where many worked, so new areas could be developed by real estate developers. Wives began to use the mule-drawn cars to come to town to buy without needing the wagon or carriage, and this also made them freer to socialize during the day. Churches could have more meetings for women. The great club movement for women began in the last two decades of the nineteenth century and flowered in the years prior to World War I. Little Rock was right there in the early part of each developing movement that came along, be it churches, schools, fine homes, or transportation. Little Rock was booming as it did after World War II.

But all this progress was not without some problems. On March 12, 1887, car No. 1 was ascending the upgrade on Rock Street near Fifteenth Street. The mule became frightened, got loose, and ran. Then the brakes gave way. The driver had left the car to go get his mule, and the car having no brakes soon began rolling back downhill. At Seventh and Rock streets right where the Lewis Cherrys and the Fletchers lived, the driver of oncoming car No. 7 saw the car rolling back towards him but could not avoid the collision. The mule of car No. 7 was caught in between the two cars, badly bruised, but finally was able to break away. Then the driver of car No. 7 left to go after his mule. Service was delayed for quite some time.

Mules could set the schedule depending upon their mood and how well they were fed. Sometimes the mules would perceive an unusually fresh-looking lawn, deliciously green, and would decide to take car and passengers over to the green grass. Then anything could happen to the car or to the passengers who could be thrown out or stranded. Passengers often had to help the driver put the car back on the track. One incident is related to an unruly mule during the heavy rush of business about Christmas time. The mule came to a stop at Eighth and Main streets and could not be started again. The passengers all climbed out, tried first to entice the mule, and then angrily got behind and tried to push the car with the mule in front. No luck. The superintendent of the line came along and devised a plan of hiring a boy to run ahead of the mule with ears of corn in his hand. He found the boy and the corn and loaded the passengers back on the car. The boy started running, and the mule got going.

A heavily loaded car was descending the steep hill down to the depot when the driver realized his brakes would not work. The mule was knocked down and run over. The passengers came to inside the car, whole and intact, saved by the heavy red clay on the south side of the street.

July 3, 1888, was a very special day. It was the day the Electric Street Railway Company began the Dummy Line. It was actually a coal-burning operation that produced the steam that ran the cars, popularly called the Dummy Line because the little cars were made to look like railroad cars — a dummy. There were two of these little steam engine cars which could pull one or two of the open air cars holding forty passengers; plus, there was a double-decker car holding forty passengers below and thirty-six passengers on top. W. B. Worthen and Judge John B. Jones were among the promoters of this line. It originated at Second and Louisiana streets, went west to Spring Street, south to Fourth Street (the horse and mule-drawn line had the right to Fifth Street), west to Pulaski, south again to Eighth, west again to Wolfe, south to Eleventh, west to Barton, south again to Thirteenth, and on to the Iron Mountain Railroad tracks. All these tracks were laid on a bed of granite rock quarried from Granite Mountain, and it was considered a very fine bed. This was the old Highland Park line.

W. B. Worthen and Judge John B. Jones were especially interested in promoting the sale of lots in the residential area that they were developing and that this line would serve. The formal opening was celebrated on July 3, 1888, with a big free excursion. The first car started at 3:30 filled with celebrities, among whom were Governor Hughes, Dan W. Jones, Thomas Fletcher, Col. Sappington, Col. J. W. House, Col. Thomas Essex, Col. A. S. Dunlop, Mayor Whipple, H. L. Remmel, Dr. C. J. Lincoln, Maj. W. E. Woodruff, George Dodge, John M. Rose,

J. E. Williams, J. W. Blackwood, Judge B. B. Battle, E. J. Butler, Professor J. L. Shinn, and Judge F. T. Vaughan. As there was no loop or means of turning around, the return trip was made by pushing the cars back to the starting point. The entire run took about an hour. Though coal was used to furnish the power to generate steam, all the people loved it, cinders and all. That first day cheering spectators lined the track waving and cheering all along the way.

July 4th, the next day, there was a baseball game between Gus Blass Company and Quinn and Gray Dry Goods Company at the ballpark at Thirteenth and High. As the ballgame was for the benefit of the Orphan's Home, the management of the Dummy Line provided free transportation. Regular fare was to be 5 cents. A waiting room was installed (for the convenience of patrons) on Markham Street opposite the old post office. At the west end of the line in a big, shady pine grove, benches were placed in the cool inviting shade. Lemonade and ice cream booths were erected. This ride provided an excellent pleasure trip.

Electricity was developing nationally. The City Electric Street Railway Company, which owned the Dummy Line, had anticipated using electricity when the company was organized by John B. Jones, M. W. Benjamin, W. B. Worthen, and Howard Adams. This company received a perpetual franchise and was permitted to use all the other streets in the city for tracks except those granted to the two horse-car companies for the limit of their franchises. In March 1890, the Capitol Street Railway Company was organized by H P. Bradford, H. G. Allis, W. N. Stannus, John M. Taylor, George R. Brown, and George Rose. They bought the two horse-car companies. Exactly one year later they leased their property to the City Electric Street Railway Company. It was all reorganized with H. G. Allis as president, H. P. Bradford as secretary-treasurer, and U. M. and George B. Rose as attorneys. At that time the company operated 3? miles of track, had 4 miles under construction, and took over 14.7 miles from the Dummy Line making a total system of 22 miles. The company had 45 cars and 308 mules and horses. The livestock were sold, but 20 cars suitable for trail cars were kept. Now all public transportation was under one control.

In August 1887, an electric car was first tried out on Fourth Avenue in New York City. In Little Rock on November 24, 1891, just four years later, electric powered car No. 55 started at the foot of Main Street full of company officials, newspaper reporters, and dignitaries. The main switch was turned, and twenty miles of overhead electric trolley wires were charged. This was the beginning of what we know as the trolley cars or streetcars. There were twenty-eight new electric cars costing $3,300 each. They operated with fifteen horsepower motors and were capable of pulling another car behind, which they did on festive occasions calling for an extra load of traffic. Thousands of people thrust their heads out of windows or stood on doorsteps and sidewalks to witness this moving phenomena — no animal to pull, no smoky engine, just a wire overhead with invisible power. The cars were painted bright yellow, electrically lighted inside, and described as magnificent rapid transit. Little Rock was far ahead of many a city. The Chinaman aptly said, "no pushee, no pullee, but run like hellee." The second car of the day was full of curiosity riders. The men in the power plant had worked so hard preparing the power plant to supply the electricity and had suffered such tension wondering if it would work perfectly that first try that they were too exhausted to operate the plant Sunday.

Now all this electric system called for was a power plant and a car barn. The site chosen for the power plant was located on the old water works site at Water and Arch streets where Zeb Ward had previously dug wells to supply the city with water at a cost of $25,000. A selling point in the selection of this site was that the Missouri Pacific Railroad's main line and a switch line ran below the north side, which eliminated extra handling of the coal used to generate the electricity. The profile of the land enabled the design to be very compact and thereby cheaper to operate. Power house and equipment when completed cost about $100,000 and the entire plant about $300,000. These fine trolley cars when not in use had to be housed, and they had to be kept in mechanically perfect condition. The barn at Chester and North streets had a turntable with seven foot pits where the mechanics could stand to work underneath the cars. It was an operation something like the round house for trains in North Little Rock.

A newspaper clipping tells that Miss Mary McCabe, a member of the Aesthetic Club and many other clubs, perfected arrangements for the Arkansas Central Power Company to have a series of luncheons at the power plant for civic and business clubs of Little Rock to see this wonderful power plant and to have it explained to them. The Affiliated School Improvement Associations (the forerunner of the P.T.A.s) were invited to a tea, and ladies of the State Federation of Women's Clubs were guests during their second annual meeting.

These first electric trolley cars of the 1890's replaced the "pokies" or mule cars and the steam Dummy Line. The growing city got its first of the 200 series of big eight wheelers in the early 1900's. On Christmas Day 1924, the 400 series appeared on the Pulaski Heights line. Little Rock got its first gasoline buses on November 29, 1936, but it continued to use some trolley cars on less traveled lines until Christmas Day 1947. But the fun and sociability was gone long before that date.

Enough of the mechanical and financial side, the human side is much more interesting. Little Rock was a city of 13,000 people in 1880, 28,000 in 1900, and 45,000 in 1910. That is an increase in population of 30,000 in thirty years, and Little Rock went from a few mule-drawn cars to large trolley cars. South Main now served a lovely residential area. Fifteenth Street was the most heavily traveled line serving a wide variety of patrons. There was East Ninth, West Ninth, Highland Park, Biddle Shop, and Pulaski Heights.

The Pulaski Heights line is typical of the relationship between transportation and real estate. Before the Heights could be developed, the train tracks had to be crossed, so the opening of the fine viaduct on West Third, still in use today, was a big celebration. The route of the line took an old Indian trail which had the least incline of any route going over those hills. Pulaski Heights was once a little incorporated town of its own. The line went first just as far as Lee Avenue and Prospect Avenue (now Kavanaugh). There Celsus Perry built his home. The Stifft family began developing Midland Heights, and the place where one caught the streetcar became known as Stifft Station. I have been told there was once one of those little square waiting rooms, open but roofed that stood there, also one at Lee Avenue and Prospect, and one at Cedar and Prospect (the Ashley Cockrill house stood on the opposite corner and had the little playhouse in the yard). St. Mary's was opened in 1907, and the line was extended on out there. Then it went on out to Forest Park, which was at what is now Kavanaugh and University opposite Corder's grocery store. There was another little waiting room at Van Buren and Prospect known as the Country Club Station. One got off there and walked to the new country club through the woods and over a swinging bridge across the ravine. The Country Club had no kitchen; one took a picnic in a basket, and according to Mrs. S. P. Davis, nice young girls were chaperoned. Just past Cedar and Kavanaugh there was once a long swinging bridge built to shorten the walk of residents on Fairview, Lookout, and Kenyon Streets; it was a long way around to Beechwood down to Hillcrest where one could catch the streetcar. There were no grocery stores at first anywhere in the Heights; one had to ride to town for everything. And men out there rode the streetcar to work and back home like New Yorkers rode the commuter trains.

Such was true all over town as this increase of 32,000 people spread everywhere, especially westward. Families chose to live near the carline. There was only one big shopping area — downtown, and many worked downtown. People rode to the Capitol Theatre which was then on Markham across from where the Marion Hotel was built in 1907. Then the Kempner Theatre was built on Louisiana between Fifth and Sixth streets; the Majestic Vaudeville House was on Main between Eighth and Ninth; Falstaff, once a fine restaurant, was on West

Markham Street; and many will remember Breier's. Peckham had an ice cream parlor on Main Street. Don't we ride to get ice cream today?

People loved the parks, they were great gathering places. There was Glenwood Park at Seventeenth and Main with beautiful flowers and a pavilion. Highland Park was at Thirteenth Street and the Iron Mountain tracks. As has been mentioned, the streetcar company set up benches in the cool, inviting pine grove there and soon lemonade and ice cream stands appeared in warm weather. There was an excellent spring out on High Street, and often people took their jugs and filled them up with drinking water. West End Park was where Central High School now stands, and it had a dance pavilion, a race track, an amphitheater, and refreshment stands. Later Kavanaugh Baseball Park was there. Think how many people must have ridden the streetcar to see the ballgames. Forest Park was an amusement park and had a big bandstand with typical Victorian gingerbread. It was the only place in town big enough for the crowd who wanted to hear the great Sarah Bernhardt. One man lived very near the Pulaski Heights line and reported watching thirty-four cars go by in an hour that night. Pauline Hoeltzel says she was left with neighbors while her parents went to hear the Great Sarah. It was three o'clock in the morning before her parents got home. The power had gotten very weak transporting so many passengers.

But the greatest tax on the transportation system came during the Confederate Reunion in 1911. There were 118,000 veterans gathered in Little Rock. It was the streetcar that transported them wherever they needed to go. Not one single accident or streetcar breakdown occurred during this reunion.

Do you think chartered buses are a new idea in our time? In May 1886, the Round Robin Club, whose members lived only on the west side of town, repaid their social obligation to the Aesthetic Club, whose members lived only on the east end of town, by inviting them to a great social function at the home of Mrs. Beverly A. Williams who lived at 1019 West Fourth (between Chester and Ringo). Both chartered carriages and a chartered streetcar were needed to get all the ladies to the big affair. In May 1900, the annual entertainment of the Aesthetic Club was in Glenwood Park at Seventeenth and Main. Eight hundred invitations were extended. How many do you suppose rode the streetcars?! A comedy entitled "Man Proposes" was the entertainment put on by Miss Daisy Deloney and Miss Molly Fletcher with Miss Lillian Hughes in charge of the music.

Mrs. Isaac Gardner, wife of the superintendent of the Arkansas School for the Deaf, who lived from 1907 to 1916 in the main building where the Deaf School still stands, was a great clubwoman and hostess. She and Mr. Gardner often entertained groups, and one account in the Aesthetic Club minutes describes a great entertainment in the springtime when the ladies chartered a streetcar to ride out there. The brave members climbed the tower to enjoy the gorgeous panoramic view, including the turbulent Arkansas River at floodtide.

Mrs. Davis says that her whole graduating class from high school chartered a streetcar and for entertainment rode all over town all day long. More recently, Raymond Rebsamen chartered a streetcar for his son's birthday party and loaded it with boys to go to White City to swim. White City was a city-owned pool that was located where the Heights Theater now stands.

Did you know that the streetcar system once had a water wagon? It was used to flush the debris from between the tracks, and it dashed water on bishop and babe with equal impunity. A strong breeze would spray water on the ladies' skirts. Big boys would torment Mr. Colton, who operated the car, and when they were grown men would guiltily come back and apologize to him. Think how many children rode the streetcar to high school, first to Fourteenth and Scott and then to Fourteenth and Park.

The last car of the day was known as the owl car. It started to the barn at eleven o'clock, which settled when one's date would be over. Three prominent young men had only one thing in common, often riding together on the owl car — Mr. J. N. Heiskell who was dating Willamena Mann, Mr. Will Rawlings who was dating Miss Winnie Bess Sappington, and George Worthen who was dating Edith Beidelman. Each gentleman married his young lady despite the time limit on courting each night

In the early 1900's ladies would ride the streetcars putting their baby buggies and go carts on the streetcars with them. The following notice appeared in the paper on February 14, 1910: "The majority of objections we have received regarding the former custom of carrying baby carriages and go carts on the platforms of the cars has come from ladies," said Mr. Hegarty, General Manager. He reported that many ladies had experienced the inconvenience of oil spots on their skirts as they passed by the axles on the carts. No complaints came from men. Here is another item dated March 5, 1912:

> Love me, love my dog. It is an ancient adage, but hereafter streetcar conductors will ignore it. The fiat has gone forth whether mastiffs, puppies, whelps, or hounds or curs of low degree, the following order was promulgated yesterday. To motormen and conductors: Your attention is called to the rule of the company in regard to carrying dogs on cars. Hereafter you will not allow anybody to board a car with a dog unless it has a chain or rope around its neck or attached to a collar. The passenger must have a permit filled out properly. The

dog must be placed on the front platform of closed cars and the rear platform of open cars. In either case, dog must be securely tied or held by the owner or one in charge of the dog.

World War I and the opening of Camp Pike put an extra load on the streetcars. There was a shortage of cars, especially on the Pulaski Heights line where there had been a great increase in population. There were not only soldiers but visitors. The streetcar company published an ad in the paper saying if the city would allow them to use the sixteen open cars until they could get the new closed cars, which had been ordered but not delivered due to the war, the situation would be relieved. The company called to people's attention the fact that the city of Denver used open cars, and the people just bundled up in their overcoats and enjoyed the fresh air. On December 15, 1917, this item appeared in the paper:

The Little Rock Street Railway and Electric Company will be forced to close its plant at 8:00 in the morning, it is predicted by C. J. Griffith, General Manager. All electric power would have been shut off last night had not John W. Dean, general manager of the Missouri Pacific Railroad, come to the rescue and given the company a carload of coal to operate the plant during the night. Darkness due to lack of electricity settled upon Little Rock for a time last night at 6:00. The streetcars had to stop running at intervals due to insufficient current. Many downtown workers had to walk home. At 7:00 several night circuits were cut off, and at 8:30 Camp Pike was in darkness. At 9:00 Mr. Griffith announced that the streetcars were about to stop running; he thought it would be necessary to cut off all lights. The carload of coal from the Missouri Pacific helped, but it takes four carloads a day.

Here are a few streetcar stories about some well-known people. Booker Worthen was sent on the streetcar from his home at Second and Gaines to his dentist at Seventh and Main. Along the way Dr. Ida Jo Brooks got on the car and sat down by Booker. She was the school doctor, a very heavy-set woman who always wore a long black dress and carried her doctor's bag. Booker was scared to death to ring the bell and have to walk in front of her, so timidly he sat until she got off at Tenth and Main to walk to her home. Booker then got off and *ran* back to the dentist's office so as not to be late.

Ewing Jackson lived on Twenty-fourth between High and Marshall. He was sent on the streetcar to take his cello lessons. He had visions of being a world-famous cellist at this time; his mother was a great musician. But in due time he had to give up this dream, since transferring every trip with his huge cello was just too much for any boy.

Mrs. Preston Davis who lived on Broadway at this time went with her friends May and Myra Thompson to take their dancing lessons. They took their dancing shoes in their slipper bag, caught the South Main car, rode to Tenth and Main Street where they got off and walked to Center Street to Peperman Hall. Gymnastics was taught at the hall too, and it was the scene of many dancing parties for young people. The Rumbaugh sisters lived on West Markham where they also had a dancing school. If a young lady went to a dancing party, she took her party shoes in her slipper bag.

Katie Haltom says she well remembers the conductor on the South Main who would allow the children to board the car at Twenty-Third and Arch, ride down to Ringo and back to Arch. This was before the loop was added.

I lived near Kings Drug Store located at Fifteenth and Gaines, and I can well remember the boys jerking the trolley off the line and enjoying watching the motorman get mad. They would also put pennies on the track so the trolley would flatten them.

Mr. Frank Pace lived at Twenty-third and Broadway in a handsome home. Long after he owned an automobile, he continued to ride the streetcar. He enjoyed the news and gossip he learned riding the streetcar.

Gertie Remmel Butler tells the story that at age six she and Phil Henson got on the Pulaski Heights open air car one afternoon with a little umbrella. They had no money with them, and when the motorman came by they just pulled the umbrella down over their little heads and kept on riding and riding. Mrs. Remmel was at home at 114 Johnson Street with a new baby and several small children. She had to call Mr. Remmel at his office to go and get Gertie and Phil off the line.

But the following is the best story of all told by Mr. Beall Hempstead, Peg Smith's uncle. He got on the South Main car one day and soon a mother with a little boy got on. The little boy's head was enormous and so wrapped up in newspaper that one could not really see the little boy. However, the newspaper began to come off, revealing a very serious problem. The youngster had stuck his head in a chamber pot, and the mother was taking him downtown somewhere to have the chamber pot cut off his head.

These are just a few of the funny and interesting stories people have remembered about the streetcars that make them such a fascinating part of the city's past. If you know of others, share them with us.

NOTES

This article first appeared in the *Pulaski County Review*, 29 (Spring 1981): 2-10.

"Traffic and Transportation — Little Rock," Clipping File, Little Rock Public Library.

Personal conversations.

THE DEVELOPMENT OF PULASKI HEIGHTS

By Cheryl Griffith Nichols

Cheryl Griffith Nichols received a bachelor's degree from Hanover College in Indiana and a master's degree from George Washington University, where she wrote a thesis on the Town of Pulaski, the Hillcrest and Pulaski Heights sections of Little Rock. In addition to this article, she assisted F. Hampton Roy, Sr. and Charles Witsell, Jr. with "How We Lived: Little Rock As An American City" and with Sandra Taylor-Smith did a study of Hillcrest architecture that supported the area's nomination as an historic district. She currently serves on boards of advisors for the Historic Preservation Alliance of Arkansas and the National Trust for Historic Preservation.

As the original portion of the city and the location of an admirable array of nineteenth century buildings, Little Rock's downtown area has received considerable attention from local historians and persons interested in historic architecture. However, that area, now commonly known as the Quapaw Quarter, is not alone among the city's neighborhoods in having a past worth exploring. A case in point is Pulaski Heights, the neighborhood that, in the early years of this century, began to usurp the Quapaw Quarter's status as the city's leading residential district. The story of the development of the Heights as a streetcar suburb of Little Rock is an interesting chapter in the history of the city and provides insight into the manner of Little Rock's growth and expansion around the turn of the century.

The development of Pulaski Heights, which began in earnest in 1903 with the opening of the Pulaski Heights streetcar line, was generally similar to the development of early suburbs of many other cities. Streetcar transportation was the primary factor enabling this suburban development to occur. Prior to the advent of the streetcar, the expansion of cities was limited by their residents' need to live within walking distance of shopping areas and places of employment, as relatively few people could afford the luxury of maintaining private transportation (that is, horses and carriages). Inexpensive public transportation, in the form of the streetcar, provided the means by which large numbers of city dwellers were able to live farther from the center city, thus allowing for the development of suburbs.

Little Rock's first streetcars, which were mule-drawn, began running in 1877. The city's street railway system was improved and expanded until, in 1891, the first electric streetcars were put into operation. With this form of transportation available, Little Rock had the means to expand into outlying areas previously considered too far from the center city for convenient residence.

Apparently recognizing the potential for suburban development in Little Rock, a group of investors initiated the development of Pulaski Heights during the 1890's. One man, H. F. Auten, played a particularly important part in the early development of the Heights. Auten was a native of Michigan, as were many of the first investors in the Heights. Like other northern entrepreneurs of that period, Auten must have realized that the South held many opportunities for investment and development, although the specific reasons for his choice of Little Rock as the location of his endeavors are not known.[1] Shortly after Auten moved to Little Rock, a paper in his hometown of St.Johns, Michigan, reported:The south is experiencing a healthy and substantial boom, and no one appreciates this fact better than St. Johns businessmen, some of whom are already interested in the southern states, and are likely to largely increase such interests.[2]Auten may have been following a precedent already established by businessmen with whom he was acquainted in St. Johns. In any event, he left St. Johns early in 1890 to begin his journey to Little Rock, where he lived until his death in 1918.

Because of the major role he played in its development, it is appropriate to begin the story of Pulaski Heights with Auten's move to Little Rock. His achievements seem to have been quickly forgotten, despite their long-lasting effects on the city.[3] Similarly, little attention has been given to history of Pulaski Heights itself.

In the fall of 1889 an article appeared in a St. Johns, Michigan, newspaper announcing that two of the town's attorneys, Henry Franklin Auten and Edgar Eugene Moss, had sold their law office. They were reported to be moving to Little Rock, Arkansas, where they would "continue the practice of law and engage in real estate business also."[4] The article spoke highly of the two young attorneys:

> They have built up a large practice, and are very successful lawyers, both in the circuit and supreme courts. Some time ago they acquired interests in the south, and propose to remove to Little Rock, Ark., in December . . . . Both gentlemen have many friends here who regret this move; but the same untiring energy, integrity and business ability, which has built up such a successful business here, will win for them a larger measure of success in their new and wider field of labor. We can heartily commend them to the good people of Little Rock.[5]

Moss left St. Johns for Little Rock on December 23, 1889 (planning to make stops on the way to visit friends and family), and Auten began his journey on

January 13, 1890.[6] By the end of January, their arrival in Little Rock had been noted by both the *Arkansas Democrat* and the *Arkansas Gazette*.[7]

Auten and Moss did enter the practice of law in Little Rock (although their partnership continued for only a few more years),[8] but it was their activities in real estate investment that would leave their mark on the city. In these activities, Auten overshadowed his partner. Moss took part in the investment plan that culminated in the development of Pulaski Heights, but it was Auten who later was called the "Father of Pulaski Heights,"[9] and justifiably so. It was largely through his efforts that the development of Pulaski Heights succeeded.

Shortly after arriving in Little Rock, Auten began laying the groundwork for this investment scheme. Perhaps realizing that sufficient investment capital was not available in Little Rock,[10] he returned to St. Johns, Michigan, in April of 1890 to line up prospective backers, some of whom then visited Little Rock to investigate the potential for investment.[11] He also entered into negotiations with Eugene H. Hillman (a real estate agent who dealt mainly in "lumber and timber lands")[12] to purchase some land, settling on a hilly and heavily wooded tract of about 800 acres to the west of Little Rock.[13] The land was owned jointly by Hillman, Charles E. Ferguson, and Harry E. Kelley (the latter of Fort Smith).[14]

Despite the early start in negotiations, it was not until March of 1891 that the land was fully acquired. More than a year had passed since Auten and Moss arrived in Little Rock. Several factors hindered the progress of the transaction: illness, the death of one of the owners of the land and the reluctance of another to sell his interest, and a law suit which clouded the title to the land.[15]

The final one-eighth interest in the desired property was acquired on March 23, 1891;[16] the total purchase price was $80,000.[17] The funds for purchase had been raised through the organization of the Pulaski Heights Land Company with capital stock of $150,000.[18] Investors had been drawn mainly from Michigan, but some Little Rock residents also participated.[19]

Soon after the land was acquired, the work of surveying and platting the property was begun.[20] The plat of the first ten blocks of the Pulaski Heights Addition was filed for recording on November 9, 1892.[21]

The growth of Pulaski Heights proceeded very slowly at first. Only eight families, including the Autens and Mosses, built homes in the area during the 1890's.[22] Due to the lack of a good transportation route from Little Rock, the Heights remained very isolated. This encouraged the development of a closely knit little community,[23] but it must have limited the profitability of the Pulaski Heights Land

Company's investment.[24]

H. F. Auten's wife later wrote of the "doubting Thomases" who could not imagine why Auten would attempt the development of Pulaski Heights: "Who would go out there to live? The idea was absurd ...."[25] When the only means of reaching the Heights was by horse and carriage,[26] the idea of its ever becoming a popular and convenient suburb of Little Rock probably did seem unlikely. Auten had foreseen the need for the extension of streetcar service into the Heights, knowing that only then would it attract residents in large numbers. Even he occasionally may have despaired of realizing his goal, however, when numerous problems developed as he worked toward having a street railway built into the Heights.

Auten reportedly had been assured by the Little Rock streetcar company that a line would be built.[27] Neither he nor the streetcar company could foresee that the panic of 1893 would force the company into receivership. Little Rock soon had another streetcar company, but still Pulaski Heights did not receive service.

A franchise granted to the Little Rock Traction and Electric Railway Company on September 27, 1901, required that the company build a street railway into the Heights if the company first was provided a graded roadway, a free right-of-way, and certain "other aid."[28] Among the other things necessary for the streetcar line to be built was the construction of a viaduct over the railroad tracks at the western edge of Little Rock. If the graded road and viaduct were not in place within two years of the date of the franchise, the right to build the streetcar line would lapse. To Auten and his fellow property owners in Pulaski Heights fell the responsibility for seeing that the necessary preliminaries to extension of the line were completed within the allotted time —that is, by September 27, 1903.

The viaduct was needed to cross tracks belonging to the St. Louis, Iron Mountain, & Southern Railroad and the Choctaw, Oklahoma & Gulf Railroad; those companies agreed to see to its construction.[29] In accordance with an agreement with several Pulaski Heights property owners, Little Rock contracted the construction of a wooden approach to the viaduct from the city side. A similar agreement with the county provided for the grading of a road through Pulaski Heights, and the necessary right-of-way for the road was given to the county by the Pulaski Heights Land Company and other landowners.[30] By the spring of 1903, it appeared certain that Little Rock and the county would meet the September deadline with their portions of the work. However, the railroads reneged on their promise to build the viaduct.

H. F. Auten then took matters into his own hands. He and F. B. T.

Hollenberg, who also had property interests in the Heights, borrowed the money to have a wooden viaduct built, and the Little Rock City Council adopted a resolution approving the construction of this viaduct "in accordance with plans prepared by the Supt. of Public Works of the city of Little Rock."[31] The viaduct was completed in July 1903, and the construction of the street railway started shortly thereafter.[32] On Thanksgiving Day of 1903, the first streetcars made the trip to Pulaski Heights, although the line was not completed in its entirety until the following spring.[33]

Despite the various problems encountered in extending streetcar service to the Heights, progress in the development of the area was not entirely deterred. Probably in anticipation of the extension of the streetcar line, in 1901 H. F. Auten, with F. B. T. Hollenberg and Charles M. Newton, incorporated another land company, the Mountain Park Land Company,[34] which also acquired land in Pulaski Heights. Late in 1902, the second group of lots in the Heights, the Auten and Moss Addition, was platted and recorded.[35]

Once it appeared certain that Pulaski Heights would receive streetcar service, its promoters (H. F. Auten, as manager of the land companies, and two real estate agents) went to work. They encouraged the purchase of property in the Heights before the street railway was completed because "the day the cars start lots will ADVANCE 25 PER CENT IN VALUE."[36] In the fall of 1903, the real estate column of the *Arkansas Gazette* reported: "The building of the Pulaski Heights electric railway has caused the eye of the investor to turn toward that section of the city, which has heretofore had but little attention on account of its inaccessibility."[37]

The promoters of the Heights obviously were counting on the new street railway to assist in attracting buyers, and they probably were not disappointed. According to newspaper accounts, the street railway was not able to handle the crowds of people who wanted to visit the Heights on the first day of streetcar service.[38]

The promotion of Pulaski Heights proceeded on a rather lavish basis for at least two years. Advertisements ran regularly in the local newspapers, enumerating again and again the desirable qualities of the Heights. Occasionally a new tactic would be used to attract the attention of prospective property buyers. During July of 1903 one of the real estate agents handling property in the Heights, Maxwell Coffin, held a contest for the best advertisement of lots in the suburb. The first and second place winners would receive $10 and $5 in gold, respectively. Coffin reported that forty-one people entered the contest, and "some of the suggestions were admirable."[39] The winning entries were published in the *Arkansas Gazette*.[40]

Another effort to gain attention was a promotional brochure, *Beautiful Pulaski Heights*, published by the Pulaski Heights Land Company, probably in 1903.[41] In both words and pictures, it recounted the many attributes of the Heights, from the sights along the streetcar line to the terms of payment for a lot.

If newspaper accounts are accurate, lots sold quickly in the Heights. The real estate column of the *Arkansas Gazette* reported that as many as twenty-nine lots had been sold in one day during the summer of 1903.[42] Early in August of the same year, Maxwell Coffin announced that "over 260 lots have been sold thus far in Pulaski Heights ...."[43] The number of lots sold had risen to "nearly FOUR HUNDRED"[44] by November of 1903, according to H. F. Auten. Lots sometimes also were sold at auctions, which were planned as festive events to attract buyers.[45]

By the early part of 1904, a park under construction at the terminus of the Pulaski Heights streetcar line was being highly touted. First referred to as "Mountain Park," it opened in the spring of 1904 as "Forest Park."[46] The purpose of this park, which was constructed by the streetcar company, was to encourage ridership on the street railway, as well as to provide a recreation area for residents of the Heights.

A 1905 newspaper article about the park described it as having extensive grounds, tastefully and beautifully laid out. Among its attractions, which the article said were "almost as numerous as those of Coney Island,"[47] were a summer theater, a roller coaster and merry-go-round, a bowling alley, a roller-skating rink, a dancing pavilion, and several refreshment stands.[48] One of the highlights in the history of Forest Park came in the spring of 1906, when Sarah Bernhardt made an appearance playing Camille in the park theater. Some 3,000 people crowded out to the park for this momentous event, taxing the streetcar system almost beyond its capabilities.[49]

Besides the opening of Forest Park, the spring of 1904 saw three new areas of lots added to Pulaski Heights: The Hollenberg Addition, the East Pulaski Heights Addition, and the Mountain Park Addition.[50] The opening of the latter was occasion for a "three day gala,"[51] on each day of which a lot worth $350 was given away. The prices of other lots sold during the celebration were reduced by 25 percent.[52] When the event was over, H. F. Auten reported that "many lots were sold to the best people of the city for homes."[53]

The rapid opening of new additions indicates that the developers were confident of the appeal Pulaski Heights held for the residents of Little Rock. After eleven years of existence without streetcar service, the suburb evidently quickly made up for lost time once that service was obtained. By the time the issue of its incorporation as a town arose in the spring of 1905, the population of the Heights was estimated to be between three hundred and four hundred.[54]

The petition for incorporation was presented to the county judge by H. F. Auten, Edgar E. Moss, and Maxwell Coffin on June 27, 1905.[55] It bore the signatures of thirty-nine Pulaski Heights residents and proposed the incorporation of an area approximately 2? miles by 1? miles in size.[56] The size of the proposed town surely was the result of some wishful thinking. Even though Pulaski Heights seemed well on its way to success, less than half of the area proposed for incorporation had even been platted. Moreover, much of it remained unplatted until well after the Heights was consolidated with Little Rock in 1916. Nevertheless, with one adjustment in boundaries to appease some property owners who did not want their land included in the town, the petition was granted, and the Town of Pulaski Heights came into being on August 1, 1905.[57]

The primary reason for incorporation was to provide public improvements. As a municipality, Pulaski Heights could establish improvement districts and charge their residents fees to finance improvements such as the paving of streets and the construction of sidewalks. Several of the first ordinances passed by the newly-elected town council dealt with the establishment of improvement districts, with street paving being the most pressing concern.[58]

The promotion of the Heights did not abate with its incorporation as a town. Another land company, the Riverside Land Company, joined the other two companies already active in the area.[59] An advertisement placed by H. F. Auten in the *Arkansas Gazette* in November of 1905 summarizes the virtues of Pulaski Heights as promoted by the developers:

DO YOU WANT AN ELEGANT HOME?

Do you want sewerage, so you can have modern bath room, closet and lavatory?

Do you want city water, with hot and cold water in every room?

Do you want both old and new telephone?

Do you want to live on the best constructed and smoothest car line in the city, with large, open cars in summer and electric-heated cars in winter?

Do you want health and pure air and beautiful scenery?

Do you want these now or have you decided you can't afford them until you are old?

A residence lot in the city which can give you these advantages will cost you from $1,500 to $3,000 each.

I have seven lots at the Oak Street Station, Pulaski Heights, for $500 each that cannot be equaled elsewhere in the city for less than $2,000 each.

These lots are within twelve minutes from Main Street.[60]

Auten's faith in the Heights proved justified. Its development continued apace; it soon had its own little newspaper,[61] a school and church, and stores catering at least to the basic needs of its residents. New additions continued to be opened: Hillcrest, West Rock, and Forest Park in 1906; Lincoln Park and the Newton Addition in 1907.[62] The residents of the Heights reportedly were elated when their town was chosen as the site for Mount St. Mary's Academy in 1907. They felt its presence "would lend much dignity"[63] to the area. The years 1910, 1911, 1912, and 1914 each saw the opening of a new addition[64] as the population, recorded by the 1910 census as 683, continued to grow.

The residents of the town, as represented by those elected to the town council, were concerned that community standards be maintained at a high level. The town council passed many ordinances designed to assure such high standards. These ordinances dealt with a wide range of topics, from the prohibition of firearms in the Heights to the prohibition of the peddling of peanuts and popcorn at Forest Park.[65] There were ordinances to protect public morals, and others to protect the appearance and environment of the town.[66]

The need for such ordinances indicates that the growth of Pulaski Heights was not without its drawbacks. It created problems that previously had not existed. Further evidence of this fact was the loss of the pine trees for which the area was known. Their rapid disappearance as a result of the "march of civilization"[67] had been noted as early as 1905. The pines continued to disappear until, in October 1915, the Pulaski Heights newspaper strongly condemned the practice of cutting down the trees. In an article entitled "Wanton Cutting of Native Trees by Suburban Homebuilders Deplored as an Act of Public Vandalism," the newspaper stated:

Pulaski Heights owes much of its fame for beauty of landscape to the pines . . . that stood . . . long before the city dwellers came hence to build their bungalows and chicken coops. . . . can anyone explain why every fellow who gets a notion to build, whether mansion, house, or shanty, first lays siege to and destroys the pine trees — the prettiest and most valuable thing he has on his stingy little piece of gravel?[68]

Even so, the newspaper apparently could not help but report in glowing terms the growth and development of the Heights. Just two months after the harangue about the pine trees appeared, the paper announced:

> Building operations in Pulaski Heights are more active this winter than at any season in the history of this rapidly growing suburb, improvements now under way and in process of promotion aggregating an outlay of more than half a million dollars. [69]

The very success of Pulaski Heights probably was a factor in its demise as a town. The fall of 1915 brought discussions concerning the possibility of consolidating the Heights with Little Rock. With its burgeoning, largely affluent population, the Heights undoubtedly was attractive to Little Rock. At a meeting on October 19, 1915, representatives of Little Rock presented a plan for the consolidation of the two municipalities to a group of residents from the Heights. Among the incentives for consolidation offered by Little Rock was the promise that a fire station would be built in the Heights.[70] Although a 1913 Pulaski Heights ordinance had established the entire town as an improvement district for the purpose of building a central fire station,[71] this had not yet been accomplished. Thus, Little Rock's proposal was appealing. Many Pulaski Heights residents quickly were won over to the benefits of consolidating with Little Rock.[72]

Besides a fully-equipped fire station, Pulaski Heights was promised twenty-five fire hydrants and twenty-five street lights. The Heights also would gain the services of all of Little Rock's various departments: health, garbage, streets, police, and so on. Further, advocates of consolidation pointed out that with the presence of a fire station, insurance premiums would be reduced.[73]

The Pulaski Heights residents active in encouraging consolidation with Little Rock were described by the town's newspaper as being "conspicuous for their social prominence and large property interests... ,"[74] Among them were H. F. Auten, Ashley Cockrill, and the man who, as the result of the consolidation, would be the last mayor of the Heights, L. H. Bradley. The campaign for consolidation was conducted with much the same zeal as the promotion of Pulaski Heights earlier had been. A mass meeting was held in the Heights on November 1, 1915, to consider the consolidation issue.[75] This was followed by a concerted effort to make sure all voters in the Heights went to the polls on January 4, 1916, to express their opinions on the issue.[76]

The campaign met with success. In Pulaski Heights the vote in favor of consolidation was 178 to 43; Little Rock voters approved consolidation by a margin of 793 to 57.[77] The mayor of Little Rock, Charles E. Taylor, announced that the vote was "a great victory for the progressive elements of both sides. Undoubtedly both will be benefited by the consolidation."[78] Mayor Bradley of the Heights expressed similar sentiments.[79] Pulaski Heights officially became the Ninth Ward of Little Rock on January 13, 1916, when the Little Rock City Council passed an ordinance to that effect.[80] A week later, voters of the new Ninth Ward elected their two representatives to the Little Rock City Council, and the consolidation was complete.[81]

In terms of its promises to the residents of Pulaski Heights, Little Rock proved as good as its word. The day the Ninth Ward aldermen took their seats in the city council, a resolution was adopted providing for immediate action on the improvements promised the Heights.[82] By the end of the year, Mayor Taylor was able to say that the city's promises to the Heights had been kept. A fire station opened in the Heights on November 1, 1916; fire hydrants were being installed; and street lights were on hand, awaiting installation. Some Pulaski Heights residents already had received refunds on their insurance premiums because of the fire station.[83] On the whole, consolidation was deemed a success.

In the first few years following consolidation, only two small additions opened in the Heights, Doyle Place in 1918 and the McGehee Addition in 1921.[84] Then the boom of the 1920's arrived, and eight additions opened between 1924 and 1930: Fairfax Terrace, Prospect Terrace, and Cliffewood in 1924; Edge Hill and Oakwood Place in 1926; and Shadowlawn, Pine View, and Normandy in 1928, 1929, and 1930, respectively.[85]

By 1930 the success of Pulaski Heights was an accomplished fact. A 1933 newspaper article about the Heights observed:

> Its 13 years of pioneering and 11 years as an incorporated town had brought forth results which convinced all of its desirability as a location, its durability and progressiveness as a community, and its exceptional character [of] residents. Today it is the choice residential district.[86]

From a hilly, wooded tract of land on the outskirts of Little Rock, H. F. Auten (with the help of Edgar Moss and many others) had created a suburb that became one of the city's favorite neighborhoods, a status it retains even today. The reasons for its continued success comprise yet another story. Suffice it to say that the origins of Pulaski Heights as a streetcar suburb provide it an important and rather unique place in the history of Little Rock. It is a segment of the city's history which deserves greater attention.

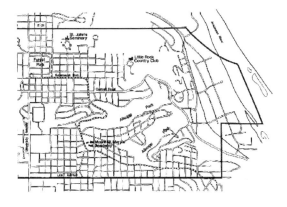

Heavy solid line indicates boundaries of the Town of Pulaski Heights (August 1905-January 1916)

Dotted line shows route of Pulaski Heights streetcar line

Map by Tim Jameson

NOTES

This article was first published in the *Pulaski County Historical Review*. 30 (Spring 1982): 2-16.

[1] Many years after his death, Auten's widow wrote that while on a train he had "picked up a little folder ... and was deeply impressed by a paragraph in it, relating to Arkansas." Mrs. Auten also reported that her husband had visited Arkansas to make "a personal inspection of resources and possibilities of their development." Mrs. Carrie C Auten, *Henry Franklin Auten* (Little Rock: By the Author, 1939), p. 3.

[2] *The Clinton Republican*, 17 April 1890 (hereafter cited as Republican).

[3] In 1939 Auten's widow wrote that he was "the forgotten man. No school, street, park or public building has honored his name." (Auten, *Henry Franklin Auten*, p. 10.) This remains the case today.

[4] *Republican*, 24 October 1889.

[5] Ibid.

[6] *Republican*, 19 December 1889; 16 January 1890.

[7] *Arkansas Democrat*, 25 January 1890; and *Arkansas Gazette*, 26 January 1890 (hereafter cited as Gazette).

8 The 1895-6 city directory of Little Rock lists Edgar E. Moss as being in law practice alone and indicates that H. F. Auten had acquired a new law partner, Wilbur F. Hill. *R. L. Polk & Company's Little Rock City Directory*, 1895-6 (Little Rock R. L. Polk and Co., 1895), pp. 81, 257, 370.

9 Mrs. Bernie Babcock, *Yesterday and Today in Arkansas* (Little Rock: By the Author, c. 1917), no page numbers.

10 Following the repudiation of several state debts in 1884, Arkansas had an extremely poor credit record that made raising capital for investment difficult. See George H. Thompson, "Reconstruction and the Loss of State Credit," *Arkansas Historical Quarterly* 27 (Winter 1969): 293-308.

11 On April 17, 1890, while Auten was visiting St. Johns, a local newspaper reported: "Mr. Auten is taking steps toward the organization of a company to buy 800 acres of suburban property at Little Rock, and it is probable that St. Johns parties will take a hand in the deal. Mr. Auten will return [to Little Rock] the last of this week or the first of next, and may be accompanied by Capt. [George F.] Marvin, Edward Brown, and Willard Potter." (*Republican*, 17 April 1890.)

During May of 1890, the newspaper referred several times to the group of St. Johns businessmen who traveled to Little Rock. The group ultimately consisted of Albert Retan, Edward Brown, Willard Potter, James Richardson, and Orin R. Rice. All but Potter eventually invested in the development of Pulaski Heights, and Albert Retan moved to Little Rock. (Republican, 8, 15, 22 May 1890; and Arkansas, Secretary of State, *Articles of Agreement and Incorporation*, Pulaski Heights Land Company, 1891.)

12 *The Arkansas Press Little Rock City Directory*, 1890 (Little Rock: Press Printing Company, 1890), p. 243.

13In choosing property west of Little Rock, the developers of Pulaski Heights helped set a precedent for future expansion of the city. As they later stated, "the city cannot grow north, nor east, nor south. It must go west." (*Gazette*, 13 December 1903.) The following explanation was given for the necessity of westward expansion: "[Little Rock] can't build north on account of the Arkansas River, can't go east on account of the bottom land which the river overflows, nor south because of Fourche Bayou, therefore MUST GO WEST." (*Gazette*, 20 April 1906.)

14 Hillman and Ferguson each owned a one-eighth interest in the property; Kelley's interest was three-quarters. Correspondence between Hillman and Kelley and, later, between H. F. Auten and Kelley sheds some light on the negotiations that led to the purchase of the land by Auten and Moss and their investors. See E. H. Hillman to Harry E. Kelley, 5, 21 March; 12, 21, 29 April; 5 May 1890; and H. F. Auten to Harry E. Kelley, 4, 9, 10, 13 December 1890, Little Rock Streetcar Company File, Small Manuscript Collection, Arkansas History Commission, Little Rock, Arkansas; and Pulaski County, Circuit Clerk, *Deed Record* 34, pp. 145-146, 272-278.

15Edward Brown, one of the St. Johns investors was ill with "the grip" in March 1890 and also lost his young son that same month to the measles. (*Republican*, 13 March 1890; and E. H. Hillman to Harry E. Kelley, 21 March 1890, Little Rock Streetcar Company File.) E. H. Hillman died suddenly and unexpectedly later in the spring of 1890. (E. H. Hillman and Company to Harry E. Kelley, 7 June 1890, Little Rock

Streetcar Company File.) Charles Ferguson did not agree to sell his interest in the property until December of 1890. (H. F. Auten to Harry E. Kelley, 4 December 1890, Little Rock Streetcar Company File.) Finally, a previous owner of part of the property, Marion J. Clay, was claiming, via a law suit against Kelley, $2,000 for his interest in the property. (H. F. Auten to Harry E. Kelley, 4, 9, 10, 13 December 1890, Little Rock Streetcar Company File.)

[16] Pulaski County, Circuit Clerk, *Deed Record* 34, pp. 277-278.

[17] The land was acquired in three transactions: three-quarters interest for $65,000, one-eighth interest for $8,000, and the final one-eighth interest for $7,000. See Pulaski County, Circuit Clerk, *Deed Record* 34, pp. 145-146, 277-278.

[18] Arkansas, Secretary of Slate, *Articles of Agreement and Incorporation*, Pulaski Heights Land Company, 1891.

[19] Ibid. The Little Rock residents among the twelve incorporators of the Pulaski Heights Land Company were H. F. Auten, Edgar E. Moss, Edward H. Leaming, and Mrs. Eugene H. (Carrie L.) Hillman. The incorporates from Michigan were Otis Fuller, Reuben M. Winston, Edward Brown, Robert M. Swigert, James Richardson, Albert Retan, Orin R. Rice, and George F. Marvin. Albert Retan eventually moved to Little Rock and built a house (which is still standing) in Pulaski Heights.

[20] Although streets were laid out when the Pulaski Heights Addition was platted in 1892, improvements did not come until the early 1900's. See Marcia Winn, "Pulaski Heights Pioneers," *Arkansas Gazette Magazine*, 5 February 1933, p. 1.

[21] Pulaski County, Circuit Clerk, *Deed Record* 40, pp. 197-199.

[22] Claire N. Moody, "Pulaski Heights Grew From Realtors' Dream," *Arkansas Democrat Magazine*, 23 July 1950, p. 4; and Winn, "Pulaski Heights Pioneers," p. 1. Based on interviews with long-time residents and former residents of Pulaski Heights, these articles both mention eight families who moved into the Heights during the 1890's. That number has been substantiated by Pulaski County Deed Records and by listings of Pulaski Heights residents in the 1893-4, 1895-6, and 1897-8 Little Rock city directories.

[23] Ibid.; and *The Heights-Land Weekly Visitor*, 10 April; 17 July 1958. All of these articles speak of the camaraderie that existed among the first residents of the Heights. This fellowship was exhibited in weekly social gatherings, a lack of enmity between residents of northern and southern origins, and "buggy pooling" into Little Rock. The little Pulaski Heights community was described as "one big happy family" by one former resident.

[24] Except for a few annual reports in the possession of Edward H. Leaming's grandson, the business records of the Pulaski Heights Land Company were not located by the author, so it is not possible to ascertain the company's financial status or profitability except by inference from certain facts and circumstances.

[25] Auten, *Henry Franklin Auten*, p. 3.

[26] Two carriage routes into Pulaski Heights were available during the 1890's but neither directly served the small enclave of houses built during those years, one road being some distance to the north and the other to the south. Two newspaper articles about

the early history of the Heights also indicate that sometime before the establishment of streetcar service, the Rock Island Railroad made a slope near the Arkansas River in the vicinity of the Heights. See Moody, "Realtors' Dream," p. 5; and the *Heights-Land Weekly Visitor*, 24 April 1958.

[27] Ibid.

[28] Little Rock, City Clerk, *Ordinance Record* 4, pp. 350-351.

[29] *Gazette*, 28 April, 10 May, 19 July 1903.

[30] *Gazette*, 30 May, 19 July 1903; and Pulaski County, Circuit Clerk, Deed Record 85, pp. 46-47.

[31] Little Rock, City Clerk, *City Council Record* N, p. 258.

[32] *Gazette*, 26 May, 25 June, 19 July 1903.

[33] *Gazette*, 26 November 1903.

[34] Arkansas, Secretary of State, *Articles of Agreement and Incorporation*, Mountain Park Land Company, 1901.

[35] Pulaski County, Circuit Clerk, *Deed Record* 72, pp. 362-365.

[36] *Gazette*, 25 October 1903.

[37] *Ibid.*

[38] *Gazette*, 29 November 1903.

[39] *Gazette*, 12 July 1903.

[40] *Gazette*, 12, 26 July 1903.

[41] The brochure is undated but contains several clues pointing to 1903 as the date of its publication. The most conclusive has to do with the park then under construction at the terminus of the Pulaski Heights streetcar line. The brochure states that the park theater "will be opened . . . not later than May 15th next. . . ." The theater opened in 1904 (*Gazette*, 7 June 1904), so the brochure must have been published in 1903.

[42] *Gazette*, 19 July 1903.

[43] *Gazette*, 9 August 1903.

[44] *Gazette*, 8 November 1903.

[45] *Gazette*, 17 November and 8, 20 December 1903.

[46] *Beautiful Pulaski Heights*; and *Gazette*, 5 December 1903 and 7 June 1904.

[47] *Gazette*, 30 July 1905.

[48] *Ibid.*

[49] *Pulaski Heights Bulletin*, 31 March 1906.

[50] Pulaski County, Circuit Clerk, Deed Record 76, pp.449-453; and *Deed Record* 84, pp. 86-88.

[51] *Gazette*, 8 May 1903.

[52] *Ibid.*

53 *Gazette*, 22 May 1903.

54 *Gazette*, 28 June 1905.

55 *Gazette*, 29 June 1905.

56 *Ibid.*

57 *Gazette*, 2 August 1905; and Pulaski County, Circuit Clerk, *Deed Record* 85, pp. 168-174. The property that was excluded from the boundaries of the town was owned by the "Feild Brothers," who protested that their land was not contiguous with the rest of the area proposed for incorporation. The Feild Brothers' land lay north of the town, as it finally was created, in the bottom land along the Arkansas River.

58 *Gazette*, 24 September, 19 November 1905; *Pulaski Heights Bulletin*, 29 December 1905, 24 February 1906; and Pulaski Heights, *Ordinance Record*, Ordinances Nos. 3,4, 5,6, The first election in the Town of Pulaski Heights took place on September 23, 1905, and resulted in the following officers: mayor - George H. Joslyn; recorder - Frank D. Leaming; aldermen - Maxwell Coffin, Charles N. Faubel, Claude Thompson, Robert O. Paul, and Edgar E. Moss. After Joslyn, four other men served as mayor of the Heights: Edgar E. Moss (1906-09), T. J. Jackson (1909-11), Charles N. Faubel (1911-13), and L. H. Bradley (1913-16).

59 Arkansas, Secretary of State, *Articles of Agreement and Incorporation*, Riverside Land Company, 1905. The incorporators of this land company were Oscar Davis, F. B. T. Hollenberg, Chris Ledwidge, and H. F. Auten.

60 *Gazette* 12 November 1905.

61 The first newspaper published in Pulaski Heights was a monthly publication, the *Pulaski Heights Bulletin*, and consisted of only fourteen issues, December 1905 through February 1907. Its successor was *The Pulaskian*, a weekly newspaper published during the years 1915 to 1922.

62 Pulaski County, Circuit Clerk, Plat Book 1, pp. 19, 20, 30, 63, 80.

63 *Pulaski Heights Bulletin*, 28 February 1907; *Arkansas Democrat*, 24 April 1938, Sec. B., p. 15.

64 The additions were as follows: 1910 - Pleasant Hill (Pulaski County, Circuit Clerk, *Plat Book* 1, p. 122); 1911 - Park View (*Plat Book* 3, p. 108); 1912 - Altheimer's (*Plat Book* 1, p.165); 1914 - Country Club Heights (Plat Book 1, p. 181).

65 Pulaski Heights, *Ordinance Record*, Ordinance Nos. 35 (firearms) and 55 (peddling of peanuts and popcorn in Forest Park).

66 Several ordinances dealt with morality and the behavior of persons in Pulaski Heights. Ordinance No. 49 prohibited "loitering, rambling, etc. after eleven o'clock p.m. on the streets, roads, etc. of Pulaski Heights." Ordinance No. 51 had to do with public nudity and "indecent or lewd dress." Ordinance No. 71 prohibited "disorderly houses, dives, dance houses, etc." Among the ordinances designed to protect the appearance and environment of the Heights were No. 7, which regulated signs, and No. 39, which regulated rendering plants, tanneries, distilleries, and similar "nuisances."

67 *Gazette*, 28 May 1905.

[68] *The Pulaskian*, 1 October 1915.

[69] *The Pulaskian*, 3 December 1915.

[70] *The Pulaskian*, 22 October 1915.

[71] Pulaski Heights, *Ordinance Record*, Ordinance No. 58.

[72] *The Pulaskian*, 29 October 1915. Consolidation with Little Rock actually had been considered likely since the time of the incorporation of Pulaski Heights as a town. At that time, it was said that it was "probable that the area later will be annexed to Little Rock." See *Gazette*, 29 June, 2 August 1905.

[73] *The Pulaskian*, 29 October 1915.

[74] *The Pulaskian*, 22 October 1915.

[75] *The Pulaskian*, 29 October 1915.

[76] *The Pulaskian*, 31 December 1915.

[77] *Gazette*, 5 January 1916.

[78] Ibid.

[79] Ibid.

[80] Little Rock, City Clerk, Ordinance Record 6, p. 483.

[81] *Gazette*, 14, 20, 21 January 1916; and *The Pulaskian*, 21 January 1916. The two aldermen elected from the new Ninth Ward were L. H. Bradley and John P. Streepey, who had served as the city attorney of Pulaski Heights.

[82] *Gazette*, 25 January 1916.

[83] Campaign brochure (untitled) issued by Charles E. Taylor, December 1916, p. 11.

[84] Pulaski County, Circuit Clerk, *Plat Book 2*, pp. 20, 78.

[85] Pulaski County, Circuit Clerk, *Plat Book 2*, pp. 152-153, 159, 197-198; and *Plat Book 3*, pp. 45, 63, 92, 108.

[86] Winn, "Pulaski Heights Pioneers," p. 1.

"WE WOULD BE BUILDING," THE BEGINNING OF THE PHYLLIS WHEATLEY YWCA IN LITTLE ROCK

By Peggy Harris

Peggy Harris was a writer for the "Arkansas Gazette" and a graduate student in Public History at the University of Arkansas at Little Rock when she wrote an M.A. thesis from which this article was drawn. It tells the story of a project carried out by the women of Little Rock's African-American population, who, as Harris makes clear, were active in civic affairs long before the end of segregation. She continued the story of the Phyllis Wheatley YWCA in a second article published in the "Review". Peggy Harris is now a reporter with the Associated Press.

In the early 1920s, when the world was recovering from World War I, a small group of black women reportedly sold dinners on the streets of Little Rock, hoping to raise money for a Young Women's Christian Association.[1] Black civic leaders had been waging small battles to provide recreational facilities for black boys and girls since at least 1913, but to no avail.[2] The women, mostly teachers or the wives of black professional men in Little Rock, would take up the cause and establish a center, with the help of the national YWCA, that would serve for more than twenty years as the only facility entirely devoted to the recreation of blacks. It would reach its peak in the late 1940s, significantly change with the coming of civil rights legislation, and then close in 1971.

Given the history of dependence among blacks since slavery and the limited opportunities afforded blacks after Reconstruction, the Phyllis Wheatley YWCA was a significant development in Little Rock's black community. While blacks suffered race hatred, lynchings, and violations of their civil rights, the Phyllis Wheatley YWCA, along with black churches and businesses, flourished along Ninth Street and provided an invaluable sense of black pride and identity.[3] Phyllis Wheatley women worked voluntarily for some fifty years to provide constructive activities for young black girls. The Phyllis Wheatley building itself, a two-story brick and block structure, became a symbol of black progress, a place where young girls learned the social graces and black women could lead without interference.

Since its beginnings in the mid-nineteenth century, the Young Women's Christian Association considered itself a pioneering movement, dedicated to democratic and Christian principles and committed to serving women and girls of all backgrounds. Segregation was not a part of its ideal plan. But for many years, the YWCA struggled with the question of how to best serve all women in a segregated world, particularly in the South.[4] Much of the struggle was the result of black women seeking equal treatment, respect and greater authority within the organization. Despite the adoption of the YWCA name by black women's groups and "unceasing efforts to affiliate with their white counterparts," the black associations were not accepted.[5] As early as 1893, a YWCA was organized for Negro women at Dayton, Ohio, and there is evidence of several Negro student associations in the late 1800s or early 1900s, as well as YWCA groups among black women in Louisville, Kentucky, Memphis, Tennessee, and Columbus, Georgia.[6] When the national YWCA was formed in 1906, it took on work already started by black women in New York, Brooklyn, Baltimore, Washington, Philadelphia and Dayton. But, at the time, there were no black YWCAs farther south.[7] In these early years, the national YWCA either affiliated already-established black YWs directly with its national board or set up "subsidiaries" of local white YWs to accommodate southern members who might be uncomfortable with the prospect of attending national conventions with black delegates.[8]

In 1915, at Louisville, Kentucky, the national YWCA held its first interracial conference, setting up a biracial committee to promote the YWCA among black women and launching a leadership training program.[9] In 1920, despite a bitter, behind-the-scenes debate, the YWCA endorsed the "Social Ideals of the Churches" at its Sixth National Convention in Cleveland, Ohio.[10] The "Ideals" originated with the Federal Council of the Churches of Christ in America and supported equal rights and justice for all, equal pay for equal work, abatement of poverty, the abolition of child labor, and "the fullest possible development of every child especially by the provision of education and recreation."[11]

Aside from black leadership and the changing views of white YWCA leaders, World War I also sparked change. Among YWCA women, the war provoked a tremendous response. Women heeded the call to provide stability at home during unstable times abroad. At the same time, according to Adrienne Lash Jones:

> Black church and club women found the YWCA model of interdenominational work most appealing. In spite of the fact that they were not welcomed as members or participants in local all-white Associations, the critical need to accommodate the migrating population [of blacks] inspired black women to proceed along the same lines as their white counterparts.[12]

In 1917, the national YWCA set up a War Work Council to meet the needs of women of all countries affected by the war and expanded its work among black women and girls with $400,000 of a $4 million government appropriation for war work.[13] Under Eva Bowles, a black woman and the national YWCA secretary for Colored Work, the number of black YWCA branches increased from sixteen in 1915 to forty-nine in 1920; the number of black staff members increased from nine paid local workers to eighty-six, and the number of national secretaries increased from one to twelve.[14] The Phyllis Wheatley YWCA at Little Rock was a part of this growth.

When May B. Belcher, a national YWCA war worker and a black woman, arrived in Little Rock in March of 1918 to launch a campaign for a black YWCA, she was impressed by the response. "The campaign served as a real dynamo to that section of the country," she reported.[15] "The inspiration and consecration which came to the women from that effort has lasted through the year. The splendid work done by the women of Little Rock, the creditable way in which they carried their responsibility has been gratifying." At the time, Little Rock was "a city of peculiar advantages, a college town for the colored."[16] Philander Smith College, Arkansas Baptist College, and Shorter College served blacks seeking education, and the public schools for black children were considered superior to most black schools in the South. A number of black fraternal and insurance organizations lined Ninth Street near downtown Little Rock and provided some economic security for blacks. Many young black women were employed in cotton mills, laundries, and railroad shops in and around the city or worked as elevator girls or waitresses.[17] Others were accountants, actuaries, secretaries, clerks, teachers, and insurance collectors.[18]

At the request of the United States War Department Commission on Training Camp Activities and the Young Men's Christian Association, the national YWCA set out to provide wholesome recreation, social programs, and job and housing assistance to more than a million young black women in the country, whose lives were changed by the war. The YWCA was interested in serving, in particular, those women and girls who lived near military camps. Little Rock, then, became a prime location to launch a campaign because of nearby Camp Pike and Fort Roots and an aviation field at Lonoke.[19]

"Miss Belcher, knowing the tremendous necessity, fairly plunged the city into a campaign for a recreation center for girls," according to one YWCA account.[20] A committee of leading women was organized under the chairmanship of Alice Crumpton Meaddough, the wife of Dr. R. J. Meaddough, a dentist and one of a small number of black professionals in Little Rock.[21] By April 1, 1918, the campaign was in full swing.

Denominational lines were forgotten and the whole colored community responded to the appeals of the organizer. Fraternal societies vied with each other in raising money "for our girls." Schools and alumnae in three colleges and the high school joined in the greatest girls' parade ever held in the city. Seven hundred girls marching, bearing the banners, "Stand behind Our Country's Girlhood," and "Our Girls, the Second Line of Defense." Over two thousand dollars in cash was raised and the girls' work was launched on a sound financial basis.[22]

During the campaign, Alice L. Harper of Louisville, Kentucky, arrived to take charge of the work, and ten neighborhood groups were organized to build up membership and interest. On July 1, 1918, Sadie B. Davis arrived and began a campaign among black girls. A narrow hallway was used as an office for the Blue Triangle Center, as it was called, and the girls met in the schools, on campus and in the homes of campaign supporters.[23] President D.J.M. Cox of Philander Smith College provided a college hall as a temporary center for the group and allowed the girls to play tennis and croquet on the college campus. A short while later, in September 1918, the group moved to "a large dwelling with double parlors and a spacious front porch, kitchen and dining room."[24] Two halls were used for gym classes. One class was held in the afternoon and one in the evening, with about sixty to eighty girls participating.

A YWCA account in 1919 described the value of the Blue Triangle Center:

As the city offers no public amusements suitable for self-respecting girls, the recreation center proved a Godsend. Segregated street cars, segregated theaters and picture shows, and the only privileges, driving through the public parks or attending un-chaperoned, questionable dance halls are conditions which girls must face here.[25]

The Little Rock Young Women's Christian Association at Fourth and Scott streets had been operating since 1911 but was used for white women and girls, despite a YWCA tradition of Christian good will, democracy, tolerance and service to all women.[26] Like many organizations throughout the country, Christian or otherwise, the Little Rock YWCA was operating in accordance with the U.S. Supreme Court ruling of separate but equal. A Young Men's Christian Association had been operating for white men since 1885, and a YMCA group formed around the 1890s for blacks.[27] But black youth had no recreational facilities, neighborhood playgrounds, parks, swimming pools, gymnasiums, summer camps, organized athletic programs, organized cultural activities, adequate libraries, or meeting places, other than what a few black churches and schools could provide.

Through the YWCA's Blue Triangle Center, black girls enjoyed hikes, outdoor sports, and a sunrise Sunday school class in the summer on a hill in Kavanaugh Park. Young women participated in club meetings, "community sings," and parties. They held a military pageant in June 1918, a pageant for the United War Work Campaign in November and a Christmas pageant that included an original play by Sadie Davis, the campaign leader. During a gas shortage in Little Rock in December and January, the girls assisted needy families by providing wood and stoves. In these early years, the center also offered a recreation program one evening a week for working girls.[28]

The YWCA's war work at Little Rock also included efforts to serve black soldiers. In December 1917, the month a Hostess House opened for white soldiers, black women in Little Rock and on the national YWCA's Committee on Colored Work began work to secure a Hostess House for black soldiers at Camp Pike.[29] A Hostess House could provide some semblance of home life to the thousands of black soldiers stationed at the camp. Hostess House workers looked after visitors and helped at the base hospital. They provided recreation to soldiers and their families and emergency assistance in personal and social matters.[30]

At Camp Pike, a few black companies entertained the men and raised money for the war effort by putting on shows and working with the War Camp Community Service Program.[31] But Camp Pike and Camp Logan, near Houston, Texas, were the only camps where the YWCA encountered significant obstacles in its efforts to establish Hostess House programs for blacks. "Most exasperating of all the prejudices to overcome was the calm assurance of officials that they, being white men, understood the negro race as no colored women could," one YWCA observer wrote.[32]

> Throughout many trials the work of securing a house progressed slowly. Promises were made and broken. Requests for the house were mysteriously held up until . . . finally it was decided months later to use the white hostess house for colored troops after building a new house for white soldiers.[33]

Of the two Hostess Houses, the smaller one was used for black soldiers but, for all practical purposes, because of the delays, ". . . the troops were leaving camp and the house was officially declared closed before it was ever opened."[34]

Other war efforts by black women and girls in Little Rock proved successful, however. Most likely, black women were involved in the running of a Colored Soldier's Club at 818 State Street through the War Camp Community Service

Program.[35] During the United War Work Campaign, some 200 high school girls gave $1,050 to the war effort. In all, $1,500 was pledged by girls of the Patriotic League, a forerunner of the Girl Reserves and Y-Teens.[36] According to a 1919 YWCA account: "One hundred and fifty sweaters, numerous socks and wristlets have been knit for the Red Cross and during the influenza epidemic many girls responded to the call for service in the Red Cross rooms."[37] For local YWCA efforts in war relief work and YWCA efforts nationwide, Governor Charles Brough declared May 18, 1919, "Y.W.C.A. Day in Arkansas."[38] In a small blurb at the end of a lengthy article by Brough for the *Arkansas Gazette*, black men of the community also were recognized for their patriotic contributions during the war.

> Our colored population, led by such representatives as Scipio Jones, Bishop [J. M.] Conner, Dr. [Joseph A.] Hooker, Dr. [J. M.] Robinson, Professor [J. G.] Ish, and others, made a noble showing of patriotic endeavor, and the percentage of colored soldiers from Little Rock in proportion to the total Negro population of the city was most incredible.[39]

On March 7, 1919, the Committee on Colored Work decided to pursue construction of a YWCA for black women and girls in Little Rock. Julia Morgan, an architect in San Francisco, California, had already developed plans for the building.[40] Two weeks later, on March 22, the national YWCA purchased two lots on the northwest corner of Tenth and Gaines streets for $4,650 as a site for the building. The property had belonged to Ada Thompson Norfleet, whose aunt was responsible for the Ada Thompson Memorial Home for elderly white women.[41] As planning progressed on the building, the committee realized it needed to limit its expenses and decided October 31, 1919, on a $40,000 budget for construction.[42] In the meantime, at least seventeen clubs operated out of the Blue Triangle Center and hundreds of girls participated in center activities. The girls had use of a private tennis court, and the women were making plans for a summer camp.[43]

It is not exactly clear what the relationship was between the Blue Triangle Center and what came to be the Phyllis Wheatley YWCA. The Blue Triangle Center involved many of the same people, and, in fact, Sadie Davis's and Alice Meaddough's names were associated with both groups.[44] Most likely, the Blue Triangle Center was operated by the Phyllis Wheatley YWCA or a group that simply took the name of the Phyllis Wheatley YWCA once the new building opened at 924 Gaines. A program for an annual meeting of the Phyllis Wheatley YWCA dates the organization back to 1917; another report says it started in 1919.[45] Various reports also mention that the group headquartered in an office building, a private home on Pulaski Street, at Philander Smith College, and in the Taborian Temple at Ninth and State before moving into the new building on Gaines Street, reportedly in 1921 or 1922.[46]

Adolphine Fletcher Terry, a longtime resident of Little Rock and one of three white women appointed as advisers to the black YWCA, provides further details:

> When the war effort was over, the black women of the town who had run such an outstanding War Camp Community Service Program and looked after the soldiers so well, were given forty thousand dollars by the National War Camp Community Service to build a black YWCA here . . . . When the black YWCA was formed, it was necessary for it to have a board of directors. The members of the board of directors of the white YWCA wouldn't touch the whole project with a forty foot pole. They would not even permit the black organization to use the name of the Young Women's Christian Association, so it was named after a black poet and became known as the Phyllis Wheatley Club. Three white women were asked by the national office of the YWCA to serve as an advisory board for the club, and I was one of them. We soon found that we weren't needed at all. The women who served as directors of the club were all well educated and leaders of their community, and they had plenty of ideas of their own. We, the advisers, got more out of the experience than we gave because we made friends among those black women who since the Civil War had never been thought of as possible friends of ours, and who had lived in a world apart. They were the wives of professional men, and they provided us with an education. We, the daughters of Confederate veterans who had heard a great deal about the white side of the war, now learned of the suffering of the black population . . . . [47]

It should be noted that while it might have been true that the Little Rock YWCA did not want the black women to use the YWCA name, more than likely the nationwide practice of using the Phyllis Wheatley name for black YWCAs was what determined the name of the group in Little Rock.[48] In fact, the Phyllis Wheatley name, in honor of the black slave who became a published poet in the 1700s, was used by many black women's groups around the country.[49] Even Little Rock had another Phyllis Wheatley Club that was distinct from the Phyllis Wheatley YWCA.[50] In any case, once the building opened, the Phyllis Wheatley Young Women's Christian Association became the established group for YW-work among black women and girls in Little Rock and the only recreational facility for blacks. Although white women may have been peripherally involved in its early stages and the majority white national YWCA owned the building, the Phyllis Wheatley YWCA was wholly separate from the white YWCA at Little Rock and remained that way until 1942.[51]

At the time the Phyllis Wheatley YWCA opened, the black community had long been aware of the need for a recreational building. A commission of prominent black men, appointed by Mayor Charles E. Taylor in 1912 to investigate the problem of prostitution among blacks, expressed concern that women occasionally visited pool rooms, known for gambling, idleness and vice. In addition, it said, "There are far more women, girls and children of the colored race who have to leave their homes early in the morning and get back late at night than women, girls and children of any other race." In numerous cases, these women and girls have been "taken advantage of" on their way to and from work. The commission reported that "100s and thousands" of black youths, between the ages of ten and twenty, were not in school nor employed.[52] "We believe that, more and more, our churches and schools must be made social centers. Outdoor sports and athletics must be provided for all young people," the vice commission said.[53]

> As it is now nothing of the sort is provided for the children of our race in this city, except as the churches and Sunday Schools give a picnic once a year, far beyond the limits of the city, where the great majority of our children cannot go . . . . There are also thousands of negro homes in which there are no front yards and very scarce back yards. All the children and youth of these schools, colleges and homes are deprived of anything like regular and frequent outing within the city limits, or anything like playgrounds and parks . . . . [54]

The commission argued that since blacks work in white establishments and homes, their welfare and character should be a concern to the white community. "The city and the community owe them such protection as will make them love their jobs and make them morally independent of all individuals and conditions tending to lead them astray," the black commissioners concluded.[55] In 1912, a Little Rock Parkways Association was formed to develop a parks system for the city.[56] In the summers of 1917 and 1918, the white YWCA provided supervised play for children on Sunday afternoons at City Park, making obvious the need for a city parks system for whites, as well. But such efforts were interrupted by the war, and it would be thirty years or so before the city would take any concrete action to satisfy the commission's recommendations.[57]

In the meantime, black men and women in Little Rock's professional class, including teachers, physicians, lawyers, and businessmen, enjoyed the activities of numerous fraternal organizations and charity clubs, started by blacks in the late 1800s with the coming of Jim Crow. Just as the better-educated and well-to-do whites had established clubs, so, too, did their black counterparts in Little Rock. Club work that provided educational opportunities and leadership training to white women held similar promise for black women. These outlets included federated clubs of the National Association of Colored Women, established nationally in 1896 and in Little Rock in 1897, the Arkansas Association of Colored Women, the Frances Harper Charity Club, established in 1907, the Sunshine Charity Club, established around 1910, and the Provident Relief Charity Club, established around 1914.[58]

In its early years, the Phyllis Wheatley YWCA fit the pattern of drawing leadership from the better-educated, better-off class of women. Besides Alice Meaddough, Elizabeth "Bessie" Stephens Thornton and Amelia Bradford Ives were among its early local organizers. Thornton was the daughter of Charlotte Andrews Stephens, Little Rock's first black public school teacher, and J. H. Stephens, a building contractor. She attended Walden College at Nashville, Tennessee, and received a bachelor's degree. She taught a few years in the Little Rock School District before marrying John G. Thornton, a physician.[59] Thornton spent her life trying to improve the lives of others, realizing that society adhered to only part of the separate-but-equal rule. "It was indeed separate but far from equal, and she spent the better part of her life trying to make them equal as well," her daughter recalled.[60] Thornton headed a community activity called Christmas Cheer that provided food and toys and, in some cases, money for needy families. She helped establish the first detention facility for black juveniles, the first playground and the first public library for blacks. When she died August 3, 1934, flags flew at half-mast in Little Rock.[61]

Ives was a native of Port Gibson, Mississippi, and came to Little Rock with her grandmother and aunt when only seven years old. She attended Fisk University, taught mathematics at Gibbs High School at Little Rock and later became principal of John E. Bush Elementary School.[62] In 1907, she became a charter member and the first president of the Frances Harper Charity Club, an affiliate of the National Association of Colored Women. Besides helping to establish the Phyllis Wheatley YWCA, she also led a fundraising campaign in 1923 to help build a sanatorium for blacks who suffered from tuberculosis, and she collected food for school children during the Depression. In 1937, Ives founded the Urban League of Greater Little Rock.[63]

Other early organizers were Annie Gillam, who held a bachelor's degree from Douglas University, did graduate work at St. Louis University, and was a longtime teacher in Little Rock, and Mary J. Caver Booker, wife of the Reverend Joseph A. Booker, who was president of Arkansas Baptist College and chairman of the vice commission in 1912.[64] Mary Booker had attended Roger Williams University and taught school in Helena three years. As was her husband, she was known for her efforts to improve the lives of blacks. ". . . the college is as much a monument to her unremitting efforts as it is to those of her able husband," one observer wrote.[65]

Just as their white counterparts, the Phyllis Wheatley YWCA women represented the best-informed, best-connected, and most capable women in the community. But their chances for equal treatment were slim to none, and their association with white women of the Little Rock YWCA was limited. Frances Thornton Poe, the daughter of Bessie Thornton, recalled some contact among the YWCA women but said, "It was primarily just a voice contact. The secretary from the Phyllis Wheatley Y might call for some reason to the secretary at the other Y, and the presidents of the boards of the two also were in some contact."[66]

In May 1917, not long before national YWCA and Little Rock black women began work on a Hostess House program for black soldiers, Ellen V. Cobb, the secretary of the Little Rock YWCA, recommended the board make the Frances Harper Club a branch. The purpose of the Frances Harper Club, also named after a black poet, was "to give service to our community with charitable projects and scholarships; to support our state, region and national programs and projects, and to help achieve for all citizens equality, justice and peace." Its membership was mostly middle-class black women.[67] But Mrs. W. S. Rawlings, a board member of the Little Rock YWCA, suggested instead that the board defer action on establishing "a colored branch" and the board agreed.[68] The status quo would not be shaken until decades later.

In the meantime, the Phyllis Wheatley would serve as a vital part of the black community. C. E. Bush, writing for the *Arkansas Democrat* in 1921, noted that the group had a membership of 851 members and said of its building:

> It is one of the most beautiful buildings in the city and sitting upon a high elevation surrounded by wide rolling courts, readily attracts the attention of the passing public. It is quite a center for all of the religious and social activities of the negroes of the city.[69]

The building stood across from St. Phillip's Episcopal Church, founded in 1885 as a Trinity Cathedral mission among blacks.[70] Taborian Hall and Mosaic Temple, landmarks of the black business district, were within walking distance, as were Philander Smith College and other black schools. United Friends Hospital for blacks would be built nearby in 1922. Black-owned insurance offices, a black newspaper office, and Dubisson Funeral Home were also in the neighborhood. The building had tennis courts behind it and space for croquet.[71]

Above the entrance door were inscribed the words "Phyllis Wheatley Club." In the 1940s, supporters would donate a large neon triangle, which would hang outside the building. The building itself was in the colonial revival style with a gable roof.[72] It was brick and block, two-stories with a basement. It had a fireplace, hardwood floors, twelve-foot high ceilings, and a large staircase. On the ground floor were the lobby, office, and meeting rooms. The second floor included a kitchen, a large bath, and a large room with folding doors that could be closed to create three meeting rooms or be left open for a large dance floor. In the basement were several showers, two bathrooms, and another large room.[73] "We had the only good tennis courts in that part of the city, and we had the only free showers," Victoria Sims, a former Phyllis Wheatley YWCA member recalled.[74]

In 1921, the first year in the new building, the Phyllis Wheatley YWCA organized thirty-five Girl Reserve Clubs, five recreational clubs, and thirty-two vesper services. It was visited by 3,318 people, including visitors from Pennsylvania, Georgia, Florida, Mississippi, Minnesota, Colorado, Kentucky, Oklahoma, Tennessee, Massachusetts, New Jersey, New York, Kansas, Missouri, Illinois, Ohio, Louisiana, Texas, and Alabama. The *Arkansas Gazette*, remarking upon this impressive out-of-state interest, argued that whites, too, should be interested in supporting the black YWCA. "It is needless to say that these visitors from other states carried away impressions that will be good advertising for Little Rock and Arkansas."[75]

For its first five years, the Phyllis Wheatley YWCA work had been supported by the national YWCA or what funds could be raised from the local black community. This support had paid off in reaching thousands of blacks in the city. The recreational clubs had an attendance of 1,184 people in 1921 and vesper services reported a total attendance of 1,481.[76] The Girl Reserve meetings, "devoted to mental, physical and spiritual improvement," had a total attendance of 3,775. Girl Reserves, led by Ethel Jones and Ethel Davis, would camp in Pankey's Addition because they could not camp where the white girls camped.[77] The girls had no permanent place to camp, one early Phyllis Wheatley member recalled:

> A Mrs. Pankey owned quite a bit of property out here on Highway 10, what's now Cantrell Road, and she had a lot of goats. You would set up

> camp out there and have your campfire out there. . . . You wouldn't care
> if those goats would come out there and knock your fire over. [78]

The Blue Triangle club met at the Phyllis Wheatley YWCA once a week after school. The girls followed parliamentary procedure, learned arts and crafts, and took hikes. They discussed a variety of topics, including manners, personal hygiene, and how to interact with boys and people in general. Other young women learned how to knit at the Phyllis Wheatley YWCA. Under an arrangement with Gus Blass, a downtown department store, if the women bought their yarn from the store, the store would send someone to the Phyllis Wheatley YWCA to teach them how to knit, since it did not allow blacks in knitting classes at the store.[79]

Agnes Hunter, a former Girl Reserve, recalled meeting regularly at the Phyllis Wheatley YWCA, going on picnics and swimming at Tillar Park, which was several miles outside of Little Rock and apparently owned by a black family. The girls enjoyed dances, which boys attended, and bunking parties, also known as slumber parties, at the Phyllis Wheatley YWCA.[80]

The early years also included "wiener bakes," Bible classes, gym classes, millinery classes, and tennis. The Phyllis Wheatley touted five-mile hikes to Echo Valley and hikes to Dripping Springs, as just some of the fun girls would not want to miss. It maintained an Employment Department, which placed ten applicants in jobs in one month and handled a total of thirty-two job applications and twelve employer applications. "Many girls and women are reached through this department that otherwise would be unknown to us. Very pleasant remarks come back about many of the applicants sent out," Sadie B. Felloston, the acting secretary for the Phyllis Wheatley in 1924, said.[81]

A board of black women and an advisory board of white women ran the Phyllis Wheatley YWCA. The national YWCA generally selected the executive director, or general secretary as they were called, to supervise the Phyllis Wheatley YWCA under the board's direction. Occasionally, national representatives would visit. Annual membership fees were fifty cents for twelve-to-eighteen-year-olds and one dollar for adults.[82] White women of the Little Rock YWCA, although they honored rare requests for visits to the Phyllis Wheatley YWCA, distanced themselves from their counterparts. During one meeting in February 1923, the Little Rock board went to the trouble of approving a recommendation "that an effort be made to correct the impression that the Phyllis Wheatley Club is a branch of the Y.W.C.A. on Fourth and Scott."[83]

Despite support from the national YWCA and funds from the black community, long-term survival of the Phyllis Wheatley YWCA depended on finding a stable source of local support that would at least take care of its financial needs. This happened in 1923, when the Phyllis Wheatley YWCA became one of the original members of the Community Chest, a forerunner of the United Way.[84] In fact, for many years, the Phyllis Wheatley YWCA was the only black organization directly served by the Community Chest, suggesting that even in the white community it had a good reputation as the only formally organized recreational and social service agency for blacks. Community Chest support meant the Phyllis Wheatley YWCA could not only serve as an outlet of wholesome recreation for young girls but also help the black community in other ways. No doubt, several Phyllis Wheatley women were also involved in a fundraising campaign, led by the Federation of Colored Women's Clubs and Amelia Ives, to build a sanatorium for blacks suffering from tuberculosis.[85] At the time, the tuberculosis death rate among blacks was three times that among whites. In 1923, the group raised $1,200. The money was used toward an option on the property, to drill for water, for traveling expenses of project coordinators and trips to secure money from the Rosenwald Fund, for shrubbery and landscaping, and for a cottage for the superintendent. The project resulted in the Thomas C. McRae Sanatorium, which opened in Alexander in 1931.[86]

The Phyllis Wheatley YWCA assisted in 1927, when spring flood waters covered nearly half of Arkansas and 143,273 people had to seek shelter in refugee camps.[87] The Phyllis Wheatley served as headquarters for Negro refugees, providing hospital space, sleeping quarters, and a food station.[88] In addition, the Phyllis Wheatley YWCA started, in 1928, "the first important movement toward instituting Negro playgrounds."[89] With the cooperation of black school administrators and teachers, the Phyllis Wheatley YWCA raised $1,000 to equip and operate summer playgrounds at Arkansas Baptist College, East End School, and Stephens School.

> The playgrounds were provided with swings, slides, seesaws, softball equipment, croquet sets and sandboxes. They were supervised by paid directors and volunteer workers. The following year more money was raised and a fourth playground opened at Bush School. Old equipment was replaced and supplemented, and a supervisor was employed to direct sports on all the playgrounds and conduct inter-playground baseball games.[90]

A need, expressed by the mayor's vice commission in 1912, had been partially addressed through the diligent efforts of this black women's group.

The Phyllis Wheatley YWCA was a source of pride for the black community. To the community, it seemed wholesome and Christian and right. It provided hope. Its founders had acted on democratic and humanitarian impulses during the war and had kept to the guiding principles of the YWCA, as reflected in this verse, often sung at Phyllis Wheatley meetings:

> We would be building, temples still undone
> O'er crumbling walls their crosses scarcely lift
> Waiting 'til love can raise the broken stone
> And hearts creative bridge the human rift.[91]

NOTES

This article first appeared in the *Pulaski County Historical Review*, 43 (Winter 1995):70-86

[1] Sue Cowan Williams, interview by author, tape recording, Little Rock, Arkansas, 16 January 1992.

[2] Rev. Hay Watson Smith, comp., *Report of the Little Rock Vice Commission May 20, 1913* (City of Little Rock, 1918). Mayor Charles E. Taylor appointed a twenty-six member biracial vice commission in January 1912. The five black members investigated the problem of prostitution in the black community and recommended, among other things, that recreational facilities be provided as a character-building measure.

[3] Many descriptions of economic, social and political conditions among blacks in the latter part of the nineteenth century and early 1900s exist. Among them are C. Vann Woodward, *The Strange Career of Jim Crow* (New York: Oxford University Press, 1966); Fon Louise Gordon, "The Black Experience in Arkansas, 1880-1920," (Ph.D. diss., University of Arkansas, 1989); and Charles C. Alexander, "White-Robed Reformers: The Ku Klux Klan Comes to Arkansas, 1921-1922," *Arkansas Historical Quarterly* XXII (Spring 1963): 8-23. There is no history of Ninth Street in Little Rock, the black business district of the 1920s, 1930s and 1940s, but partial information is available in various works. See Tom Baskett Jr., ed., *Persistence of the Spirit: The Black Experience in Arkansas* (Little Rock: Delta Cultural Center, Arkansas Department of Heritage, 1991); *Arkansas A Guide to the State*, comp. Workers of the Writers' Program of the Work Projects Administration in the State of Arkansas (New York: Hastings House Publishers, 1941); and Jim Lester and Judy Lester, *Greater Little Rock* (Norfolk, Va.: The Donning Company, 1986).

[4] For a discussion of black women and the YWCA, see Jane Olcott. comp., *The Work of Colored Women* (New York: Colored Work Committee War Work Council of the National Board of Young Women's Christian Association, 1919); Gerda Lerner, ed., *Black Women in White America, A Documentary History* (New York: Random House, 1973); Nancy F. Cott, *The Grounding of Modern Feminism* (New Haven and London: Yale University Press, 1987); Juliet O. Bell and Helen J. Wilkins, *Interracial Practices in Community Y.W.C.A.'s* (New York: National Board Young Women's Christian Association, 1944); Gladys Gilkey Calkins, "The Negro in the Young Women's Christian Association" (Master's Thesis, George Washington University, 1960); Paula Giddings, *When and Where I Enter* (New York: William Morrow and Company, 1984); Sharlene Voogd Cochrane, " 'And the Pressure Never Let Up': Black Women, White

Women, and the Boston YWCA, 1918-1948," in *Black Women in United States History*, ed. Darlene Clark Hine (Brooklyn, N.Y.: Carlson Publishing Inc., 1990), 259-69; Jacquelyn Dowd Hall, Revolt Against Chivalry: *Jessie Ames and the Women's Campaign Against Lynching* (New York: Columbia University Press, 1974 and 1979); Mary S. Sims, *The Purpose Widens 1947-1967* (New York: National Board Young Women's Christian Association, 1969).

[5] Adrienne Lash Jones, "Black Women and the YWCA," 1992 draft manuscript for *Encyclopedia of Black Women's History*.

[6] Lerner, *Black Women in White America*, 478; Mrs. A. W. Hunton, comp., "Beginnings Among Colored Women," 1913, YWCA of the U.S.A., National Board Archives, New York.

[7] Bell and Wilkins, *Interracial Practices*, 3; Lerner, Black Women in White America, 477-478.

[8] Lerner, *Black Women in White America*, 477-478; Jones, "Black Women and the YWCA."

[9] Lerner, *Black Women in White America*, 477-478.

[10] "Y.W.C.A. News 1920-1921," 18 August 1920, 2-3, Bess Chisum Stephens YWCA records, Little Rock, Arkansas. Hereafter cited as Bess Chisum Stephens YWCA records.

[11] "Y.W.C.A. News 1920-1921," 5 May 1920, Bess Chisum Stephens YWCA records.

[12] Adrienne Lash Jones, "Struggle Among the Saints: Black Women in the YWCA, 1860-1920," Paper prepared for the Organization of American Historians, Louisville, Ky., April 12, 1991, 2.

[13] Olcott, *Colored Women*, 5; Adrienne Lash Jones, "Black Women and the YWCA," 1992 draft manuscript.

[14] Lerner, *Black Women in White America*, 477-478.

[15] Olcott, *Colored Women*, 67.

[16] Ibid., 66.

[17] Ibid., 67.

[18] Victoria Sims, telephone interview by the author, Little Rock, Arkansas, 2 August 1992.

[19] Olcott, *Colored Women*, 5, 67.

[20] Ibid., 67.

[21] Ibid.; E.M. Woods, *Blue Book of Little Rock and Argenta* (Little Rock: Central Printing Co., 1907), 60-61.

[22] Ibid.

[23] Ibid.; a blue triangle was an early symbol of the YWCA Girl Reserve, which originated in the fall of 1918 and became Y-Teens in the 1940s. It also came to symbolize sisterhood in all lands and to represent the unity of body, mind and spirit.

[24] Ibid., 68.

[25] Ibid.

[26] Peggy Harris, "The Bringing in of the Kingdom of God: The Young Women's Christian Association at Little Rock, 1911-1991," Unpublished manuscript, Seminar in Public History, 1991,University of Arkansas, Little Rock.

[27] Carl Moneyhon, "Black Politics in Arkansas During the Gilded Age," *Arkansas Historical Quarterly*, 44 (Autumn 1985): 225.

[28] Olcott, *Colored Women*, 68, Appendix.

[29] Olcott, *Colored Women*, 14; "Minutes Board of Directors of the Young Women's Christian Association 1913-1918," 12 December 1917.

[30] "Y.W.C.A. News 1918-1919," 24 July 1918, Bess Chisum Stephens YWCA records.

[31] Adolphine Fletcher Terry, *Life Is My Song*, Also, unpublished manuscript, n.d., 130, Special Collections, Ottenheimer Library Archives, University of Arkansas, Little Rock.

[32] Olcott, *Colored Women*, 14.

[33] Ibid.

[34] Olcott, *Colored Women*, 14; "Information on Y.W.C.A. Building," Records of Mrs. Charles F. W. Loewer, Bess Chisum Stephens YWCA records.

[35] Little Rock and North Little Rock City Directory (Little Rock: Southern Directory Company, 1919).

[36] Olcott, *Colored Women*, 68.

[37] Ibid.

[38] "Y.W.C.A. News 1918-1919," 23 April 1919, Bess Chisum Stephens YWCA records.

[39] Charles Brough, "Little Rock During the World War," *Arkansas Gazette*, Little Rock Centennial Edition, 7 November 1931, Part IV, 5.

[40] "Minutes of the Colored Work Committee, March 7, 1919," YWCA of the U.S.A., National Board Archives, New York.

[41] Pulaski County Circuit Clerk, *Deed Book* 139, 55-56, Little Rock, Arkansas.

[42] "Minutes of the Colored Work Committee, October 31, 1919," YWCA of the U.S.A., National Board Archives, New York.

[43] Olcott, *Colored Women*, 68-69.

[44] Ibid., 67; *Arkansas State Press*, 27 April 1951, 5; Sue Cowan Williams interview.

[45] "Phyllis Wheatley Branch YWCA Twenty-Ninth Annual Meeting and Dinner January Tenth, 1946," a program in the author's possession; "Minutes Board Meetings 1942," 11 November 1942, Bess Chisum Stephens YWCA records; Ozell Sutton, "Y Center For Negroes Is Popular," *Arkansas Democrat*, 19 April 1953, 6 (A); *Survey of Negroes in Little Rock and North Little Rock*, comp. Writer's Program of the Works Projects Administration in the State of Arkansas (Sponsored by the Urban League of Greater Little Rock, 1941), 92.

46 Sutton, "Y Center For Negroes"; *Survey of Negroes*, 92; Frances Thornton Poe, telephone interview by author, Little Rock and New York, 27 May 1992. Poe, the daughter of Elizabeth Thornton, one of the founders of the Phyllis Wheatley YWCA, said that a Mrs. Bessie [probably Maggie] Ashford allowed the group to use her home on Pulaski Street between 15th and 16th streets in its early years; Sutton says the Gaines Street building opened in 1921, but Little Rock city directories do not list the Phyllis Wheatley YWCA at 924 Gaines until 1923.

47 Terry, My Song, 130-131.

48 *The Little Rock Survey: A Four Weeks Study of Public and Private Social Work in Greater Little Rock Arkansas April 1939* (New York: Association of Community Chests and Councils, Inc., 1939), 180.

49 Adrienne Lash Jones, "Phyllis/Phillis Wheatley Clubs and Homes,"1992 draft manuscript for the *Encyclopedia of Black Women's History*. Jones says the Phyllis Wheatley name became almost synonymous with residences for old and young black women and was a popular nomenclature with the organization of the national black women's club movement in the late 1800s. She says that at some point, the correctly spelled "Phillis" was updated to "Phyllis."

50 *The Arkansas State Press*, a black newspaper at Little Rock, mentions another Phyllis Wheatley Club from time to time during its publication in the 1940s and 1950s, and Phyllis Wheatley YWCA members remember the club as being separate from the YWCA. Apparently, it was a small group of women who met socially on a regular basis.

51 C. E. Bush, "Little Rock Negroes Have Made Much Progress in Business Activities," Arkansas Democrat, 6 November 1921, 8. Bush says the Phyllis Wheatley YWCA was started by "local negro women aided by members of the white 'Y'."

52 Smith, Little Rock Vice Commission, 25-27.

53 Ibid., 25-26.

54 Ibid.

55 Ibid., 26.

56 *Survey of Negroes*, 55.

57 "Y.W.C.A. News," 7 July 1920, Y.W.C.A. Minutes January 1919, Bess Chisum Stephens YWCA records.

58 Fon Louise Gordon, "Black Women in Arkansas," *Pulaski County Historical Review* 35 (Summer 1987): 26, 28-30.

59 Frances Thornton Poe interview; Woods, *Blue Book*, 61- 62. Woods says Thornton taught four years. Poe said her mother taught two years.

60 Frances Thornton Poe interview.

61 Ibid.

62 "Urban League of Arkansas, Inc. Golden Anniversary Celebration 1937-1987" (Little Rock: Urban League of Arkansas); Gordon, "Black Women," 29-30; the *Arkansas Survey*, a black Little Rock newspaper, lists a Mrs. A. B. Ives as its city editor

and reporter in a September 20, 1924, issue. Most likely, this is the same Ives who helped start the Phyllis Wheatley YWCA.

[63] Gordon, "Black Women," 29 - 30; Erle Chambers, "The Tuberculosis Sanatorium for Negroes," n. d., Special Collections, Ottenheimer Library, University of Arkansas, Little Rock; "Urban League Golden Anniversary," 12; Terry, My Song, 131.

[64] *Arkansas State Press*, 8 December 1950, 8; *Arkansas Gazette*, 3 November 1959, 7 (B); *Arkansas State Press*, 27 April 1951, 5; Smith, *Little Rock Vice Commission*, 3, 27; G. P. Hamilton, *Beacon Lights of the Race*, Vol. I (Memphis, Tenn.: P. H. Clarke and Brother, 1911), 173-174; *Arkansas State Press*, 27 April 1951, 5.

[65] Hamilton, *Beacon Lights*, 173-174.

[66] Frances Thornton Poe interview.

[67] Gordon, "Black Women," 29-30.

[68] "Minutes Board of Directors Young Women's Christian Association 1913-1918," 9 May 1917, Bess Chisum Stephens YWCA records. The minutes that day also mention that the board approved a motion to aid the Patriotic League during the war, but it is unclear whether this was a black girls' or white girls' group.

[69] Bush, "Little Rock Negroes."

[70] Louise Patterson, "The Diocese of Arkansas 1838-1951," Unpublished manuscript, n.d., Special Collections, Ottenheimer Library, University of Arkansas, Little Rock.

[71] Bernice McSwain, interview by author, tape recording, Little Rock, Arkansas, 13 January 1992.

[72] "Y Notes," *Arkansas State Press*, 3 March 1944, 7; "Appraisal Report For Arkansas State Highway Department, Little Rock, Arkansas," Project No. 1-630 - 2 (94) 140, Job No. 6873, June 29, 1972; also, Bernice McSwain has a photograph of the front entrance, which shows the inscription.

[73] "Appraisal Report"; Victoria Sims, interview by author, tape recording, Little Rock, Arkansas, 6 March 1992; Bernice McSwain interview.

[74] Victoria Sims interview.

[75] "Little Rock and the Phyllis Wheatley Club," *Arkansas Gazette*, 27 February 1922, 4.

[76] Ibid.

[77] "Little Rock and the Phyllis Wheatley Club," *Arkansas Gazette*; Victoria Sims interview.

[78] Mattie Davis, interview with author, tape recording, Little Rock, Arkansas, 6 February 1992.

[79] Bernice McSwain interview.

[80] Agnes Hunter, interview by author, tape recording, Little Rock, Arkansas, 10 February 1992; Bernice McSwain interview.

[81] *Arkansas Survey*, 20 September 1924.

[82] "Little Rock and the Phyllis Wheatley Club," *Arkansas Gazette*, 27 February 1922, 4; *Arkansas Survey*, 20 September 1924; Frances Thornton Poe interview.

[83] "Resolutions/Minutes 1924-1931," 10 March 1926, Bess Chisum Stephens YWCA records. Lila Ashby, executive secretary of the Little Rock YWCA, announced she would meet with the Phyllis Wheatley Club as requested. "Minutes, Board of Directors of Young Women's Christian Association 1919-1923," 14 February 1923, Bess Chisum Stephens YWCA records.

[84] "A History of the United Way," United Way of Pulaski County records.

[85] Arkansas Tuberculosis Sanatorium Files, Special Collections, Ottenheimer Library, University of Arkansas, Little Rock.

[86] Ibid.

[87] Fred Berry and John Novak, *The History of Arkansas* (Little Rock: Rose Publishing Company, 1987), 187.

[88] *Survey of Negroes*, 92.

[89] Ibid., 56-57.

[90] Ibid.

[91] "Phyllis Wheatley Branch YWCA Twenty-Ninth Annual Meeting and Dinner."

The Work Projects Administration in the Pulaski County District, 1935-1943

By Lynda B. Langford

Lynda B. Langford had been a social studies teacher in Jonesboro, Arkansas, before moving to Little Rock and taking a position as educational coordinator at the Arkansas Territorial Restoration (now Historic Arkansas Museum), where she was when she wrote this article. She went on to study law and was a legal advisor for the Arkansas State Workers Compensation Commission until her retirement five years ago. Among other virtues, this article illustrates the highly-important role played by New Deal programs in Arkansas during the Depression.

"It will be a ticklish job . . ." remarked W. R. Dyess, the new state administrator of the Works Progress Administration as he addressed his staff on July 8, 1935. Dyess was in charge of transforming what had been the Arkansas Emergency Relief Administration that had provided aid, relief, or welfare to the unemployed into a federal agency that provided jobs and paid work. "We will dictate the operation of the program," said Dyess, "yet at the same time, the various local governmental agencies must sponsor our projects and make a contribution . . . That is the picture . . . let's get organized and get going."[1]

In this manner the Works Progress Administration began a work relief program in Arkansas. The program reached all sections of the state through eight district offices and continued until July 1, 1939, when it was succeeded by the Work Projects Administration. (Hereinafter, WPA is used for both agencies.) The WPA continued work relief programs until it was liquidated on May 1, 1943. Established by executive order in April 1935, the WPA was designed to get the federal government out of direct aid (leaving this field to the states and municipalities) and into a system of work relief, by providing jobs for the unemployed[2] The federal government ended all direct relief payments on November 30, 1935, and the individual states were responsible for such payments after that date.

The Works Progress Administration provided an organizational structure to channel approximately $50 million in assistance to the state. This figure represented the amount Arkansas was to receive from the $4 billion relief fund established by the Congress in 1935. Arkansas received the assistance, not by monthly grants, but by requisitions for materials, administration, labor, and equipment against a designated monthly amount.[3] Because of the restrictions placed on these funds in the beginning, however, even tools and materials could not be purchased to carry on work projects, though labor could be made available to state and local government agencies for various work projects. Unfortunately, towns and cities were nearly bankrupt and could not afford to buy materials for projects of permanence. It was during these early months of federal assistance that various WPA projects were described as being in the "leaf-raking era."[4]

With the high concentration of people in central Arkansas, and the resulting heavy relief burden, Pulaski County became a part of the Works Progress Administration district with the largest quota of jobs for the unemployed. Those counties in District Three (hereinafter called Pulaski) were Pulaski, Faulkner, Garland, Grant, Hot Spring, Lonoke, Prairie, and Saline counties. Over one hundred construction projects involving repairs or new construction and hundreds of non-construction projects were completed between 1935 and 1943. Several construction projects in Pulaski County were unique. Thus, the WPA, in the Pulaski County district, 1935-1943 is the focus of this paper.

By November 1935, the WPA work relief program was well underway. Some 30,720 persons (6,000 in Pulaski County) were on the payrolls, and approximately 2,500 more were at work but had not received their first paychecks.[5] A total of 1,418 projects had been approved statewide by November 1935 with sixteen of those projects approved in November for Pulaski County.[6] Those sixteen projects were approved at an estimated cost of $400,000. As will be seen, bridges, storm drains, streets, curbs, water mains, and community service activities were on the list of projects slated for assistance.

Five thousand women had been placed on 214 projects by November 1935. Blanche Ralston, southern regional director of the Works Progress Administration women's division, reported that Arkansas was the first of twelve southern states to assign all women who met the eligibility requirements to projects allotted to the states.[7] Over 4,000 women were assigned to 123 sewing projects. The remainder were placed in clerical projects, library and book binding jobs, playground projects, historical surveys, nursing projects, and the writers' project. Pulaski County ranked second in the job placement of women in 1935 with 753 women placed in jobs, led by the Pine Bluff district with 903 women placed.[8]

In November 1935 the WPA Arkansas Writers' Project began. This project was "set up to employ writers, editors, historians, research workers, art critics, architects, archeologists, map draftsmen, geologists, and other professional workers to prepare material for an American Guide and to accumulate new research material on matters of local, historical, art and scientific interest in the United States."[9]

As a part of the Writers' Project in Pulaski County, local writers prepared

annual reports for the various departments of city government for recommendation to the mayor or council of aldermen. For example, the Little Rock Fire
Department report for January 1, 1936 - January 1, 1937, recounted that the fire
department answered 1,868 alarms in 1936, of which 1,707 were actual fires.
There were 949 fire hydrants in Little Rock and 26,450 feet of hose in service.
One fatality occurred to a fireman as he fell through the pole hole at the station
while preparing to respond to an alarm.[10]

The annual report of the Parks and Sanitation Department for Little Rock
cited the work of the Works Progress Administration by saying:

> This organization has rendered us valuable assistance in adding sev-
> eral thousand yards of gravel to low streets, and has aided material-
> ly to our yardage of paved streets and footage of curb and gutter.
> WPA constructed twenty-four bridges with permanent bottoms and
> sidewalls.[11]

In addition to annual reports, local writers produced historical writings about
Arkansas, wrote biographical profiles of famous citizens, prepared statistical
information, worked on putting the city ordinances in digest form, organized
newspaper clippings, and produced documents. (A nine-page checklist in the
Writers' Project file dated April 8, 1937, included thirty-two categories of documents for production with a space for the title, date, copies, and notes.)[12]

Personal tragedy occurred in the administrative hierarchy of the WPA in
Arkansas in January 1936 when W. R. Dyess, returning from Washington, was
killed in a plane crash at Goodwin, Arkansas. Floyd Sharp, the Deputy
Administrator, was then appointed as head of the agency. Sharp, the fourth
administrator for federal relief programs in Arkansas brought considerable
administrative experience to the position.[13] In addition to his experience as
deputy administrator of the WPA and as executive secretary of the Emergency
Relief Commission, Sharp also worked for the Arkansas Department of Labor,
the First Reconstruction Finance Corporation, and the Civil Works
Administration. Those last two agencies combined had been responsible for
nearly $42 million in federal funds.[14]

Concerns for civic improvement were evident from the work projects promoted by the Little Rock city government. With the help of WPA labor, surveys
were made in an attempt to find another good, dependable source of water for
the city. The logical conclusion, following the survey, was the Alum Fork of
Saline River. The city's first movement to obtain a water system began in 1877
when a group of businessmen formed the Home Water Company. However, at
the time, ordinary citizens were still convinced that city cisterns would be the

source of water for many years to come. In 1889, the Home Water Company sold its franchise to Arkansas Water Company, which operated the system until 1936 using wells, reservoirs, and water from the Arkansas River. The city then purchased Arkansas Water Company for $3,850,000 in 1936, financing the purchase with the sale of revenue bonds. Final approval for a loan and grant from the Public Works Administration for $3,080,000 came that same year. Work then began on laying pipes to the Saline River for a new water supply.[15] The system was operational in 1939.

Another example of WPA action came in the form of improvements to the Fair Park Municipal Zoo in 1935-36. This work was unique to Little Rock, which had the only municipal zoo in the state. Projects included completion of the cat house for $30,000 and a monkey house for $65,000, plus the widening of the streets through the site. The 200-acre park easily accommodated the Sunday crowds that averaged 5,000 in summer with 500 of those being out-of-town visitors.[16] The Little Rock Parks and Sanitation annual report had this to say about other park improvements:

> The WPA is doing a wonderful job of beautification. We are fortunate in having their assistance in the construction of the golf course, club house, caddie house, new grass greens, and set off at Ball Park and the paving and widening of all roads.[17]

A report from Mayor R.E. Overman to the 1937 council of aldermen outlined ten major needs in Little Rock that required attention. Six of those listed were areas for which the city sought WPA assistance – parks, paving, jail, a digest of city ordinances, elimination of streetcars, and a municipal auditorium. The report went on to say that on January 26, 1937, the citizens of Little Rock voted three to one in favor of constructing a new municipal auditorium with a 45 percent grant from the Public Works Administration. The projected cost of the building was $650,000. Paving for the parking area and landscaping for the structure were to be provided by the WPA.[18]

By December 1937, construction was underway on the Greco-Modern style building that began to rise at the northeast corner of Markham and Broadway. The building was designed to seat three thousand people in the main auditorium; the arena located in the basement below the main auditorium was designed to seat eight thousand people. The height of the building was the equivalent of a ten-story building and the facility was completely air-conditioned.[19]

By August this impressive facility was known as the Joseph Taylor Robinson Memorial Auditorium. In that month, "a committee composed of Harvey Couch, utilities magnate, Mayor J.V. Satterfield, Jr., Mrs. Joe T. Robinson and former Alderman Jack Pickins,"[20] left for Washington, D.C., to confer with national WPA officials about a $50,000 additional federal grant to properly complete and equip Robinson Memorial Auditorium. The building was completed in late December, and city officials held an open house in January 1940 to allow visitors to inspect the new auditorium. Four thousand people attended the open house where Boy Scouts served as escorts through the newly completed structure.[21]

Nineteen thirty-nine was a year of change for the nation, downtown Little Rock, and the WPA. For the nation, change occurred in the growth of the economy as the reverberations from the European war began to affect the country's industrial output; for downtown Little Rock, change occurred as the restoration of old, dilapidated buildings transformed an eyesore into an historical park; for the WPA changes occurred when the new work relief act of 1939-40 ended the Works Progress Administration and provided for its successor, the Work Projects Administration to continue work relief with different regulations. All of these changes, moreover, were linked directly or indirectly with the WPA and its activities.

In Little Rock positive signs of change occurred for the downtown area as a small group of public-spirited, local citizens began a series of meetings in January 1939. Calling themselves the Arkansas Host and Historical Society, this group wanted to improve the state's tourist industry. They offered "a constructive plan for building the fame and fortune of Arkansas."[22]

One of those citizens was Louise Loughborough (Mrs. J. Fairfax Loughborough), vice-regent of the Mount Vernon Ladies Association of the Union, the commission in charge of restoring and preserving George Washington's home in Virginia. Mrs. Loughborough, a member of the Little Rock Planning Commission, was cited in a 1939 newspaper article as an "authority on architecture and furnishings of early Arkansas buildings."[23] As a member of the Planning Commission, Mrs. Loughborough had advance information about the condemnation of the old buildings along Cumberland and Third streets. The article continued,

> A historical restoration project of interest to the entire state will be undertaken during 1939 by a committee of Little Rock citizens in an effort to prevent loss to the city and the state of historically valuable and important property between Second and Third Streets on the west side of Cumberland Street.

> All buildings of no historical interest on the half-block of the ground will be removed and the grounds planted in relation to the period in

which the buildings were erected. The resultant park is only a few blocks from hotels, bus stations and bus and streetcar lines. Efforts to acquire the property are underway, and a WPA project for carrying on the work has been established. The National Park Service has promised technical aid in architecture, engineering and landscaping.[24]

With the public announcement of the restoration project, Work Projects Administration of Arkansas, Project Number 6892-3 began. But the project number served as only one of many identifying names for the restoration. Lumber companies and manufacturers, as determined by five representative invoices, could not agree on a name for this project. Leird Lumber Company named the project "Territorial Restoration" on its invoice but listed the address as Third and Rock streets.[25] Dyke Brothers, a manufacturer and wholesaler with branches in seven states according to the invoice heading, called the project "Committee to Restore Ark. Territorial Capital" [sic][26] with the address correctly stated. The same kind of error appeared on both the typed and the handwritten invoices from the Arkmo Lumber Company, which named the project "Committee on Restoration of Territorial Capital" [sic].[27] Enterprise Lumber Company gave the project the garbled name "Committee to Restoring Territorial Property" [sic].[28] This particular invoice bore a circled, one-word notation in the lower right corner – "rejected!"

However, Mrs. Loughborough's appeal to the Arkansas General Assembly for $30,000 was not rejected. With $17,500 she bought the half-block portion along Cumberland of Block 32 for the State of Arkansas. The WPA supplemented that amount with a $37,000 appropriation for labor costs. In August 1939, restoration began on the entire half block between Second and Third streets along Cumberland. According to an Arkansas Gazette feature article in 1950, "the WPA uttering glad cries over being able to do something more substantial than rake leaves took over the demolition job." [29]

Such a flurry of restoration and construction also generated a flurry of paperwork for the project's sponsor, the Territorial Restoration Commission. An individual account for bookkeeping purposes was established for each WPA project. Each month a report was prepared itemizing the federal funds expended for payroll, for purchase of materials, for rental of equipment, and for other items. Payroll numbers had to be further subdivided to indicate the dollar amounts paid to relief workers (those certified as eligible for relief assistance by the WPA) and to non-relief workers. For example, from January 8 - January 31, 1941, $290.96 in federal funds was spent on the Restoration project but only $57.68 of those funds went to non-relief workers. Roughly, 80 percent of those federal funds went to the relief workers while only 20 percent went to non-relief workers. For the same reporting period, the sponsor's contribution to the Restoration was $214.87 or 42 percent of the total of $505.83 expended.[30] In addition, the sponsor had to complete WPA Form 710 called "Certification of Sponsor's Contribution (Materials, Supplies, and Equipment)," which had to be signed by the sponsor, the project supervisor, and a WPA reviewing official.[31]

The Restoration project had been slated for completion in about a year; however, it was two years before the doors were officially opened on July 19, 1941, at 2:00 p.m. The buildings were open Tuesday-Sunday, from 9:30 a.m. to 5:30 p.m. and 1:00 to 5:30 p.m. on Mondays. Admission was twenty-five cents a person except for soldiers and children who were admitted for ten cents.[32] The cooperative venture between the Territorial Restoration Commission and the WPA, financed by the Arkansas General Assembly and private donations, brought a great change in Block 32 of the Original City of Little Rock.[33]

The Works Progress Administration (WPA) came to an end on June 30, 1939. A new agency called the Work Projects Administration (WPA) succeeded the old WPA as President Roosevelt signed the legislation into law. Floyd Sharp was appointed administrator of the new organization. One of his first actions was to reappoint "administrative employees of the old WPA on active pay status to the same position with the new WPA."[34]

Some of the changes under the new legislation included abolition of the hourly rate for the project workers; the substitution of a 130-hour per month work schedule for all workers; a reduction of the monthly quota of workers; cancellation of employment for thirty days for workers continuously employed for more than eighteen months; the limitation of the WPA allotment for constructing federal and non-federal public buildings; the requirement that contributions by project sponsors equal 25 percent of the project cost; and cancellation of the non-security wage. According to Sharp, the most far-reaching requirement of the new act was the one affecting the 130-hour per month schedule, which hit skilled workers the hardest. The skilled WPA workers in Little Rock earned $1 per hour; their work was limited to 66 hours resulting in a security wage of $66 for the month. Under the new act, their security wage remained the same but their hours were increased to 130 hours per month. Unskilled workers locally were affected little by the new regulation since their monthly hours of work averaged about 130 hours. Professional/technical workers in Pulaski County also worked more hours than the skilled workers with their hours ranging from 104-137 per month.[36]

Within days, a nationwide reaction set in to the changes in the work relief law. WPA workers in six northern and eastern states walked off their jobs by the hundreds to man picket lines in protest. Conflicts between labor and management leaders resulted in several injuries and at least one fatality. Leaders of the American Federation of Labor were divided as to whether they should encourage the strikes or appeal to Congress to restore the wage rates to WPA workers.[37] The newsletter of the Congress of Industrial Organizations asserted that longer hours were only one factor in the dispute. Other factors cited were the starvation layoffs for any WPA worker on the payrolls for eighteen months or more and the impending layoffs of one million workers decreed for the coming year.[38] By the time the strikes ended in mid-July, some 18,000-20,000 WPA workers had been dismissed on orders from WPA headquarters; these were strikers who had been on strike and away from the job for five days or more. From newspaper accounts during July 1939, it appeared that there were few strikes in Arkansas and Pulaski County. One obvious reason was the announcement by F.C. Harrington, national administrator of the WPA, that wages in the South would be increased while those in the North and West would be decreased under the legislative provision of the new act that called for a readjustment in the geographical differentials of the workers' pay.[39] Strategic labor relations actions by WPA officials coupled with an absence of strong labor organizations served to create a relatively tranquil labor atmosphere in Pulaski County and the state among WPA workers.[40] According to the WPA Final Report:

> About the time the WPA started several efforts were made to organize the workers in various labor organizations. After one such organization had caused a strike in the city of Fort Smith, . . . we decided to inaugurate a system of labor relations which has never been printed in the book of rules.

We employed as labor relations officials two members of the typographical union, both of them getting somewhat up in years who were known for their staunch loyalty to organized labor and fairness. These men did not act as undercover officials. They joined every organization where money would buy a membership, including "Share-The-Wealth" Clubs in rural communities. They attended meetings of the workers and when some uninformed person would take the floor and make a great spellbinding effort to agitate the minds of the workers, one or both of these old gentlemen would follow by giving the facts and assuring the workers that all was being done that could be done under existing regulations and that any grievance presented to them would get a hearing. Under this procedure our labor difficulties disappeared.[41]

The effects of the legislative provision requiring thirty-day layoffs of WPA workers continuously employed on projects for eighteen months were felt in November 1939. Little Rock and Fort Smith were the hardest hit with 4,315 workers dropped from the rolls in Little Rock and 4,255 laid off in Fort Smith. Statewide the displacement amounted to 15,062; [42] however, these numbers were offset somewhat by additional employment authorized in eleven states where crop failures or floods had caused unusual distress in rural areas. The quota for Arkansas was 3,000 additional workers due to drought conditions in north-west Arkansas.[43]

Despite the layoffs, October and November were busy months in Pulaski County for the WPA projects. The dedication of the Helen Keller Memorial Building of the new Arkansas School for the Blind was held in October with Helen Keller as honored guest. Harrington, the national administrator, attended and commented that the new building would be "one of the best of its type undertaken by the WPA." [44]

Workers, also, conducted a survey sponsored by the Pulaski County Planning Board and the cities of Little Rock and North Little Rock. Survey results showed that nearly 48 percent or 15,101 of the 31,490 dwelling units in the county were substandard (needed major repairs) or were unfit for use, had no private toilet and bath, or were occupied by more than two persons per room.[45] A supplementary project was approved for improving a park and recreation area at the auxiliary dam of the Little Rock Municipal Water Works on Highway 10 west of Little Rock.[46]

The University of Arkansas Medical School and University Hospital were improved by the WPA beautification project that began in November 1939. The project included relocating driveways, constructing four tennis courts at Thirteenth and McGowan streets, building additions to a workshop and a storage room, and adding parking spaces for sixty-five automobiles.[47]

November 1939 marked the beginning of another WPA program that touched the lives of more people than any other program with the exception of the Recreation Program. The School Lunch Project, under the joint sponsorship of the WPA and the State Board of Health, began employing more than 3,000 adults and providing hot lunches for 75,000 school children. It also provided families with important information on the proper nutrition for school-age children. The project had widespread approval among school principals, the parent-teacher association, social workers, and other agencies.[48]

A federal food stamp plan began in mid-December 1939 under the auspices of the new Federal Surplus Commodities Corporation. Jacob P. Austin directed the program for Pulaski County. Direct grant recipients from the State Welfare Department and those persons eligible for WPA jobs but who had not been assigned work received the special blue stamps free. Orange stamps were sold to WPA workers and others with sufficient income to purchase the orange stamps.[49] The WPA certified 5,591 families eligible to purchase orange stamps in Pulaski County.[50]

The Recreation Program operated from September 1935 to March 1943. Early participation was limited because Arkansans had little experience with organized recreation. Accusations were made in Arkansas, as in other states, of "paying people to play." However, the Recreation Program came into its own in 1940, the year an army camp was established at Camp Robinson. Through volunteer contributions promoted by the City Recreation Council of Little Rock and the newly organized Civilian Military Council, $50,000 was raised to provide adequate recreation for the soldiers and their families. The WPA was asked to furnish the recreation leadership. A staff of twenty-two workers assisted the WPA supervisor who worked cooperatively with the Young Men's Christian Association (YMCA) director.[51]

The project was located in the old National Bank Building at Third and Main streets in Little Rock. The downtown center, furnished attractively, provided lounges, game rooms, classrooms, and reading rooms for soldiers whose attendance plus that of civilians ran as high as 615,000 in a typical month. In one weekend period, 23,000 persons went through the center.[52]

The WPA staff worked with civic clubs and other groups to organize and arrange entertainment for the soldiers. Regular Saturday night dances were held at the City Auditorium and the Women's City Club with other civic clubs assisting. Military dance bands and the WPA orchestra provided the music.

Later, when the United Service Organization (USO) came into existence in 1941, this recreation project was well established. The building was then purchased with federal funds and its operations transferred to the USO.[53]

In 1942 the Recreation Council and the State Council of Defense cooperated to provide a Community Service Center for military personnel, defense workers, and civilians of Greater Little Rock. Dances were held nightly for war workers and servicemen with Saturday night dances held exclusively for servicemen. Swing-shift dances and breakfast dances were held exclusively for war workers. Qualified dance instructors conducted dancing classes for both soldiers and civilians. Technicolor films were shown occasionally by the Parks Commission, and such games as ping pong, shuffle-board, bridge, checkers, dominoes, and other small board games were also popular.[54]

The WPA Music Project, begun in September 1940, was designed to teach music to low-income groups as well as copy and bind music for use in the project classes and in the public recitals given by the performing units. In March 1942, this project and the Recreation Project merged; the combined program operated until 1943. Activities in Pulaski County for the 24,000 soldiers at Camp Robinson began in January 1941. The following month, the Music Project performance unit, the Little Rock WPA Orchestra, began serving Camp Robinson. That was the first military area in Arkansas to benefit from the various programs and dances. Concerts were also given at institutions such as the Florence Crittenden Home, the Little Rock Boys' Club, the Confederate Home, and University Hospital to name a few; musicals were also given at community festivals in the area. Musical entertainment was provided weekly at the Base Hospital at Camp Robinson.[55]

The WPA turned its attention to national defense in 1940. WPA officials announced "because of the serious world situation, top priority will be given to projects contributing to the national defense."[56] Construction of municipal airports, highways, and armories were listed as projects important to the national defense. A long-hoped-for improvement program for runways, drives, parking areas, and an administration building began at Adams Field, the Little Rock Municipal Airport; Little Rock voters had approved a $75,000 bond issue for this WPA project. Dedication of the airport project came on Armistice Day, November 11, 1941.[57]

Early summer 1941 brought good economic news for Pulaski County. Two defense plants were announced for the towns of Jacksonville and Marche, both within a fifteen mile radius of Little Rock.[58] The fuse and detonator plant at Jacksonville (Arkansas Ordnance Works) and the smaller plant at Marche (Maumelle Ordnance Plant) employed 9,000 workers when completed.[59] In December 1941 following the Pearl Harbor attack and the declaration of war on Japan, those workers donated a day's work at the two plants and saved the government nearly $40,000.[60]

The National Industrial Conference, meeting December 23, 1941, predicted a general labor shortage. Employment for 1941 was 93.5 percent of the normal labor force. Expansion of the armed forces by two to three million soldiers would completely absorb the available workers in the market. The need was so great, according to the Conference reports, "that an extended work week and the entrance of new people into the work force, i.e., housewives, students of working age, and retired workers, can not be long postponed." [61]

The death knell had begun to sound for the WPA following the peak years of 1935-1940. On June 6, 1942, the Civilian Conservation Corps (hereinafter CCC) ended after the House Appropriations Committee called for Congress to dissolve the agency. When the House of Representatives rejected funds for the CCC, it was all over for the nine-year-old agency. Only days later the WPA bill survived in the House by a vote of 277-52; however, the appropriation was limited to $336 million. This was a fraction of the funds expended in the peak year 1939 when three million persons were on WPA rolls and the agency spent $2.23 billion.[62]

Six months later in December 1942, President Roosevelt, citing wartime increases in private employment that had made the agency unnecessary, ordered states to liquidate their WPA state agencies by February 1 or as soon as possible. Sixteen were liquidated by February 1. All were to be completed by June 30, 1943.[63]

In Arkansas, liquidation plans were to be completed by May 1, 1943. Clients were dropped rapidly to effect an orderly and speedy liquidation.[64] No consideration was given for their need of employment; no new workers were assigned; no new projects were undertaken. Twenty building projects were to be completed by May with crews transferred from project to project to speed completion. Among those were three projects in Little Rock and one in Pulaski County. These were the State Hospital, Little Rock High School, the School for the Blind, and Pulaski County Hospital.

Editorials in several newspapers around the state reflected on the passing of the agency with phrases that suggested a tone of "good riddance."[65] The *Marked Tree Tribune* said the WPA had outlived its usefulness three years ago. The *Camden News* hoped that other government agencies in the "bleeding hearts" category would be dragged away from the feeding trough known as the national treasury.[66] Only the *Arkansas Democrat* acknowledged the achievements of what it termed the greatest social and economic experiment in the United States; however, it hoped that the WPA would never be revived.[67]

> John Grover of the Associated Press wrote as the headline for his feature article "WPA DIES UNMOURNED AND NO FUNERAL SERVICE." He went on to say the tombstone might read:

> WPA killed by war prosperity, May 1, 1943, aged seven years . . . . Construction work accounted for most of WPA activity but cultural and community service enterprises ridiculed as "boondoggling" caused the most controversy.

> The WPA left a permanent imprint on the culture of the nation with

2,500 mural paintings, 16,500 pieces of sculpture, 108,000 easel works for public buildings. No other agency ever gave such a boost to struggling artists. Theatre projects pumped new life into legitimate theatre. In construction of public buildings, the WPA made important contributions to present day life with 664,000 miles of highway, 5,700 new schools, 200 new hospitals, 140 new libraries, and 8,100 new parks, 950 sewage-treatment plants, 16,000 miles of water mains and 15,000 miles of drainage ditches.

Military authorities will argue that the airport building program (800 in all) made the WPA worth its salt. Almost without exception, they are in military use today.[68]

In Pulaski County alone, the following list includes a general summary of the physical accomplishments of the Operations Division of the WPA and the non-construction accomplishments of the Service Division.

OPERATIONS DIVISION - Pulaski County

Structures Completed

Educational 10

Non-educational (sponsored by State of Arkansas) 22

Non-educational
(sponsored by Little Rock and Pulaski County) 25

Buildings Repaired or Enlarged

Educational 19

Non-educational...83

Building operations expenditures for the above equaled $1,707,200 for a total of 159 buildings. Twelve of the buildings included in the 159 structures were buildings at the Territorial Restoration.

County Roads improvements (paving or grading or application of gravel) - 322 miles.

Little Rock and North Little Rock street improvements - 52 miles.

Road improvements expenditures for the above: $6,976,800 for a total of 374 miles.

The total WPA funds spent in Pulaski County for these construction projects of the Operations Division totaled $13,914,500. Statewide, there were 3,073 projects listed in this division.

SERVICE DIVISION - Pulaski County

In the Service Division there were 138 total projects statewide but no break-down was given by counties for these; however, from related newspaper articles, it appears that there were over 100 local units of these projects in Pulaski County.[69]

Floyd Sharp said his good-byes in a letter to the WPA employees. "All things must end and our number has been called . . . . All citizens must turn their minds, hearts, and hands to the tasks that are most urgent in our crises."[70] The task that had begun in the Depression crisis of the 1930s with a challenge from W. R. Dyess, the first state WPA administrator, had now ended in the war crisis of the 1940s with a similar challenge from Floyd Sharp, the last state WPA administrator. The work of the WPA was now a part of the history of Pulaski County, Arkansas, and the nation.

NOTES

This article first appeared in the *Pulaski County Historical Review*, 35 (Spring 1987): 2-15.

[1] Work Projects Administration, "Final Report of Arkansas Report of Arkansas Work Projects Administration, In Liquidation, March 1, 1943," Little Rock, Arkansas, unnumbered.

[2] Calvin D. Linton, ed., *The Bicentennial Almanac* (New York: Thomas Nelson, Inc., 1975) p. 336.

[3] Clipping, June 26, 1935, Work Projects Administration Scrapbook, No. 5, 1935, Floyd Sharp Collection, Arkansas History Commission, Little Rock, Arkansas.

[4] Work Projects Administration, "Final Report."

[5] Clipping, November 23, 1935, Sharp Collection.

[6] Ibid., October 6, 1935.

[7] Ibid., November 14, 1935.

[8] Ibid., November 22, 1935.

[9] Work Projects Administration, "Final Report."

[10] Work Projects Administration, Pulaski County Source File, 1935-43, Arkansas History Commission, Little Rock, Arkansas.

[11] Ibid.

[12] Ibid.

[13] "Sharp's predecessors were W. A. Rooksberry, Edward I. McKinley, Sr., and W. R. Dyess. Clipping, August 28, 1928, Sharp Collection.

[14] Ibid.

[15] Work Projects Administration, Pulaski County Source File.

16 Ibid.

17 Ibid.

18 Ibid.

19 Ibid.

20 *Arkansas Gazette*, August 6, 1939.

21 Work Projects Administration, Pulaski County Source File.

22 Bulletin, Box XXIX, 1939 Small Manuscript Collection, Mrs. J.F. Loughborough, Arkansas History Commission, Little Rock, Arkansas.

23 *Arkansas Gazette*, January 1, 1939.

24 Ibid. Members of the committee were James H. Penick, Fred W. Allsopp, Mrs. Mahlon D. Moorhead Wright, Gordon H. Campbell, and Mrs. Loughborough, chairman, all of Little Rock.

25 Leird Invoice, 1940, Arkansas Territorial Restoration, Invoice Collection, Arkansas Territorial Restoration (renamed Historic Arkansas Museum), Little Rock, Arkansas.

26 Ibid., Dyke Invoice, 1940.

27 Ibid., Arkmo Invoice, 1939.

28 Ibid., Enterprise Invoice, 1939.

29 Clipping, 1950, Arkansas Territorial Restoration Scrapbooks, Book I, 1941-1957, Arkansas Territorial Restoration (renamed Historic Arkansas Museum), Little Rock, Arkansas.

30 Ibid., Monthly Report, 1941.

31 Ibid., Form 710, undated.

32 *Arkansas Gazette*, July 16, 1941.

33 Governor Carl Bailey signed the 1939 legislation authorizing $30,000. The bill had been proposed by Senator I. N. Moore of Dumas, Arkansas Territorial Restoration Scrapbooks, Book 1, 1941-1957, Arkansas Territorial Restoration (renamed Historic Arkansas Museum), Little Rock, Arkansas.

34 *Arkansas Gazette*, July 2, 1939.

36 Ibid.

37 Ibid., July 16, 1939.

38 Ibid., July 13, 1939.

39 Ibid., July 16, 1939.

40 Ibid., July 13, 1939.

41 Work Projects Administration, "Final Report."

42 *Arkansas Gazette*, November 15, 1939.

43 Ibid., November 14, 1939.

[44] Ibid, November 3, 1939.

[45] Ibid., November 8, 1939.

[46] Ibid., November 19, 1939.

[47] Work Projects Administration, "Final Report."

[48] Ibid.

[49] *Arkansas Gazette*, December 2, 1939.

[50] Ibid, December 30, 1939.

[51] Work Projects Administration, "Final Report."

[52] Ibid.

[53] Ibid.

[54] Ibid.

[55] Ibid.

[56] *Arkansas Gazette*, May 19, 1940.

[57] Clipping, November 11, 1941, Sharp Collection.

[58] *Arkansas Gazette*, June 6, 1941.

[59] With the influx of defense workers, the population of Pulaski County increased from 156,085 to 176,000 between April 1940 and May 1942, an increase of 12.8 percent. Ibid., December 2, 1942.

[60] Ibid., December 20, 1941.

[61] Ibid., December 23, 1941.

[62] Ibid., June 12, 1942.

[63] Ibid., December 5, 1942 and December 4, 1942.

[64] Ibid., December 16, 1942.

[65] Clipping, December 10, 1942, Sharp Collection.

[66] Ibid., December 15, 1942.

[67] Ibid., December 6, 1940.

[68] Ibid., April 30, 1943.

[69] Work Projects Administration, "Final Report."

[70] Clipping, December 17, 1942, Sharp Collection.

DR. J. M. ROBINSON, THE ARKANSAS NEGRO DEMOCRATIC ASSOCIATION AND BLACK POLITICS IN LITTLE ROCK, ARKANSAS, 1928-1952 [PART I]

By John Kirk

John A. Kirk was working on a doctoral dissertation at the University of Newcastle-Upon-Tyne when he published this article. The dissertation was later published as "Redefining the Color Line: Black Activism in Little Rock, Arkansas, 1940–1970", and Kirk has since written a number of articles and books on civil rights in the United States. This article appears in a collection of his essays, "Beyond Little Rock: The Origins and Legacies of the 1957 Little Rock School Crisis", published by the University of Arkansas Press in September 2007. Kirk is now senior lecturer at Royal Holloway, University of London. The "Pulaski County History Review" published this article in two parts, only the first, telling the story through 1944, is reprinted here.

The following is not an attempt to provide a comprehensive biography of Dr. J. M. Robinson, a complete history of the Arkansas Negro Democratic Association (ANDA) or a definitive exploration of black politics during the era 1928-1952.[1] Rather, what follows is a brief outline of political trends and events in black politics in an oft neglected era of Arkansas history. It uses as a narrative focus a man and organization whose political fates were very much linked in fortune and experience and who stood at the heart of the black political struggle during the 1930s and 1940s. In advancing the cause of black Democratic politics from the late 1920s, which marked a decline in the activities of the city's black economic elite, to the early 1950s, which saw the emergence of a new black political leadership, Dr. Robinson and ANDA filled a vacuum left between these eras and shared traits found in both.

Dr. Robinson and ANDA were indelibly marked by the era in which they had roots. They stood for a participation in politics led mainly by the educated few. They mobilized their forces in a separate organization which was for the most part happy to co-exist with a "white" Democratic Party. There were no appeals for social equality or mass participation by blacks in politics,[2] nor a strategic use of the black vote at elections. In this sense they reflected the more "accommodationist" and non-conflict seeking models associated with black leaders and organizations of the time.

However, having said this, Dr. Robinson and ANDA (albeit reluctantly) pioneered the struggle for black participation in politics through the Arkansas courts. They were the first to initiate the idea of blacks gaining real power via the ballot box since the period of Reconstruction politics, encouraging payment of the poll tax and building a reservoir of qualified black voters in the process. They also helped lead the way for the idea of a black organization forming a political grassroots network throughout the various state counties, a new and important innovation. Many of these approaches are associated more with "protest" leadership models, which were prevalent in much later years.[3]

While reflecting the more limited forms of black expression which existed in the 1920s and 1930s, Dr. Robinson and ANDA went a long way in providing blueprints and laying the groundwork upon which a new leadership could build, extend and develop in later years. Although ANDA did develop over time, trying to adapt to a changing social and political climate, it failed to do so quickly and comprehensively enough to stave off its eventual demise.

John Marshall Robinson was born in Pickens, Mississippi, around 1880, son of Mr. Amos G. and Mrs. Isabelle Robinson. After being educated in the public school system, he attended Rust College, entering Meharry Medical College at Nashville, Tennessee, in 1898. After passing the Arkansas Board of Medical Examiners he went on to practice medicine in Newport from 1901 to 1904, returning to school again at Knoxville Medical College, where he graduated as a valedictorian. He resumed practice at Newport for a year before finally moving to Little Rock, where he practiced at Seventh and Main streets.[4]

After his final move to Little Rock, Dr. Robinson seems to have been active in community affairs and organizations. In 1905 he helped organize the Pulaski County Medical, Dental and Pharmaceutical Association, a black medical society which still exists to this day.[5] However, unlike other leading members of Little Rock's black professional community at the time, what might be regarded as Little Rock's black ruling elite, he does not seem to have had a close involvement with the fraternal groups to which most of these people belonged. Instead, the first organization in which he took an active interest was the NAACP. He was one of the founding members of the local branch in Little Rock when it applied for a charter from the national organization on July 4, 1918.[6]

The early years of the NAACP in Little Rock were fairly uninspiring as far as concrete achievements go. Its membership was made up of recognizable names from the well-to-do black elite, like A. E. and C. E. Bush, I. T. Gillam, G. W. Ish, and J. A. Booker (among others),[7] many of whom were already members of fraternal organizations, most notably the Grand Mosaic Templars of America.[8] It seems that while it may have been felt prestigious to belong to the NAACP, nothing but lip service was paid to it as a new organization in town. The more established fraternal organizations seem to have been the primary concern of these leaders and the initial interest in the NAACP soon faded away.[9]

Most of the politically active members of the Mosaic Templars, the largest black organization of the time, were Republicans. Scipio Jones, one of the foremost leaders from the black community associated with the Republican Party, practiced law out of the Mosaic Templars building and acted as the organization's attorney. Jones had fought a long battle throughout the 1920s to regain a place in the party for blacks which had been usurped by "lily white"

Republicans. Although in 1928 a compromise had been effected to restore black participation in the party, the relationship between black and white Republicans continued as the less-than-blissful political "marriage" it had always been.[10] In the same year that black Republicans had regained a place in their party, Dr. Robinson set about on a radically different course, seeking participation in the party of the South, an alliance with the Democrats.

It is interesting to speculate as to the reasons why the formation of ANDA came about in 1928. It is likely that the Nixon v. Herndon decision, which gave blacks a constitutional precedent for gaining the ballot in Democratic primaries, was a particular motivation,[11] especially in a national context. On the local level, however, this move also may have been a reaction to events in the Republican Party that year. On the one hand, events there may have encouraged blacks to try to join forces with the Democrats too.[12] On the other, it might have reflected a disillusionment with what these black Republicans had been able to achieve in their struggle since becoming part of that party and convinced some to look elsewhere for a political voice. That political voice, it seems to have been decided, could only have an impact by aligning with the Democratic Party. Since all political power in the South emanated from this base, with Arkansas in particular developing as a paradigm of the "purest" one-party state, it might be seen as an "obvious" choice.[13]

The sense of urgency in gaining some say in the political power structure may have also been motivated by other changes in the local situation. The previous year had seen one of the worst incidents of racial violence ever to occur in Little Rock, the macabre burning of a lynched man on West Ninth Street. The ceremonial parading of a lynched, bullet-riddled black body, through black downtown neighborhoods, to be finally burnt on a pile of pews plundered from a leading black church (of which Dr. Robinson was a member), in the heart of the black business community, must have provided not just a slight but a humiliation to the city's black leadership. This leadership had always claimed Little Rock to be a place of "good" relations between the races.[14]

Surely at this point the question must have been asked, after fighting for representation in the Republican Party, forming strong fraternal organizations, and trying to cultivate relations with the white community through goodwill and informal petition, just what had been achieved? This shock to the black community led many to vote with their feet and move out of the city altogether. Some accepted it as an "anomaly" in a city which usually could expect "good" race relations. Dr. Robinson was obviously touched and affected by the situation; he sent his son to college, away from the city, in the wake of the lynching.[15] Dr. Robinson stayed, however, and attempted to exert pressure in a new and different way to empower the black community.

The burning on West Ninth Street marked a speeding up in the gradual decline of Little Rock's black economic elite as an influential "political" power. Although they still continued to be active in community affairs, tenaciously clinging to their status within the black community, the barriers of Jim Crow, the increasing hostility to blacks across the South, together with the Depression of the late 1920s and early 1930s, all served to erode the social and economic influence base of these black leaders.[16]

Perhaps there was no better nor more opportune time for the formation of an organization which took a new direction for black advancement. As the fraternal organizations buckled under the weight of the Depression,[17] a new organization, relatively small and centered around the leadership of one man, emerged. The ANDA was to be a new-vehicle of black political expression through lean years, sustaining a forum of protest as times got tougher, bridging the decline in activity of this economic leadership to the rise of anew political leadership which would become more clearly pronounced in the later 1940s and early 1950s.

The origins of ANDA seem to lie in a meeting held at England, Arkansas, on September 18, 1928. Here seventy-five blacks organized a Smith-Robinson Club in support of the Alfred Smith-Joe T. Robinson Democratic ticket for the White House that year. At the meeting, Dr. Robinson was duly initiated as state president declaring that blacks were "no longer slaves of the Republican Party" and that "labor, thought, concentration, understanding between the races is the possible solution of our progress." Further, he stated: "The Southern white man lends us money, feels our sorrows and helps bear our burden. He extends business courtesies and to a large degree makes possible our success. When we want a favor, we go to him and usually get it."[18]

If this sounds a lot like rhetoric of an "accommodationist" black leader, just like any other at the time, it is worth bearing in mind that alienating the white power structure would have made any real chance of progress, certainly in making headway into the Democratic Party, impossible. Note that cooperation and "understanding" were seen as "possible" solutions, not the only ones. Only through a double-pronged approach, of conciliation and appeals to reason on one hand, and a determination to succeed in gaining a say, with power to act on the other, would advancement of any kind be achieved. If offering an olive branch and genuine support for the cause could not bring the desired ends, other methods and devices of petition were to be available too.

It took only a month between the formation of the Smith-Robinson Clubs and the drawing up of a constitution for the Arkansas Negro Democratic Association. On October 28, 1928, Dr. Robinson, along with P. H. Jordan, I. T. Gillam, F. A. Snodgrass, J. C. Gray and George G. Walker, founded the association and drafted the constitution, of which Article II laid down their three primary goals:

(a) Unite Negroes who believe in the principles of the Democratic Party and who will work to promote its best welfare and expansion;

(b) Encourage them to qualify as voters; and

(c) Educate them in the philosophy of government and the mechanics of voting.[19]

It took less than a month after the organization of ANDA for it to win its first victory. On November 27, 1928. Judge Richard M. Mann of the Second Division Circuit Court, sitting in the absence of Chancellor Frank H. Dodge in the Pulaski County Chancery Court, upheld an application by Dr. Robinson et al for an injunction against the Democratic Party to prevent them from barring blacks from voting in primaries. Denying black participation had previously been done under the Section 5 clause of the party constitution which stated that only "qualified white electors" could cast their ballots. The injunction restrained election officials from preventing "persons qualified to vote from exercising their right of franchise in the Democratic City primary ... on account of race, color, or condition of previous servitude."

Surprisingly, the immediate reaction from Democratic leaders was reported to be "likely they will not offer further opposition to the petition" under threat that it would be taken to the Arkansas, and even United States Supreme Court, if violated. However, the ruling by Judge Mann that as a "precautionary measure" ballots cast by blacks were to be separated at the primary polls, in case of appeal, seems to give some indication as to the expected outcome of events.[20] Nevertheless, incredible as it may seem in the context of the times, blacks held the constitutional right to vote in Democratic city primaries for almost a year, during which time some were actually able to exercise that right. It would be a long battle before they could do so again.[21]

On August 30, 1929, Chancellor Dodge, after studying the suits for several months, during which time officers of the State Central Committee as well as the city Democratic Party had been included in the suit, dismissed the restraining order for want of equity. He cited as precedent the ruling of Justice J. C. Hutcheson of Houston, Texas, in July of 1928, which had claimed that prescribing membership rules of the Democratic Party as "white electors" did not interfere with the casting of black ballots. Rather, it was a rule of affiliation to a privately funded organization which was entitled to make its own membership rules.[22] There may have been a precedent allowing blacks to vote in a federal court ruling in Virginia which had granted blacks the ballot in Democratic primaries, but in Virginia those primaries were financed by the state, whereas in Arkansas primaries were funded by the Democratic Party. Also in Virginia, it was given specifically to the State Committee to draw up membership rules, while in Arkansas no such provision existed. In any case the ruling in Virginia was to be appealed further.[23]

It was this Virginia case that the Arkansas Negro Democrats had looked to for a ruling of precedent before continuing to press their case. In the meantime, Dr. Robinson commented that he felt "that I and my colleagues have been buffed about in a manner unbecoming of Democratic citizens. I feel that we who qualify as Democrats have a right to vote in the primary and that anything less is a reflection upon the integrity and confidence of Democracy in Arkansas."[24] However, his lawsuit, filed as *Robinson v. Holman*, which sought the vote, only led to disappointment. The Arkansas Supreme Court upheld the Democratic Committee and on November 24, the United States Supreme Court refused to entertain the case with no other explanation than "it failed to raise a constitutional question."

The central bone of contention again was whether the Democratic Party could be considered a private organization, which could prescribe its own membership rules. If it was, as the courts contended, then no state laws were violating the rights of blacks to cast their ballot and no crime was being committed. The counter argument of the plaintiffs was that the Democratic primaries constituted public elections, since they chose who would be elected to office, rather than the general election, which became a formality of ratifying the Democrats already chosen to stand. This central issue was to be debated for the next two decades.

Dr. Robinson was philosophical about the outcome of the suit. He noted that "no great height is reached in a day" and urged his people to be "patient." In spite of this he still recognized that: "The race without funds and ignorant of their objectives, cannot get anywhere." It was to be ANDA that made sure that a focus on the objectives remained clear and intact throughout the long haul ahead.[25]

When the Great Depression struck in 1929, it brought many changes. Overnight, seemingly everyone became poor, many losing everything they had. The prevailing politics became the politics of survival on a day-to-day basis. The Depression and its repercussions hit the black community hardest. Black fortunes lost were harder to get back than white. Less-well-off blacks, who made up the majority, found themselves as always at the bottom of the economic pile and hardest hit by disaster. New Deal recovery programs did help in evening out local prejudices, but more often than not as the Southern economy was "reconstructed" again, it was usually under Jim Crow's auspices.[26]

Just what did happen to Dr. Robinson and ANDA during the tumultuous times of the Depression is sketchy. We do know that they campaigned and petitioned for the establishment of black Civilian Conservation Corps Camps and, thus, it seems remained functioning in some form throughout the decade.[27] One of the most important things that we know is that ANDA did not, like many other local black organizations, go out of existence. It managed to remain intact and ready to fight when the time for opportune action came around again.

The impact of the Second World War on the struggle for black equality was considerable. Many blacks saw opportunities open for new jobs and new responsibilities and a chance to partake in the relative affluence which the war brought about. This was accompanied by a demand for a larger stake in the affairs of country and community, for which many black members were giving their lives on the battlefield. The battle for recognition of that role increasingly intensified as the war progressed. In Little Rock, the beginnings of protest were timid, but as the war progressed and climaxed, so black influence correspondingly grew greater, aided by a similar national trend in black affairs.[28]

ANDA resumed its battle for participation in the primary system at the beginning of the war years but with a more cautious challenge to the Democratic Party rules than before. In December of 1940 Dr. Robinson, on behalf of Negro Democrats, again petitioned the new Democratic State Committee. It was the same plea he had made to the outgoing Committee in the spring of the year before: to modify its rules to allow blacks to vote in Democratic primaries. This time he added the reassurance that ANDA did not seek "mass voting" by blacks, but asked only that those blacks qualifying to vote "under challenge" be allowed to do so. The Committee took this to be an invitation to institute a literacy test to make sure "undesirables" did not vote. Whether this was the intention, and, if so, a ploy to water down the demands which had been refused before with an attempt to get a foot in the Democratic Party door, is unclear. Robert Knox, the Committee Chairman, referred the matter to a subcommittee with the acknowledgment that last year's outgoing Committee had taken a "favorable attitude" but had not acted directly upon it, preferring instead to pass a more ambiguous resolution empowering the Democratic State Committee "to make such rules as may be needed for the good of the party."[29]

Another two years passed. Then, a glimmer of hope came. A Supreme Court case in Louisiana seemed to offer a constitutional precedent allowing blacks to vote in federal and state primaries, a decision which Dr. Robinson saw as "distinctly clarify [ing] our position in the coming political enigma." Arkansas Negro Democrats began to discuss voting procedure. Dr. Robinson advised them "to avoid sidewalk and barber shop politics" insisting "we are on trial and we must practice decorum."[30] A letter was written to United States Attorney General Francis Biddle asking for his support in allowing blacks their proper voting rights. It claimed that a petition to secure such rights had been ignored by the Democratic Party in Arkansas.

In July 1942 ANDA met to discuss their tactics. Again it reiterated: "We make no effort for mass voting of negroes, no repetition of the 1870s." Instead, it was claimed: "We only want orderly, liberty loving, loyal negro Democrats to vote for congressional and senatorial candidates." In reply, June Wooten, secretary of the Pulaski County Democratic Committee, simply stated that "under party rules, they can't vote in the primary." Governor Homer Adkins, when questioned, replied that the issue was "clearly a matter of party regulations" with the party having an inherent "right to make their own rules." Joe C. Barrett, chairman of the Democratic State Committee, felt that the burden for enforcement fell on the election judges and clerks in each precinct, adding, however, that "the party rules speak for themselves in the matter" and that he was confident that they would be "complied with."[31]

Dr. Robinson was buoyed by a reply from Attorney General Biddle's office which stated that although it was not within the Attorney General's bounds to offer opinion on the matter "the denial of the right to Negro voters to participate in the primary elections has been the subject of a series of conferences within this department" and recommended that he confer with Thurgood Marshall, with whom they had been speaking. In the wake of this encouragement Dr. Robinson declared: "There is no question but that we shall go to the polls

Tuesday and vote for candidates for Federal office."[32] This sentiment was emphasized again at a meeting attended by "more than 100 well-dressed Negroes" at Dreamland Hall at Ninth and State streets and broadcast over the radio waves by KLRA.

However, ANDA cautioned black voters to avoid conflict, insisting "we want no rabble in the Democratic Party." They were advised: "If any [primary election] judge denies you the right to vote, I suggest that you bow politely and leave the booth without ado." In spite of this advice, Dr. Robinson did not anticipate "any trouble" nor expect "any denial" of the vote. ANDA Secretary J. H. McConico told the gathered crowd: "We are not asking pity or any special favors, we are simply seeking to exercise those rights and privileges guaranteed to free men in a free country." White party officials remained adamant that blacks would not vote in primaries, although one was willing to admit that the New Deal court and the current mood of the Justice Department might invalidate the outcome of the primary if blacks were prevented from voting.[33]

Tuesday, the day of the first primaries, came. The first black voter to attempt to cast a ballot was a Baptist minister at Peabody School, who was duly refused the privilege. A further request by the minister just to see a blank ballot was also denied. Similar events occurred throughout the city, with an estimated 75-100 blacks being sent away from the voting booths. This group included Dr. Robinson, P. H. Jordan, I. T. Gillam (the principal of Gibbs School), T. W. Coggs (the president of Arkansas Baptist College) and J. H. McConico, secretary of ANDA, who was refused the ballot at the same place where he claimed he had been allowed to vote without hindrance in Democratic Primaries since 1926. There were no reports of any violence at any of the polls. In fact, Dr. Robinson claimed that he had been treated "very courteously" by election officials, who had received a memorandum on election day reminding them that the only persons qualified to vote were "WHITE DEMOCRATS." Blacks had similar experiences at Pine Bluff and Conway. However, a few blacks in Camden did vote in the primary, as they apparently had always done in the past.[34]

In the wake of the election Dr. Robinson filed a report on events with the NAACP and its attorney Thurgood Marshall. Dr. Robinson commented: "They made their decisions and made it stick. We'll just have to let things cool off for a while until everybody gets level headed again."[35] It was not long, however, before the next action was taken. An ultimatum was laid down by ANDA that, if blacks were not allowed to vote in the following Tuesday's second primary, they would "appeal to the federal courts for relief."

Still, Dr. Robinson was reluctant to take the case to court. In a letter to the

Democratic State Secretary, Harry Combs, he stressed: "We hope you understand that this will be a friendly suit, with no financial or penal objectives," again repeating that "we have no desire for court action." Court was the last resort. All along, Dr. Robinson had hoped that by appealing to reason, goodwill and the principles of American Democracy, namely equal suffrage for all, that some resolution to the situation would be found. Combs simply replied: "The same rule that applies to the first primary applies to the second primary." As far as white Democrats were concerned, this was, had been, and would continue to be the bottom line: no blacks allowed.[36]

Since this position of stalemate existed at the local level, with one side insisting it had the right to vote and the other denying the exercise of that right, the decision had to rest, finally, with an outside arbiter. This was to be the U.S. Supreme Court. In 1944, a set of cases like the one existing in Arkansas came before the court. The ruling in *Smith v. Allwright*, based on the Texas primary system (which was identical to that of Arkansas), stated that the all-white primary was unconstitutional. June Wooten, secretary of the Pulaski County Democratic Committee, conceded that the ruling would mean that blacks would be able to vote for federal offices the following summer. However, she was still thinking of denying blacks the vote in state elections, while in federal elections providing segregated ballot boxes. Although the Supreme Court had this time provided a clear mandate for blacks to vote in Democratic primaries, Dr. Robinson remained cautious in saying that he was "hopeful" that the committee would "grant us the privilege" of voting.[37]

More hope came when the U.S. Assistant Attorney General Cleveland Holland declared a more liberal interpretation of the Supreme Court's ruling than white Arkansas Democrats had. He emphasized the "state and national" clause of the written judgment, which he held to mean that blacks could vote not just in senatorial and congressional races but may be able to vote for state and local offices as well.[38] With such encouragement, ANDA held another meeting at Dunbar High School, to discuss plans for voting in the following summer primaries. This time, in his letter of invitation to the meeting, Dr. Robinson felt confident that now "a definite understanding with the majority group" had been reached.[39]

Such optimism was borne out by the announcement on May 17, 1944, that the Democratic State Committee would meet the next morning at the Hotel Marion to amend party rules, allowing full participation by blacks in Democratic Party primaries. By the simple action of removing the word "white" from Rule No. 2, which read that only "all eligible and legally qualified white electors" could vote in Democratic primaries, the long struggle by blacks to gain that vote would be over.[40]

It was that simple and that complex. After all the positive signs, the issue of black voting was avoided at the Committee's meeting. Ostensibly, it seemed that the move toward black Democratic primary suffrage had been blocked by Governor Adkins, who, in a letter to the meeting, stated that such a move "does not coincide with my views in any respect" and urged that "no action" be taken, "as it is entirely a matter for the convention and legislature to settle." Another chance for a smooth transition had been lost.[41]

Governor Adkins further initiated action to prevent blacks from voting in the Democratic Party primaries. Seeking to dodge the Supreme Court decision, in June of 1944, he advocated barring black voters from the primaries on another "basis than that of race or color." What he had in mind was a "loyalty clause," denying the vote on the basis of participation with the Republican Party. This general theme was then taken up by Democratic State Committee Chairman Joe C. Barrett, who suggested that the "white" restriction be removed to make way for rules allowing wider "freedom" to prevent black voting.[42] Such a policy was put into effect the following month when the party amended two rules to its constitution.

First, a clause stressing the "good faith" of prospective voters replaced the "white electors" clause and sought to bar blacks on the grounds that they knew "nothing about the principles and policies of the Democratic Party" and that their only motivation was to "want a voice in the affairs of the dominant political party." It instituted a requirement that voters in primaries be "not only in sympathy with the principles and policies of the Democratic Party, but with their practical application in government affairs."

Essentially hiding behind this highly subjective and ambiguous clause was a Catch 22 for the black voter. Wishing to vote, he must first agree wholesale with Democratic principles. Since included in these principles was the creed of racial exclusion, the potential voter, to qualify, must have had to believe in his own exclusion from the party. By agreeing to such, he was agreeing in the principle that he should not vote in the primaries and, if truly acting in "good faith," would then not insist on voting in the first place, since doing so contravened party principles!

As if this were not enough, Rule No. 3 was altered to read that qualified electors only consisted of the following: a) those "eligible for membership in the Democratic Party" (blacks were not); b) those not "affiliated with the Republican Party or with any other political organization that is opposed to the Democratic Party" (since membership in the Democratic Party was outlawed, blacks had only had the Republican Party to join); c) only those who had "openly declared allegiance to the principles and policies of the Democratic Party" (which worked in the same way as the "good faith" clause); d) those who had not voted against a Democratic nominee within the last two years, or supported anyone who espoused an anti-Democratic cause or who was not in sympathy with the success of the Democratic Party, again, in all "good faith."

These tests were to be administered by (white Democratic) election judges, who must reach a "majority decision" in deciding whether the voters were allowed to cast their ballot or not. The parameters were drawn so wide and contained so many subjective clauses, providing so much discretion, that anybody could have been prevented from voting, if interpretation of the rules were stretched far enough. However, for all the jargon, these rules meant the same as the word "white" in "electors only" which it replaced. Further, the Democrats decided to try to get the legislature to change the prescribed political party rules allowing them the right to "prescribe the qualifications for its own membership" and "to prescribe qualification for voting in its party primaries."

At the same meeting, Dr. Robinson was called upon to state his point of view. He declared that when the law dictated such, blacks had "stayed away from the polls" but now that the law was on their side, he expected white Democrats to be "equally subservient to the law." He reminded the members of the meeting that his organization had been "Democrats true and tried since 1928" and emphasized the fact that "we seek no racial equality," simply the privilege of voting, which was guaranteed under the constitution.[43]

This did little to persuade the Democrats. Later that month, when Dr. Robinson announced ANDA's support of Governor Adkins for the forthcoming election, Governor Adkins replied that the endorsement was "neither wished or solicited by me." He went on to say that "the Democratic Party in Arkansas is the white man's party and will be kept so. ... If I cannot be nominated by the white voters of Arkansas I do not want the office."[44] While the loophole existed between the passing of the new party rules and their being ruled constitutional by the Arkansas Supreme Court, Democrats did allow blacks to vote again in the city primaries. Again, this right was to be short-lived.[45] In January 1945, the Trussell Bill ratified the constitutional changes to Democratic Party membership rules and the Moore Bill initiated a complex segregated "double primary" system to disenfranchise black voters.[46]

A direct denouncement of Dr. Robinson's support indicated that things were getting personal. In September of 1944, Dr. Robinson's standing was directly attacked again. Secretary of State C. G. Hall claimed that Dr. Robinson was not eligible to vote in the general election because of a 1911 conviction for manslaughter, for which he had served two years in the penitentiary. Hall claimed that Dr. Robinson had never been pardoned for the offense and thus was not a qualified voter. It appeared that Hall was correct, although Dr. Robinson had been under the impression that a pardon had been granted by Governor George W. Hays.[47]

Clearly the issue was brought out at an "opportune" time, just after the Supreme Court decision allowing blacks to vote in the primaries, serving as a veiled warning or threat to the ANDA leader. It would mean that although Dr. Robinson had been able to vote in the Democratic primary, now he would be denied the vote in the general election. If this was an attempt to put the "frightners" on Dr. Robinson, it clearly worked. In exchange for the restoration of his citizenship rights, Dr. Robinson offered not only to resign as the president of ANDA, but to also "permanently cease and terminate all my activities, political or otherwise" linked to the organization.[48] It fell to Governor Adkins to issue the pardon or not. Possibly because he felt that the point had been taken and the lesson learned, Governor Adkins issued a pardon, but only after the elections had gone by and he was re-elected, without apparently holding the doctor to his word.[49] Nonetheless, the activities of Dr. Robinson and ANDA seemed to wane for some time after.

NOTES

This article was first printed in the *Pulaski County Historical Review* in two parts. The first, reprinted here, PCHR 41 (Spring 1993): 2-16 and the second, 41 (Summer 1993), 39-47.

[1] Considering the fact that the papers of Dr. Robinson seem to have been lost some time ago, it would take an extensive set of interviews, with a wide-ranging set of people, to piece together an account of all of Dr. Robinson's activities. Likewise with ANDA, to comprehend the full story of the organization would depend upon tracing those involved in the various county branches, as well as the leading members in Little Rock. The difficulty in both these cases is not so much finding who these people were, but finding them still alive: many, like Dr. Robinson, have unfortunately now passed on, taking their story with them. The whole area of black politics during this era requires much more research and study before anything approaching a definitive work can be done, Here, issues are raised which give an indication of the possible directions and themes that further research on these topics might follow up on.

[2] Dr. Robinson was primarily concerned with gaining the vote in Democratic Party primaries. Unlike many of the other Southern states. Arkansas had never formally disenfranchised its black citizens by the use of literacy tests or "grandfather" clauses. Rather, it relied upon the poll tax and the white primary system to prevent blacks from having voting influence. The one dollar poll tax was not too heavy a burden on professional, urban blacks. It was the all-white primary system which formed the greatest barrier to black political power. The full story is even more complicated. Although formally

barred from Democratic primaries, enforcement of this policy was dependent on "local custom or inclination rather than party rule" (Boyce Drummond, "Arkansas Politics: A Study of a One Party System," Ph.D. diss., University of Chicago, 1957, p. 75). In some places blacks could vote in primaries, in some not. Where blacks were allowed to vote, it was often largely due to a political machine or influential planter who could control this vote and use it to self advantage, (ibid., pp. 75-76).

3 Gunnar Myrdal, in his classic study *An American Dilemma: The Negro Problem and Modern Democracy* (New York: Harper. 1944, 3rd ed.) introduces the idea of "accommodation" and "protest" types of leaders. The former he describes as "static" in that they affirm the status quo and previous behavior patterns between the races. The latter provide a "dynamic" form of leadership, disrupting and challenging these previous modes and patterns of behavior (p. 720).

4 *Arkansas Gazette*, July 21, 1970.

5 *Arkansas Democrat-Gazette*, March 26, 1992.

6 *Papers of the NAACP: Part 12: Selected Branch Files, 1913-1939. Series A; The South* (University Publications of America, Bethesda. Maryland, 1991). Reel 4, Group I, Series G, Branch Files: Group I. Box G-12. Little Rock. Arkansas pp. 0735-0786. Fifty names, including Dr. Robinson's are on the founders membership list.

7 Ibid.

8 A. E. Bush and P. L. Dorman, *History of the Mosaic Templars of America - Its Founders and Officials* (Little Rock, Ark: Little Rock Central Printing Co.. 1924).

9 In its early years the NAACP was sustained mainly by women secretaries like Mrs. Carrie Sheppardson (see NAA CP Papers, p. 0856). Mrs. E. I. Copeland (ibid. p. 983) and Mrs. H. L. Porter (ibid. Reel 5. p. 0003). There is various correspondence between national and local branches indicating that pledges of monetary support were not forthcoming from the more influential black citizens over the years. This is summed up in a letter sent by Mrs. H. L. Porter to Roy Wilkins, Assistant Secretary of the NAACP, November 14, 1933. which read: "The professionals I find to be a very slow bunch in turning loose a little money. My success financially, depends upon the common people, I find them more liberal with their little means . . ." ibid. p. 0039-0041.

10 See Tom W. Dillard, "Scipio A. Jones," *Arkansas Historical Quarterly*, Vol. XXXI, Autumn 1972. No. 3 and Tom W. Dillard, "To The Back Of The Elephant: Racial Conflict In The Arkansas Republican Party,"*AHQ*, Vol. XXXIII, Spring 1974, No. 1.

11 See Darlene C. Hine, *Black Victory: The Rise and Fall of the White Primary in Texas* (Millwood, NY: KTO Press. 1979) Chapter IV and Chapter V, p. 96; C. Calvin Smith, "The Politics of Evasion: Arkansas Reaction to Smith v. Allwright 1944." *Journal of Negro History* Vol. LXVII, Spring 1982, p. 42; C. Calvin Smith, *War and Wartime Changes: The Transformation Of Arkansas, 1940-1945* (Fayetteville: University of Arkansas Press, 1986), particularly Chapter 5 on "Black Arkansans: The Quest For Home Front Democracy." These three pieces closely follow the same narrative line of the struggle by ANDA through the courts in 1930 and early 1940s to gain a say in the white primaries as I do later. What I write about them is an expansion of what Smith has written, which is in turn an expansion of what Hine has written. However,

although they cover in part the same material, the various accounts are significantly different. This is due to the fact that they are written with different motives in mind. Hine follows the cases in a distinctly national context, relating them to a national movement in the courts at the time. Smith's interest is in putting the cases in a statewide context of black political empowerment, specifically as regards the *Smith v. Allwright* Decision, linking it also to black social change in the state and nation during the war years. My interest will be to explore the cases in terms of the motivation of its plaintiffs in a distinctly local situation, following it as part of a more comprehensive overview of local black politics of the period, introducing more detail concerned with the personal aspect of political mechanics. It is interesting to compare and contrast these different accounts: they are complementary to each other in that each offers its own distinct perspective of the same events, each adding its own particular verve to the same story. My interest in local community politics follows trends established by civil rights scholars in recent years who have attempted to show that focusing on the local situation can significantly illuminate what is often missed by taking a wider national perspective. For example, see William Chafe, *Civilities and Civil Rights: Greensboro, North Carolina and the Black Struggle for Freedom* (New York, Oxford University Press, 1980); David R. Colburn, *Racial Change and Community Crisis: St. Augustine, Florida 1877-1980* (New York: Columbia University Press, 1985); Robert J. Norrell, Reaping the Whirlwind: *The Civil Rights Movement in Tuskegee* (New York: Alfred A. Knopf, 1985).

12 It seems "Republican Clubs" had been setup in a meeting presided over by Scipio Jones at the Masonic Temple on February 27 earlier that year (W. H. Flowers Papers, Pine Bluff, Arkansas). Later that year, as already mentioned, blacks in the Republican Party managed to effect a compromise with the "lily-whites." This success might have inspired a similar response by black Democrats to gain a say in their party.

13 V. O. Key, *Southern Politics in State and Nation* (New York: Vintage Books, 1959). However, given that it was also a bastion of white supremacy, it might not. In associating itself with the Democrats, ANDA was way ahead of its time. It was not until after the New Deal that blacks became part of the Democratic coalition, on a national basis. The two occurrences stemmed from very different modes of thought, although they both moved toward the same end, a black Democratic alliance.

14 Accounts of the burning of John Carter can be found in, Marcet Haldeman-Julius, *The Story of a Lynching* (Girad: Haldeman-Julius Publications, 1927); James Reed Eison, "Dead, But She Was in a Good Place, a Church," *Pulaski County Historical Review*, Volume XXX, Summer 1982, No. 2. There are also accounts in the local press (*Arkansas Gazette* and *Arkansas Democrat*, May 4-7, 1927. A brief account is given in *Survey of Negroes in Little Rock and North Little Rock*. Compiled by the Writers' Program of the Works Project Administration, 1941.

15 Interview with Mrs. I. S. McClinton and Mrs. Mattie Davis 9/10/92.

16 The accounts of this particular era of southern history form quite a body of literature. Among the more essential reading arc C. Vann Woodward's *The Strange Career of Jim Crow* (New York: Oxford University Press, 1956) and Origins of the New South 1877-1913 (Baton Rouge, La.: Louisiana State University Press, 1951); George B. Tindall, *The Emergence of the New South 1913-1945* (Baton Rouge, La.: Louisiana State

University Press, 1967); Robert Haws (ed.), *The Age Of Segregation: Race Relations in the Urban South* (Oxford, Miss.: University Press of Mississippi, 1978).

[17] See *Survey of Negroes in Little Rock and North Little Rock, 1941*. The Mosaic Templars went into receivership in 1930 (see WPA Federal Writers Project, Box 5, Folder 7: Societies and Associations, November 1935, p. 18, Arkansas History Commission, Little Rock, Arkansas).

[18] *Arkansas Gazette*, September 19,1928,

[19] "Constitution and By-Laws and Order of Incorporation of the Arkansas Negro Democratic Association of Arkansas," Governor Sid McMath Papers, Box XXVI, File 296, Folder 1: "Black Matters," Arkansas History Commission, Little Rock, Arkansas. This booklet refers to the "Petition for Incorporation" which was granted, note the year, March 12, 1949. It was not until this time that ANDA would become a recognized incorporated political body. However, the constitution ratified at that time was the same one drawn up in 1928, Note the membership consisted of many leading members of the Mosaic Templars. The fraternal organization not only straddled membership of both Republican and Democratic parties, but also provided its building as a meeting place for both.

[20] *Arkansas Gazette*, November 27, 1928.

[21] During this year a total of eight black Democrats voted in a segregated ballot. Hine, *Black Victory*, p. 96,

[22] Hine, p. 115.

[23] *Arkansas Gazette*, August 30, 1929; Hine. pp. 94-96, The case in Virginia, *West v. Biley*, eventually succeeded in gaining the right for blacks to vote in Democratic primaries. However, as would have been the case in Arkansas, this only resulted in a very few blacks taking up the right to do so. The apathy was due to the fact that many blacks felt alienated from the Democratic Party at this time anyway. Others did not want to antagonize the "good white people" by trying to vote, and the low voter registration figures for general elections indicated that the vast majority of blacks did not have a stake in being interested in party politics in the first place.

[24] *Arkansas Gazette*, March 26,1930.

[25] *Arkansas Gazette*, November 25, 1930; Hine, p. 96-99. Hine points out that the NAACP begrudgingly gave support to the case, but that the local attorneys working on its behalf maintained that most Little Rock blacks saw the case as a "political rather than racial fight." The driving force came from Dr. Robinson on the local level but the shortage of funds was a significant factor, of which the NAACP was to be a crucial provider in later years. The same sentiment as in Richmond, Virginia, seems to have existed, in that many blacks did not identify a political struggle to gain a say in the Democratic Party with race.

[26] For a recent overview of these years see Tony Badger, *The New Deal: The Depression years 1933-1940* (MacMillan, London, 1989). Black issues are looked at in more detail in Harvard Sitkoff's, *A New Deal for Blacks: The Emergence of Civil Rights as a National Issue, Vol. 1: The Depression Decade* (Oxford University Press. 1978) and Raymond Wolters, *Negroes and the Great Depression: The Problem of Economic Recovery*

(Greenwood: Westport. 1970).

[27] *Brinkley Argus* (Newspaper), Brinkley, Arkansas, May 2, 1935. Clipping, Floyd Sharp Scrapbooks 1933-1943, No. 11 Civilian Conservation Corps (CCC) (1933-1935). Although in the wake of these protests black CCC camps were set up, it appears this had more to do with federal pressures than local protest. Still, the voice of local protest could always be cited as a latent black interest in such matters by the federal government, and it could also keep the community aware of what issues were being, and should be, addressed.

[28] For an account of national events during the war, perhaps the best book is Neil Wynn's *The Afro-American and the Second World War* (New York: Homer and Meier, 1976). For a more localized view of the impact of the war see C. Calvin Smith, *War and Wartime Changes.*

[29] *Arkansas Gazette,* December 8, 1940.

[30] *Arkansas Gazette,* April 12, 1942, Hine, pp, 202-207. The Louisiana case, *United States v. Classic,* was not strictly concerned with black voting, but rather corrupt primary practices. However, it laid important precedents and ground rules followed up on by NAACP lawyers in other cases, eventually leading to the 1944 *Smith v. Allwright* decision.

[31] *Arkansas Gazette,* July 22, 1942.

[32] *Arkansas Gazette,* July 23, 1942.

[33] *Arkansas Gazette,* July 24, 25, 27, 1942.

[34] *Arkansas Gazette,* July 29, 1942.

[35] *Arkansas Gazettee,* July 31, 1942.

[36] *Arkansas Gazette,* August 4, 1942.

[37] *Arkansas Gazette,* April 4, 1944.

[38] *Arkansas Gazette,* April 11, 1944.

[39] *Arkansas Gazette,* April 22, 1944.

[40] *Arkansas Gazette,* May 17, 1944.

[41] *Arkansas Gazette* May 18, 1944; *The Commercial Appeal,* Memphis, Tennessee, May 18, 1944.

[42] *Arkansas Gazette,* June 4, 1944.

[43] *Arkansas Gazette,* July 9, 1944.

[44] *Arkansas Gazette,* July 20. 1944.

[45] *Arkansas Gazette,* July 26, 1944.

[46] See Smith, *War and Wartime Changes,* p. 98-99. The Trussell Bill prevented blacks from being members of the Democratic Party, but it was a double primary system which effectively disenfranchised the black Democrat. Since Smith v. Allwright had clearly ruled that preventing blacks from voting for federal offices was illegal, but had not been specific about all other offices, it was from the latter elections which white Democrats

tried to block the black vote. Four primary elections plus a general election had to be administered to cancel out this black vote. The first two primaries would be for all white Democrat voters only, in preferential and runoff races, for all offices other than federal positions. The second two would be Democratic federal primaries, in which blacks could vote, but only at segregated polls. Then there was the federal election, in which anyone who had a poll tax receipt could vote, regardless of race. For a more detailed account of the double primary system in Arkansas see Henry M. Alexander, "The Double Primary," Arkansas Historical Quarterly, Vol. III, Autumn, 1944, No. 3.

[47] *Arkansas Gazette*, September 17, 1944.

[48] *Arkansas Gazette*, September 23, 1944.

[49] Arkansas *State Press* (Little Bock based black newspaper, owned and edited by L. C. Bates), November 17, 1944.

PULASKI COUNTY HISTORICAL SOCIETY

Collecting, Preserving and Publishing Local History Since 1951

Publishers of the Quarterly Pulaski County Historical Review

P. O. Box 251903 - Little Rock, AR 72225

http://www.pulaskicountyarkhistory.org/

Presidents
of the
Pulaski County Historical Society

C.C. Allard, 1951,1952
Louise Porter, 1953
James H. Atkinson, 1954, 1955
David D. Terry, 1956, 1957
Kenneth Hanger, 1958
Harvey Young, 1959
Walter L. Pope, 1960, 1961
Guy Amsler, 1962, 1963
Sidney S. McMath, 1964, 1965
Pauline Hoeltzel, 1966, 1967
Alonzo Camp, 1968, 1969, 1970
Arthur L. Mills, 1971
Duane Huddleston, 1972
Fred O. Henker III, M.D., 1973
C. Fred Williams, 1974, 1975
Tom W.Dillard, 1976
William B. Worthen, 1977, 1978
Lucy Robinson, 1979
Inez Martin, 1980, 1981
Richard B. Dixon, 1982, 1983
Rev. R.E.L. Bearden, 1984, 1985
Col. A. J. Almand, 1986, 1987
Aubrey F. Williams, 1988, 1989
Sybil Smith, 1990. 1991
Edwina Walls, 1992, 1993
Mary F. Worthen, 1994, 1995
Richard B. Clark, M.D. 1996, 1997
James Bell, 1998
Carolyn LeMaster, 2000, 2001
Ellen Grey, 2002, 2003
James E. Metzger, 2004, 2005
Jonathan J. Wolfe, 2006, 2007
Sandra Taylor Smith, 2008